Public Policy Issues and
Latin American Library Resources

Published for

SALALM Secretariat
Memorial Library
University of Wisconsin—Madison

Public Policy Issues and Latin American Library Resources

Papers of the Twenty-Seventh Annual Meeting of the
SEMINAR ON THE ACQUISITION OF
LATIN AMERICAN LIBRARY MATERIALS

Washington, D.C.
March 2–5, 1982

SALALM SECRETARIAT
University of Wisconsin–Madison

UCLA LATIN AMERICAN CENTER PUBLICATIONS
University of California, Los Angeles

Cover design by Serena Sharp, Los Angeles Publication Design

Library of Congress Cataloging in Publication Data

Seminar on the Acquisition of Latin American Library
   Materials (27th : 1982 : Washington, D.C.)
   Public policy issues and Latin American library resources.

   The seminar was held in conjunction with the 10th
National Meeting of the Latin American Studies Associa-
tion.
   Bibliography: p.
   Includes index.
   1. Acquisition of Latin American publications—
Congresses.   2. Latin America——Cultural policy——
Congresses.   3. Libraries and state——Latin America——
Congresses.   4. Library resources——Latin America——
Congresses.   I. Latin American Studies Association.
National Meeting (10th : 1982 : Washington, D.C.)
II. Title.
Z688.L4S46   1982   025.2'9'8   84-8526
ISBN 0-917617-01-0

Contents

Annual SALALM Bibliographies

Specialized Bibliographies and Reference Aids

Editor's Note

It was indeed flattering and a surprise to be asked to edit the XXVII SALALM *Papers* for publication—a surprise that has evolved into a most pleasant experience.

The variety of topics discussed herein has proved most interesting, especially those addressing current trends toward economic cutbacks for education and cultural patrimony. Of particular importance in this collection of papers figures the section on "National Policies and Cultural Patrimony" for which the greatest number of papers were contributed.

Reflecting a change in the basic contents of the *Papers*, initiated in 1981, rapporteurs' reports are generally not included. However, two rapporteurs' reports are reproduced here for those sessions for which few or no papers were made available to the editor.

SALALM is very grateful to the panelists who participated in the annual meeting and to those who submitted the following papers and bibliographies. Appreciation is also extended to Colleen Trujillo, Principal Editor, and other members of the UCLA Latin American Center editorial staff for their assistance in producing this volume.

Pamela Howard

Preface

The theme of the XXVII annual Seminar, "Public Policy Issues and Latin American Library Resources," arose from the exceptional opportunity to meet in Washington, D.C., in conjunction with the tenth national meeting of the Latin American Studies Association (LASA). Graciously hosted by the U.S. Library of Congress, the first joint conference in SALALM's history provided a stimulating forum for the discussion of major current policy issues of concern to Latin Americanists throughout the world.

The full program of panels, workshops, and roundtable discussions, highlighted by two days of combined sessions with LASA, was attended by nearly 200 participants and twenty-one exhibitors, representing almost 40% of SALALM's personal membership.

The papers presented at the Seminar fall into three broad categories: international policy issues, the role of library resources in the formation of public policy, and strategies for developing a national policy for Latin American Studies programs and library resources in the United States.

The first papers deal with the sensitive issues of censorship and propaganda. National media policies can strongly influence the kinds of information that are printed and distributed in a country and the way in which that information is presented through the media. Papers by Laurence Hallewell and Elizabeth Mahan discuss government control of the press and media in Brazil and Mexico, the rationales for intervention, and effect of controls on the flow of literary production and factual data.

National patrimony laws, which reflect the concern of Latin American governments to preserve their rich cultural heritage, can be expected to have an increasingly strong impact on the ways in which research on Latin America is conducted and research materials are accessed. These laws raise a number of legal and ethical questions regarding the purchase and ownership of historical artifacts, documents, and books by foreign institutions, as well as important issues concerning the preservation and accessibility of collections in Latin American libraries and museums. Because of its far-reaching implications and its importance to libraries and academicians alike, National Patrimony was the topic of two joint SALALM/LASA panels, which are represented here in papers by Robert Etchepareborda, Frederick W. Lange, Cecilia Isaacs, Randal

Johnson, Ramiro Matos, M. Salem, Claudio de Moura Castro, and Alan Jabbour.

Throughout Latin America strong national library development policies have supported the growth of many new bibliographic databases and networking systems. These computer capabilities, which can be expected to revolutionize library activities in Latin America, also present tremendous possibilities for international resource sharing. A paper by Juan Freudenthal discusses the current status of library automation and databases in Chile; another by Henriette Avram examines the effect of MARC on the development of international networking systems and the role of the U.S. Library of Congress in the creation of international databases.

The availability and use of full, accurate information is clearly essential to responsible policy formation. The resources used by policy-makers in the United States and, specifically, the impact of academic publications on their policy decisions was the topic of a panel entitled "Scholarly Communication and Public Policy for Latin America," synthesized here in a report by Charles Fineman. Another panel investigated ways in which quantitative data are used and manipulated to form and influence public policy. A summary report of that session by Sonia Merubia is followed by James W. Wilkie's paper, "Management and Mismanagement of National and International Statistical Resources in the Americas."

The final papers treat the issue of developing a national plan for the support of Latin American library collections in the United States. In recent years inflationary pressures, economic recession, and changing national priorities toward education have combined to force budget cuts that have resulted in reduced book buying power, hiring freezes, and the limitation of many desirable programs and services. Despite strong recommendations during the Carter administration for the establishment and funding of a national plan to meet the library development needs of area studies programs, Title VI funds for international studies have continued to decrease each year. Papers by Carl W. Deal and William E. Carter, John Finzi, and John Risso Jones address these problems and propose strategies for implementing the recommended program. Deborah Jakubs' paper discusses the need for increased cooperation among educational institutions in collecting and disseminating information and the problem of database compatibility that must be overcome to accomplish this goal.

Diverse and thought-provoking, the papers of the XXVII SALALM reflect the views of many respected U.S. and Latin American government officials and representatives of international organizations, as well as a distinguished group of professors and librarians closely attuned to the Latin American political sphere and to Latin American policy-making in the United

States. Together, they provide a valuable compendium of current thought on the primary policy issues confronting the Latin American academic and library communities in the early 1980s.

Barbara G. Valk
President, SALALM, 1981 – 1982

Censorship and Propaganda

1. Censorship in Brazil

Laurence Hallewell

The freedom permitted at Speakers' Corner in Hyde Park, London, is often cited as an example of the truly liberal spirit of Victorian England. To me it is far greater evidence of the arrogant self-confidence—to the point of complacency—that characterized the ruling classes of that England. It is from this angle that I would have you approach the whole question of censorship. It is always a manifestation, as well as a measure, of *insecurity*: political, social, religious—or even economic (as when a Third World country fears for its "image," lest an unfavorable impression deter potential foreign investors).

Since all societies and all governments are, to some degree, insecure, censorship in some form and to some degree is, and ever will be, always with us. Not only is the degree of censorship a good indication of how insecure a particular society or government feels, but its precise direction and emphasis can be even more revealing. The same Victorian England that was so contemptuous of political criticism still felt the need for criminal law to defend itself against the dangers of blasphemy, while the threat posed to the traditional social order by the changing position of women led to restrictions against the discussion of sexual matters of a severity unknown to any previous generation.

There is also the important consideration of the audience. Those whose socio-economic position gives them a vested interest in the status quo can clearly be entrusted with that which might have unforeseen consequences if it were to reach the less privileged. One thinks of the foreign-language material available to Soviet academicians that would never be made available to the public in Russian translation, or the convenient distinction so often made between "mere" pornography and the usually higher priced erotica "with literary merit" which, it is fondly believed, only the intelligentsia will read. A gentleman in Victorian England might import Zola in the original, but the publisher who dared produce a version in English for the less well educated was immediately prosecuted. But that at least was action after the event.

Books, which the buyer may be expected to consume in the social isolation of his chamber are less threatening than the public performance of a play or motion picture, where the theatergoer will receive not just the message, but also the highly dangerous awareness of how his neighbors are reacting to it. For this reason the London theater and, when it arrived, the cinema were subject to the close control of police licensing of their premises and *censura prévia* of their productions. Even poor Dom Pedro II, who allowed so much freedom to the press that it encompassed the downfall of his regime, recognized the need, in the interests of social decorum, for close supervision of the theater.

3

The Authorities

Until the accession of João Figueiredo in March 1979, censorship in Brazil had always been a federal matter, exercised under the Republic by the Justice Minister, who, in recent years, acted through the Federal Police Department's *Divisão de Censura de Diversões Públicas* (Division of Censorship of Public Entertainments), or *DCDP*. Figueiredo's choice for the Justice portfolio, Petrônio Portela, refused to accept responsibility for censorship. He is said to have cherished presidential ambitions and was loath to have his public image tarnished. He considered the onus to be more appropriately foisted upon Education and Culture, but his namesake there, Eduardo Portella, proved obdurate. Eventually, in October 1979, a special Conselho Nacional de Censura (National Council on Censorship) was created, independent of any ministry, thus returning to the situation of 1939–1945 under the *Estado Novo* dictatorship, when the Departamento de Imprensa e Propaganda (Department of Publishing and Propaganda) was directly subordinate to the Presidency of the Republic. Actual physical enforcement of censorship still devolves upon the Justice Ministry, chiefly through the Federal Police Department (DPF, formerly the Federal Department of Public Safety, DFSP), but only as part of its general law enforcement duties.

It is always tempting to think of "government" as a unified organism with a single soul and a single brain, but it is, of course, anything but that. This is especially true in a country as vast as Brazil with a long tradition of decentralization and a high degree of personalism in administration, to say nothing of its enormous regional disparities in wealth, sophistication, and administrative efficiency. In the mid-nineteenth century, when freedom of the press in Rio de Janeiro was a model for the entire hemisphere, a wretched printer in São Luís do Maranhão was arrested by the provincial police on a trumped-up charge concerning property administration, and released from jail a year later when he was dying of prison-induced malnutrition, just for publishing the local conservative opposition party newspaper. Soon after the 1930 revolution—among whose avowed aims was a free press—a justice minister resigned in a huff because he could not control the federal *interventores* in the individual states and their interference with freedom of expression. During Vargas's period as dictator (effective from about 1935) the harshness of repression varied considerably from state to state. Within three years of the restoration of democracy in 1945, the local authorities in Bahia were apprehending whatever publications they disliked, including works by Monteiro Lobato. Moving the federal capital out to Brasília led to a *de facto* decentralization of theater and motion picture censorship. The organ responsible for this, since 1928 the Censura das Casas de Diversões (Censorship of Houses of Entertainment), had always come under the police of the federal capital. When the police powers of the old

Federal District were transferred to the new state of Guanabara, the censorship department was included by a simple legal oversight. Thereupon, other states instituted local organs to control theaters and cinemas which functioned until the promulgation of the constitution of 1967, which formally reserved all censorship powers to the Union. Nevertheless, from the 1964 revolution until the early 1970s, Rio de Janeiro endured an appreciably stricter censorship than São Paulo, particulary of books of periodials, due to the less lenient attitude of those in effective control there—particularly the local army commander. Even now, the climate of censorship in the individual states depends very much upon the attitude of the local chief of federal police, who can act on his own initiative "whenever the matter is urgent."

The Material Controlled

The farther down the social scale any material is likely to reach, the greater becomes its importance in social control. And it is still true, even in the age of electronic communications, that the ballad singer (*cantador, repentista, poeta de bancada*) and his printed equivalent, the chapbook (*folheto de feira, literatura de cordel*), retain the highest penetration range among the poor in the most backward—and, therefore, to the Maoist at least, the potentially most revolutionary—regions of the country. Even *telenovelas* (serial dramas) are reproduced in chapbook form because that is the only way they can be fully comprehended in some parts of the outback. It must also be remembered that the consumption of chapbooks is also relatively high among *nordestino* (northeastern) migrants to the big cities of the South, perhaps to assuage their *saudades de pátria* (homesickness).

In the 1930s, when the chapbook was much more significant in the life of the Northeast, the Vargas dictatorship solved the problem, despite the enormity of the task, by subjecting all such publications to censura prévia. A requirement to see the text of an intended publication or recital is still not unknown. Franklin Maxado relates how, subsequent to a public improvisation of verse by two *pelejistas* on "O salario minimo" (the minimum wage) in Natal in 1976, the local chief of federal police had both singers briefly detained and let it be known that in future he would expect the submission of a text in advance.[1]

Intimidation of the humble chapbook publisher—unsophisticated, barely literate, and legally defenseless—is relatively easy, occasions no publicity, and probably secures a wide degree of automatic self-censorship. "What people like most are broadsheets [*sic*] about shortages or the cost of living. But who is brave enough to write about that? They put you inside for it," has been quoted of one popular poet in Recife.[2] Maxado, however, thinks that the government now finds it more effective to encourage the "right" type of chapbook by awarding prizes, giving subsidies, and sponsoring publications. Some university presses are now providing outlets for popular poetry in which content may or may not be a factor in choice. Now that the chapbook is respected as a manifestation of Brazilian culture, it is even possible to find commercial sponsors if the poet is willing to extol their products or services. Most of all, control is being aided by economic factors. The traditional chapbook—hand composed by letterpress in the back street of a small northeastern town, usually by the poet himself—cannot compete with the glossier product being mass produced on modern machinery for nationwide distribution by Editora Luzeiro of São Paulo.

Television now reaches into all but the poorest families. Fully one-half of all Brazilian households are now blessed with it. The authorities watch carefully over programs according to their lights, but to this foreign observer they seem not to have grasped the true nature of the problem. It has been suggested that the greatest single common factor in nurturing a sense of dissatisfaction with their colonial status among the peoples of Asia, Africa, and the Caribbean during the 1930s, 1940s, and 1950s was the vision Hollywood presented of the white man's life style. The interminable (and universally popular) *telenovelas* of the Brazilian gogglebox are equally dangerous social dynamite. Not merely do they show every *favela* (shantytown) dweller how monstrously well provided for in all material goods are the upper middle classes, but they compound their crime by demonstrating what (apparently) dissatisfied, spoilt and miserable lives they live: a veritable education in how to envy one's betters, and despise them at the same time. What is needed is something analogous to Britain's Granada network's "Coronation Street":[3] the day-to-day life of a contented favela. Unfortunately this would never be tolerated by the vocal middle-class viewers, and would conflict with the generally held conviction that only the "positive" and "developed" aspects of Brazilian life should ever be acknowledged on something as public as television.

Approved television and radio programs are given an age-suitability rating which determines when they may be broadcast, on the ingenuous assumption that ten-year-olds go to bed at seven o'clock, twelve-year-olds at eight, fourteen-year-olds at nine, and sixteen-year-olds at ten. Similar but broader categories (the over eighteen, over fourteen, over ten, and unrestricted) are applied to films, but here age separation can be enforced and greater permissiveness shown in material released for the older age groups. In fact, in the over-eighteen category, almost anything now goes, including full frontal nudity. The pioneer in this respect was *Como era gostoso o meu francês*,[4] where a sixteenth-century Tupi Indian setting provided the desire for authenticity as an excuse for the total nudity of both sexes.

Theater is treated similarly to the cinema, except that the age categories are those of broadcasting. Naturally, by virtue of being live, it is more vulnerable to censorship by terrorism, as occurred in 1968. I am unaware of any such incidents since then.

Legislation regarding songs, musical composition, and recorded sound dates from 1946 and is expressly concerned with "trechos musicais cantados em linguagem imprópria à boa educação do povo," but the textbook by Coriolano de Loyola Cabral Fagundes—a "técnico de censura" (technician of censorship)—has the reassurance that the censorship is "incabível quanto à música em si, pois a melodia não tem condições de ser considerada obscena, ofensiva a quem quer que seja, ou desinteressante para a segurança e a dignidade nacionais."[5]

Fagundes devotes 286 pages to the censorship of broadcasting and public spectacles (cinema, theater, etc.) but only 69 to that of the press, which is perhaps a fair gauge of the relative unimportance of newspapers and magazines from the authorities' viewpoint. Readership does not extend far down the social scale. Even middle-class Brazilians are not great newspaper readers, as anyone who has experienced the low response to classified advertisements in provincial newspapers will be aware. The censura prévia was only imposed on the press at a moment of great political tension (and shortly after the staid *Jornal do Brasil* had published the manifesto of guerrilla leader Carlos Marighela) in December 1968: four and a half years after the military take-over. It was formally abolished in early 1979, when it had already been inoperative for some time. Fagundes gives his section on the press a forty-six–page supplement on Watergate, which is portrayed as an anti-capitalist plot led by "dois abutres da imprensa irresponsável, vingativa e desumanamente cruel." It may give some idea of the outlook of some of those with responsibility for censorship in Brazil to mention his conclusion that if "a simples invasão da sede central do partido da oposição, com fins de espionagem de campanha política" had really been enough to justify hounding the President from office, what statesman anywhere in the world would be safe?

If newspapers are little read, books are even less so. Fagundes barely mentions them at all. The censura prévia was not extended to them until February 1970, and even then it applied only to works that treated of "temas referentes ao sexo, moralidade pública e bons costumes." According to Jorge Amado, the government had wished to censor all books before publication, but retreated in the face of a concerted threat by an "enormous" number of authors to publish all their future works abroad. One could, however, interpret the government's readiness to make such a concession as evidence of the small importance it placed on books in the context of censorship.

Subjects of Sensitivity

The history of Luso-Brazilian censorship shows a much greater preoccupation with morals than with politics. When in February 1821, following the Oporto revolution, the Cortes enacted the abolition of censorship throughout the Portuguese empire, the vote to end political censorship was a decisive

70—8, but religious censorship was only abolished by the narrow majority of 46—32. The criminal code of the Empire, in listing subjects forbidden to the press, mentions blasphemy, attacks on the Roman Catholic religion and breaches of christian morality ahead of incitement to rebellion. Flávio Suplicy de Lacerda, the minister chosen by Castelo Branco to direct the seizure of offensive publications immediately after the 1964 Revolution, was a former rector of Paraná University who had made a name for himself by banning Zola, Pérez Galdós, Eça de Queiroz, and Guerra Junqueira from its library. The one censorship case analyzed in detail by Fagundes was the January 1967 banning of an edition of the magazine *Realidade* devoted to "today's Brazilian woman," which gave publicity to various non-traditional female life styles, included detailed anatomical drawings of the female body, and had a photograph of the actual moment of childbirth. Geisel's justice minister Armando Falcão, whose period in office marked the beginnings of the intellectual *Abertura*, was anything but liberal when morality was involved. For better or worse, this is all now ancient history. I have already mentioned nudity on the screen. Books and magazines are equally free. A 1970 law requiring anything "erotic, or treating of crime, violence, amorous adventure, horror or bawdy humor" to be displayed in opaque, sealed wrappings marked "forbidden to be sold to under eighteen-year-olds" is still obeyed, except that the wrappings—in the interests of effective merchandizing—are now transparent.

Concern to suppress unacceptable political ideologies dates from Bernardes' Repression of Anarchism Act of 1923. It was at its most intense under the Estado Novo and immediately after 1964. But protests against the banning of purely theoretical works were made very soon after the 1964 coup and these have now been tolerated for many years. Anything discussing the actual practice of communism in other than condemnatory terms has had a more difficult time gaining acceptance. Even under the Populist Republic, Jorge Amado's East-European travelogue, *O mundo da paz* (1951) was banned. The turning point was the August 1978 publication of Fernando Moraes's *A ilha*, a best-selling account of Castro's Cuba.

Direct criticism of Brazilian government policy was unacceptable for a long period after 1964, although it was often permitted in the guise of fiction, such as the novels of Antonio Callado. This was probably just inefficiency on the part of the censors. Ignacio de Loyola Brandão's *Zero* (1975) and Renato Tapajos's *Em câmara lenta* (1977) were both on the best-seller list for months before it was realized that they mentioned such taboo subjects as police torture of the children of detainees and the guerrilla war in the Amazon. The Abertura may be said to have arrived in this area with the 1979 publication of Fernando Gabeira's detailed account of torture in *Que é isso, companheiro?* By the end of 1979 it was even possible to openly publish the Moscow-line *Hora do povo*, which, despite blatantly provocative headlines, has suffered no more than the seizure of occasional issues. What is even more remarkable has been the freedom with which the opposition press has felt able to discuss the recent resurgence of right-wing terrorism. This began with incendiary attacks on newsstands in São Paulo which sold left-wing newspapers and magazines. An article in *Isto é* claimed that no organized body in the country existed that was capable of coordinating the attacks other than the security forces themselves. Later, press discussion of the Rio Center affair (in which two air force security personnel were wounded, one fatally, by a bomb explosion outside a left-wing nightclub) made the scarcely veiled allegation that the victims had been "hoist with their own petard."

The one remaining area of sensitivity is anything that might tarnish Brazil's image abroad. *O país de São Saruê*, a full-length documentary film of life in the arid outback of Paraíba (one of Brazil's most backward regions), made in 1971, has only just been released for general exhibition. Despite several invitations to enter it for foreign film festivals, its export is still forbidden. Perhaps in this case the authorities are justified. Although interesting and accurate in its content, as a film it is extremely amateurish; any prize it might win would clearly be awarded for political reasons. Less justified, but typical of official paranoia in this area, was the interception by the post office of a Brazilian university library's duplicates exchange list on its return from abroad. This list was then forwarded to the university administration with a covering letter suggesting that several of the duplicates requested were not the sort a foreigner should have access to, because of the negative view of Brazil they presented.[6]

The Means of Control

While addressing the 1934 Constituent Assembly, Francisco Antunes stated that the new constitution should contain provisions against any acrimonious criticism of government; pejorative remarks about any of its ministers; news that might threaten public order or cause alarm, even in financial matters; personal attacks on anyone whatsoever; any criticism of foreign governments, and any tendentious reporting that was unsubstantiated. The delegates were unimpressed, choosing a much more liberal wording for the section on press freedom, but undermined their good work by allowing full discretionary powers of seizure "in urgent cases" to local police chiefs. Within a year the position had been drastically modified by a draconian national security law. This forbade war propaganda, or propaganda that actively threatened the social or political order, a concept as all-embracing perhaps as the offense of "conduct to the prejudice of good order and military discipline" in the United Kingdom Army Act.

This law was repealed in 1953, but reenacted in very similar terms. The present law dates from March 1967 and is particularly wide ranging, forbidding "the spreading of false information that could imperil the good name, authority, credit or prestige of the Brazilian republic, besmirch the honor of the president of any of the three branches of the union, provoke war, subversion of the political and social order, collective disobedience to any law, animosity between the armed forces, conflict between the social classes, interruption of public services or racial hatred or discrimination, and any "subversive propaganda or incitement to perpetrate any crimes against national security." As all such activities are held to be a threat to that national security, action lies in the military and not in the civil courts. Action on other grounds is currently covered by a constitutional amendment of 1969 which states inter alia: "não serão toleradas a propaganda . . . de subversão . . . de preconceitos de religião . . . e as publicações e exteriorizações contrárias à moral e aos bons costumes."

Studying the text of the law can be misleading. Brazilian governments, none more so than the post-1964 ones, tend to gird themselves with far more extensive powers than they expect to need, so that the potential of the law is always far more onerous and restrictive than its actual, normal enforcement. Conversely, of course, the authorities may act beyond these limits and impose a reality *more* restrictive than the legal text. This may be achieved under the legal cloak of declaring a state of siege (the favorite gambit of Bernardes in the 1920s and Vargas in the 1930s), or power can be exercised arbitrarily, as in the 1890s and, on frequent occasions, in the 1964–1973 period. As an editorial in *O Estado de São Paulo* of February 22nd 1970 expressed it, although the government had given itself all sorts of powers, it preferred to act "sigilosamente, pelas ordens verbais, pela coação psicológica, pelas ameaças verbais."[7] Finally, there is censorship by intimidation practiced by unofficial groups: the pro-government mobs of the 1830s, the right-wing terrorists of 1968 and more recently.

So much for the "stick." Government can also influence the media with the "carrot" of patronage, and this is often made much of by leftist critics. The case of *cordel* has already been mentioned. A considerable number of books are published nowadays through the *co-edição* system, whereby some public body subsidizes an edition by undertaking to buy a large proportion of it. The overwhelming majority of such cases relate to either the University of São Paulo or to the National Book Institute, so that any discussion of policy must reflect on the two directors involved: Mario Guimarães Ferri, head of the São Paulo University Press since 1963 and Herberto Sales, director of the INL since 1974. Both have pursued the purposes of their respective organizations without any noticeable political bias. They have cooperated with publishers who were not in the government's graces and, a surer test, they have sponsored books which later fell foul of the censor. The other source of patronage which might or could be used to reward cooperative authors and publishers is that of the educational textbook. The choice of textbooks is made by individual schools at the elementary level, and by individual teachers at the secondary and higher levels; however, choice is often restricted to titles approved by state education departments. There have also been several moves in the past (none successful to date) to secure the economy of large-scale purchases through standardization at the federal level. The dangers here are obvious.

NOTES

1. Franklin Machado. *O que é literatura de cordel*. [Por] Franklin Maxado, Rio de Janeiro, Codecri, 1980: 115.
2. Mária da Gloria. "Mutilating the written word," *Index on censorship 4 (Special issue on Brazil):30 (1979)*.
3. A long-running saga of life in a back street of a working-class district of an industrial city in northwestern England.
4. *How Tasty Was My Frenchman*; the context is anthropophagic.
5. Coriolano de Loyola Cabral Fagundes. *Censura & liberdade de expressão*, São Paulo, Taika [distributed by Record of Rio de Janeiro, 1974?].
6. Antônio Agenor Briquet de Lemos: "Qual é a importância da censura nas bibliotecas brasileiras?", paper presented to the Painel Censura, Congresso Brasileiro de Biblioteconomia e Documentação, X, Curitiba, 22−27 July 1979: *Anais*, Curitiba, Associação Bibliotecária do Paraná, 1980: iii, 1162.
7. This theme is elaborated on in: Paolo Marconi, *A censura política na imprensa brasileira (1968−1978)*, São Paulo, Global, 1980.

FURTHER READING

Costella, Antônio F. *O controle da informação no Brasil*. Petrópolis: Vozes, 1970.

Johnson, Peter T. "Academic Press Censorship under Military and Civilian Regimes: The Argentine and Brazilian cases, 1964−1975." *Luso-Brazilian Review* 15(1) (Summer 1978), 3−25.

Martins, Wilson, et al. "Painel censura." Congresso Brasileiro de Biblioteconomia e Documentação, X, *Anais*. Curitiba, 1980. Pp. iii, 1150−1166.

POSTSCRIPT

Barely a week after SALALM, President Figueiredo made his televised mid-term address to the nation. After a passing acknowledgement of Brazil's current economic woes (all the work of OPEC) he launched into an attack on pornography and the need to protect Brazilian youth which occupied the rest of his speech. I found this a truly amazing performance. Not only does the Government have more than ample powers to deal with the situation, but the person directly responsible for the exercise of those powers is the President himself. Brazilian friends have suggested three possible explanations. The least convincing is that, desperate to divert public concern from the depressed state of the economy, and having no Falkland Islands to conquer, a moral crusade has been chosen as a convenient gimmick. Another suggestion has been that, in election year, pornography seemed as good an issue as any other: a terrible indictment, if true, of the government's estimation of both the electorate's gullibility and its conservative outlook. The third, and in my view most likely, explanation is that Figueiredo wished to give the media a broad hint that government tolerance of what they have been producing since the Abertura is now wearing thin: ''pornography,'' in this context, being any progressive views on any subject.

Time, of course, will tell, but three consequences have followed to date (3 April 1982). The governor of Pernambuco immediately secured some easy publicity by threatening the news vendors (as the weakest link in the distribution chain). Then the popular illustrated weekly *Manchete* got into the act in its issue of the same date with a three-page spread of interviews with the prominent, all lauding the President's great stand for the christian family and Brazilian civilization. Now the head of the National Film Company, whose officially backed policy had been to secure an international reputation for Brazilian movies with no holds barred, has suddenly resigned. I find much of what is presently displayed on Brazilian newsstands quite offensive, but I fear very much that ''pornography'' is just the cloak to cover a retreat from the Abertura in the face of steadily worsening economic conditions.

2. State Controls on Private Commercial Broadcasting in Mexico

Elizabeth Mahan

It is often assumed that Mexican mass media are subject to extensive state control.[1] This assumption appears to be related to the proposition that the regime type, or form of government, predicts the type and extent of government control of mass media. Thus, a representative, pluralist political regime (such as that of the United States, Canada, or many of the countries of Western Europe) is assumed to control its mass media less rigidly than a so-called authoritarian (one party or totalitarian) state such as Mexico, Cuba, or the USSR. This hypothesis seems plausible because policy processes and outcomes do differ from regime to regime and generally reflect characteristics of the political system which produced them.

There are three problems with this approach to understanding state control of mass media in Mexico, however. The first concerns the concept of the authoritarian political regime. According to Purcell, an authoritarian political regime is characterized by the limited autonomy of interest groups, a low level of political mobilization, and a patrimonialist (e.g., top-down) leadership style.[2] However, while it is possible to delineate the characteristics of an ideal-type authoritarian regime, the fact is that few, if any, regimes fit the model exactly. Rather, there is a continuum along which authoritarian regimes range, so that while Mexico meets the formal criteria of the authoritarian model, the Mexican political system is clearly less authoritarian than, say, that of the Soviet Union or Cuba. This means that we can reasonably expect to encounter variation among the types and extent of controls which authoritarian regimes impose upon mass media systems. Therefore, conclusions about the nature of state control of mass media in one authoritarian regime are not necessarily applicable to other authoritarian regimes.

The second problem concerns the concept of mass media when this refers both to printed and broadcast media. In many countries, there are different sets of standards for each type of medium and different degrees and types of state-imposed controls. In the United States, for example, First Amendment guarantees to the printed media are not automatically extended to the broadcast media.[3] There is reason to believe that in Mexico, too, the printed media are subject to different, and perhaps greater, state control than are the broadcast media.[4] Therefore, unless one specifically divides the discussion into printed and broadcast media controls, broad statements about state controls on mass media may be misleading. As indicated in the title, discussion in this paper is limited to the question of state controls on broadcast media in Mexico.

The third problem revolves around the concept of control. In studies of mass media—state relations, control has generally been equated with censorship or other efforts to supress or distort information. This, however, may be an unnecessarily simplistic view of control, which overlooks the fact that controls can both promote and inhibit the dissemination of information. Furthermore, this view of state control is rather narrowly conceived, reflecting an Anglo-American view of media—state relations, in which the proper role of the press is to be the watchdog of government.[5] One can argue, however, that the proper role of the press (or mass media) is perceived differently in different societies and that the adversary relationship with government which is the hallmark of Anglo-American journalism is not the standard for press—state relations in Latin America.[6]

This discussion proceeds from the assumption that all political regimes impose both formal and informal controls on mass media, which serve both to limit and promote the dissemination of information. Formal controls are those mechanisms, established in law and other legal instruments, which affect the structure and operation of mass media industries and define their formal relationship with the state. Informal controls are found within the culture or are by-products of a particular administrative system.

In the first category—those within the culture—are social perceptions of what constitutes news, what is appropriate to report, what constitutes obscenity, what kinds of criticisms of which individuals and institutions will be tolerated, etc. These have been variously referred to as news values or the manifestations of self censorship, depending on the perspective of the observer.[7] Foremost among informal controls which are by-products of political administration is the reliance on official press releases for information about government activities.[8]

While informal controls establish one set of rules to guide media practitioners, their effect on the dissemination of information is difficult to measure concretely. The emphasis in this discussion, therefore, is on the demonstrable effects and effectiveness of state controls. With this in mind, the study of mass media controls involves three areas of inquiry: 1. the structures of control, or the mechanisms and formal objectives of state controls; 2. the processes of control, or how the controls are exercised; and 3. the measurable effects and effectiveness of controls, that is, whether they accomplish their formally stated purposes and if not, why not and what they actually accomplish.

The Structures of Control on Mexican Broadcasting Media

The private commercial broadcasting industry in Mexico consists of 634 AM radio stations, 168 FM stations, 8 shortwave stations, and 124 television stations, for a total of 934 stations.[9] Ownership, particularly of television stations, tends to be concentrated in the hands of a few economically powerful groups, notably Televisa, which owns radio and television stations, as well as productions facilities.[10] Concentration of ownership in the radio industry is less than in television despite the fact that most radio stations affiliate with a network or commercial representative which sells time for them and provides programming. Private broadcasters earn the majority of their revenues from the sale of air time to advertisers, a group which includes the Mexican government.[11]

Formal State Controls on Broadcasting Media

The formal structures of control on Mexican broadcasting media are created primarily in the Constitution of 1917, the 1960 Ley Federal de Radio y Televisión (Federal Law of Radio and Television) and its 1973 *reglamento* (ruling), and a number of decrees and acuerdos (agreements) promulgated since the late 1960s.[12] These legal instruments establish the basic social rights and responsibilities of broadcasters vis-à-vis the state, the formal institutional regulatory apparatus, and the formal rules and regulations to which broadcasters are subject. Legal instruments create formal controls, but do not necessarily indicate if or how those controls are to be exercised. However, before attempting to analyze the operation and effects of state controls on broadcasters, it is necessary to describe the limits of the formal control or regulatory system.

The basic social rights established in Articles 6 and 7 of the Constitution of 1917 which affect broadcasters are freedom of expression, the right to information, and freedom to publish (and, by extension, to broadcast) without previous censorship, except when public order and morality are threatened. Note that these are broad social rights rather than guarantees that these rights belong to individuals. The state is given the legitimate power to interfere with the exercise of these rights when their exercise is harmful to society at large. Restrictions on the content of commercial, entertainment, and news broadcasts are not, therefore, necessarily inconsistent with the exercise of the social freedoms granted in Articles 6 and 7.

The structure of the formal broadcasting regulatory system is quite complex, involving nine government ministries,[13] two intersecretarial organizations, the Cámara Nacional de la Industria de Radio y Televisión (CIRT), and recognized trade unions. Despite the fact that nine ministries have formal roles in the broadcasting regulatory process, two are of primary importance: the Secretaría de Comunicaciones y Transportes (SCT), which formally sets and polices technical standards for broadcasting operations, and the Secretaría de Gobernación, which is responsible for the regulation of program content. This function is carried out primarily by the Dirección General de Radio, Televisión y Cinematografía (RTC), which was created in 1976 as part of López Portillo's administrative reform. The intersecretarial organizations are authorized to perform advisory and coordinating functions. One of them, the Consejo Nacional de Radio y Televisión, coordinates the regulatory initiatives of SCT, RTC, the Secretaría de Educación Pública (SEP) and the Secretaría de Salubridad y Asistencia, while the other, the Comisión de Radio-difusión, whose membership is almost the same as that of the Consejo, is responsible for authorizing the production and purchase of programs which the state broadcasts over privately owned stations.

Formal regulations cover technical aspects of broadcasting (e.g., licensing, frequency allocation, transmitter power, etc.), restrictions on the broadcasting of certain messages (e.g., false or deceptive advertising, foreign programming, content which can disrupt public order, offend morality, or harm children), and requirements that broadcasters make air time available to the state free of charge.

Objectives of Formal Controls

Formal controls on broadcasting in Mexico create a framework for strong and pervasive state control. The objectives of the controls are related to broadcasting as a technical phenomenon and to the perceived potential of broadcasting as a means of communication which can promote national integration and social development. Thus, technical regulations have as their objective the maintenance of standards which ensure the transmission of clear signals and permit the industry to take advantage of innovations in technology, but which also protect the public from disruptions in services caused by changes in technology.[14] Content regulations aim at protecting and promoting Mexican culture; the entire regulatory system (which consists of the interplay of formal regulations, government agencies, broadcast licensees, and workers) has as its objective the protection of the public interest, that is, society as a whole as it is affected by broadcasting. Formal objectives, however, are based on formal rationales for state regulation of broadcasting and on formal structural arrangements. They do not necessarily represent the actual operation or effects of state controls.

Processes of Control

Three different control mechanisms, established in law to enable the Mexican government to regulate broadcasting, will be examined here. The first, content regulation, concerns attempts to affect the dissemination of information, but goes beyond the issue of censorship. The second is sometimes overlooked as a control mechanism. This is the Cámara Nacional de la Industria de Radio y Televisión, which serves both the industry and the state in the broadcasting regulatory process. The third, the requirement that private broadcasters make free air time available to the state, is sometimes viewed as a control mechanism, but often one-sidedly seen as an attempt by the state to dictate which information must be disseminated to the public. [15]

Content Regulation

There is apparently a division or office within RTC for monitoring both radio and television programming on private commercial stations. It is concerned primarily with excessive violence in programs (particularly television programs) and infractions of advertising laws. When violations are observed, violators are notified by letter and given five days to respond. If they do not respond, or if the response does not result in the dismissal of the charge, sanctions established in the 1974 Decreto por el que se Reforma y Adiciona la Ley Federal de Radio y Televisión (Decree which Reforms and Adds to the Federal Law of Radio and Television) are applied. Such content-related inquiries can also be handled through CIRT. [16]

While broadcasters are occasionally required to withdraw offensive programming, it does not appear that this happens very often. There seems to be more evidence that program regulations which are ostensibly intended to protect the cultural heritage of the Mexican people, particularly those regulations which aim to maintain the purity and primacy of the Spanish language, are either ignored or easily circumvented. For example, Article 75 of the Ley Federal de Radio y Televisión requires that Spanish be used in all transmissions, with exceptions to be made in special cases by the Secretaría de Gobernación; Article 65 prohibits the retransmission of foreign programming. Nevertheless, a number of U.S. films are broadcast over Televisa channels as well as over the state-owned Channel 13. In addition, U.S.-originated television series are broadcast over Televisa's Channel 2 and a *convenio* signed by SCT and Televisa in 1980 permits Televisa's subsidiary, Cablevisión, to transmit programs which originate in the United States and which are taken directly from the air and broadcast intact, for example, with English-language commercials for products sold in U.S. markets. Finally, several radio stations broadcast a good deal of international, primarily U.S., rock music. [17]

There was an instance of the suppression by RTC of a political broadcast by one of the socialist parties during the fall of 1981. This notwithstanding, the preponderance of U.S. music on radio and U.S.-originated series and films on television despite legal provisions which discourage, if not prohibit, them attests to the inconsistent and perhaps half-hearted enforcement of content regulations. In light of this, it is unclear to what extent and with what effect the content monitoring division within RTC functions.

Attempts to regulate content do not focus entirely on the elimination of messages viewed as harmful to the society (or the state). The Mexican government also attempts to regulate program content through cooperation with private broadcasters in the production of programming and through the operation of its own broadcasting facilities. With regard to the former, since 1975, Televisa has cooperated with the Universidad Nacional Autónoma de México (UNAM) in the production of university-level educational programs, which it also broadcasts over its own Channels 2 and 5. Under this arrangement, technical and academic assistance is provided by UNAM, while Televisa manages the actual production and broadcasting of as many as twenty-seven programs.[18] Televisa also cooperates with a number of government ministries, most notably SEP, in the production of soap operas, or *telenovelas*. The objective of this cooperation, which is primarily at the story planning stages, is to bring the social values conveyed in telenovelas in line with those which the government wants to promote.[19]

Televisa spokesmen acknowledge that this cooperation is more formal than substantive in that it really involves only the planning of themes and not the details of production or broadcasting. Thus, the incorporation of government-sponsored social themes into telenovelas is not allowed to interfere with the realization of Televisa's own goals of providing entertainment that will attract as large an audience as possible (and thus enhance the value of the commercial time sold during the telenovela). Nor is the incorporation of such themes permitted to alter the structure of telenovelas so as to diminish the number of spots which can be sold for commercials during each broadcast.[20]

This type of cooperation at the planning stages also forms a facet of the state's content monitoring apparatus. Story ideas, which may or may not have been worked out with SEP or another agency, are submitted to RTC for approval before any segments are produced.[21] These are either approved or disapproved, in which case they are usually changed and resubmitted. Once approval has been obtained, production proceeds. The amount of control which this gives RTC is more apparent than real, however, for producers often change story ideas during the production phase without resubmitting them to RTC.[22]

In addition to its formal regulatory jurisdiction over program content on private broadcasting stations, the Mexican government, acting through RTC, operates its own broadcasting system. At the present time, the state broadcasting system consists of Channel 11, a noncommercial educational and cultural television station which broadcasts primarily in Mexico City;[23] Channel 13, a commercial station which offers primarily entertainment programming and which has approximately twenty-seven repeaters throughout the country;[24] Televisión de la República Mexicana (TRM), a network which distributes educational and cultural programs, sometimes by videocassette, to its own stations and low-power relay stations, mainly in areas not profitable for commercial television; one AM radio station in Mexico City, three FM stations, and three shortwave transmitters.[25]

Early state radio broadcasts were expressly political in nature.[26] More recently, state radio programming has served political purposes, but also emphasizes the dissemination of educational and cultural information. Similarly, Channel 11 has always been devoted to educational and cultural programming. When the state acquired Channel 13 in 1972, however, a change was introduced because 13, which had been a private, commercial, entertainment-oriented station, continued to sell time to commercial advertisers and continued (indeed, continues) to broadcast programming which largely replicates that of the private television channels, including imports from the United States.[27] TRM is officially characterized as a cultural and educational network and the majority of its programs are in that vein. It can and does, however, take programs produced for and broadcast on commercial television and retransmit them to its affiliates. The only restriction on the use of programs taken from commercial television for rebroadcast over TRM is that they be retransmitted in their entirety, including commercials and credits.[28]

State broadcasting has rarely, if ever, attracted audiences to rival those of the private broadcasting industry. There is, however, a great deal of rhetorical support for the system. This notwithstanding, the state has never adequately funded its broadcasting endeavors.[29] Therefore, much of the state's potential to influence the content of programming received by the public remains unfulfilled.

The Role of CIRT

By law, almost all Mexican businesses and industries must organize into industrial chambers. Formally, these semi-autonomous organizations serve as a communications channel between the industry and the state. They have been traditionally viewed as a means by which the state asserts control over the private entrepreneurial sector, which is formally excluded from the organization of the ruling Partido Revolucionario Institucional.

Before the formation of the Cámara Nacional de la Industria de Radio y Televisión in 1941, radio broadcasters had already organized themselves into the Asociación Mexicana de Estaciones Radiodifusoras, many of whose functions were the same as those which the new CIRT was to carry out.[30] The Asociación itself was an outgrowth of earlier efforts to promote the growth of the broadcast industry through the organization of the Liga Central Mexicana in 1923.[31] From the beginning of broadcasting in Mexico there has been a fair amount of cohesion among broadcasters which has contributed to the industry's ability to withstand government initiatives aimed at altering its structure.[32]

CIRT does not always prevail in dealing with the state over regulatory matters. For example, in 1975, its opposition to the passage of a state-supported contract law to establish industry-wide wage and working conditions did not prevent the measure from passing. Furthermore, the state has ultimate authority over the organization. Its by-laws can be reformed by the Secretaría del Patrimonio y Fomento Industrial (SPFI) or by the membership, with the approval of SPFI. However, the by-laws which spell out members' obligations to both the organization and the state are not enforced by CIRT itself, but by the government, acting through RTC or SPFI, although CIRT is obliged to report infractions of by-laws to the government.[33] The potential for state control of the broadcast industry is, thus, somewhat dependent upon the willingness of the organization to cooperate with such efforts.

CIRT is a formal participant in industry—state interactions over regulatory matters which have industry-wide impact. In addition to its involvement in the contract law negotiations, CIRT serves as a mechanism for disseminating information to broadcasting licensees. For example, when the reglamento to the 1960 Ley Federal de Radio y Televisión was promulgated in 1973, the Director General de Información of the Secretaría de Gobernación, the agency responsible for enforcing the reglamento, met with officers of CIRT to explain the new legislation.[34] Similarly, when government agencies wish to organize industry cooperation with their efforts to disseminate information about government programs, they work through CIRT.[35]

CIRT also serves as the primary forum for public interaction between private broadcasters and representatives of the state. CIRT holds a weekly luncheon which is attended by one or more high-ranking government officials. Similarly, the yearly Semana de la Industria de Radio y Televisión (Radio and Television Industry Week), while providing an information-exchange forum for broadcasters themselves, also serves to bring broadcasters, representatives of the organized entrepreneurial sector (e.g., the president of the Confederación de Cámaras Industriales), and government officials (the President and members of his cabinet) together and into the public eye. Government officials address sessions which are more or less social events, as opposed to working sessions of the meeting. Their remarks acknowledge the contributions the broadcasting industry makes to the achievement of national goals and urge broadcasters to continue to provide high quality service to the Mexican people.[36] All these interactions are shown or heard over the broadcast media and reported in the press.

Such essentially social contacts occur at times other than the yearly celebration of the Semana de la Industria de Radio y Televisión. For example, after the signing of the contract law in 1975, CIRT officials, labor leaders, and government officials celebrated at a breakfast at which Carlos Gálvez Betancourt, the minister of Trabajo y Previsión Social, praised the broadcast media in the name of President Echeverría for their high level of consciousness, which, he asserted, had helped to raise the consciousness of the Mexican people. The broadcasters, for their part, praised Echeverría and attributed their progress during his *sexenio* to his democratic and liberal policies.[37]

More recently, Margarita López Portillo and the president of CIRT joined in an awards ceremony which honored members of the radio and television industry who had supported the Colegio Nacional de Educación Profesional Técnica. This was again the occasion of speeches by both the private broadcasters and representatives of the state which exhorted and promised continued excellence on the part of the broadcast industry.[38]

These kinds of contact between CIRT and the state serve to enhance the image of private broadcasting by drawing attention to the fact that there is a fair amount of cooperation of various kinds between the industry and the state. They also permit the government to go on record as publicly commenting on the quality of private broadcasting and reminding licensees that their primary function is to promote the achievement of national social goals.

State Use of Broadcast Time on Private Stations

The Mexican government is legally entitled to use a portion of each private commercial station's broadcast day free of charge. Articles 59, 60, and 62 of the Ley Federal de Radio y Television establish what is known as "official time": thirty minutes per day for the dissemination of public service-type messages, the "National Hour" (a weekly radio program), and the time required to disseminate messages of national significance or of an emergency nature. The state is also entitled to use 12.5 percent of each broadcast day above what it is entitled to as "official time." The 12.5 percent allotment is known as "fiscal time," and is actually a tax on broadcasters—or, more precisely, a means by which they can pay one of their taxes to the state. Fiscal time is to be used for the transmission of programs, as opposed to announcements, produced or purchased under the auspices of the Comisión de Radiodifusión and made available for broadcast by RTC. Like official time, fiscal time provides the state with a means of communicating with the people for the promotion of its own programs and goals.[39] Theoretically, it also gives the state the opportunity to balance the programming offered by commercial stations.

The use of time on private broadcasting stations has only been a moderately effective means to regulate programming. The state does use more than thirty minutes a day for public service announcements; the "National Hour" is broadcast weekly, albeit rather late on Sunday nights when the audience is likely to be smaller. There has never been sufficient programming produced or purchased to fill the 12.5 percent fiscal time. When this is viewed with the failure of state television (especially Channel 13) to offer an alternative to privately produced programming, the use of broadcasting time by the state can only be seen as a mildly effective mechanism for content control.

The Effectiveness and Effects of State Controls

The framework of state control of broadcast media in Mexico is clearly biased toward state dominance. Both the Constitution of 1917 and the currently prevailing radio and television law establish a framework for strict control. However, an examination of the processes of control—how controls are implemented—reveals that, despite its formal dominance, the state does not exercise the controls at its disposal with the strictness which the law permits. Content regulations are intermittently enforced. CIRT's legal role as the channel between the industry and state has not prevented its development into a strong, independent industry advocate. The state's failure to use fiscal time and its own broadcasting system to disseminate programming which provides an alternative to the content offered by private stations indicates a lack of commitment to the development of state broadcasting and the relative ineffectiveness of the use of time as a control measure.

Although these control mechanisms seem not to be used to their maximum potential, does their operation nonetheless accomplish the formal goals of state regulation? To reiterate, the three goals of broadcast regulation which were derived from Mexican broadcasting law are 1. the maintenance of technical standards which ensure good service and allow the industry to take advantage of innovations in technology; 2. the protection of the cultural heritage of the Mexican people; and 3. the protection of the public interest, that is, society as a whole as it is affected by broadcasting.

Technical standards in Mexican broadcasting are generally high, although the quality of productions varies.[40] Radio has been available throughout most of the country for some time. With the installation of a new satellite system, it appears that television will be similarly available before too long. The state has been buying production and transmission equipment for its own use and for use in some cases by the private broadcast industry. Televisa not only effectively dominates national television, but has expanded overseas, dominating Spanish-language television in the United States and providing programming to television systems in most other Latin American countries. It appears, therefore, that technical regulations, if they have not themselves been responsible for the technical excellence of Mexican broadcasting, have at least permitted the industry to develop both the range and technical quality of the services it offers to national and international audiences.

The question of whether regulatory and control initiatives have protected the cultural heritage of the Mexican people is harder to assess. To begin with, this is a subjective matter, particularly in the absence of a concrete standard which establishes minimum amounts of programming types or specific themes which, by definition, promote cultural values. The presence of educational and cultural programming on commercial stations indicates that some efforts are being made to use broadcasting to disseminate information about Mexican history and culture. However, without an operational definition of Mexican cultural values and without data on how audiences use the information they receive through broadcast programming, it is difficult to judge the extent to which Mexican cultural values are being reinforced.

The radio and television law, however, does not specifically prohibit the broadcasting of foreign programs, music, or languages, but rather discourages it as being counter to the development of Mexican culture. The presence of foreign programming in itself is not sufficient to warrant the conclusion that programming controls have failed to protect the cultural heritage of the Mexican people. The temptation to infer that cultural values are not promoted through the operation of state controls on broadcast programming is increased when one considers that part of the regulatory apparatus which can be used to affect programming, for example, the state broadcasting system (conceived broadly as the use of time on private stations and the operation of the state-owned infrastructure), is indisputably underused.

Whether or not broadcasting regulations have served to protect the public interest as it is affected by broadcasting is more difficult to assess. There is a great deal of controversy in Mexico over just how the private broadcast industry and the state, either in cooperation or as adversaries, organize broadcasting so that it serves its formal social—as opposed to de facto commercial—purposes.[41] Leaving aside the question of how the social purposes translate into programming, it is clear that the state's view of its role as a regulator and a broadcaster is predicated on a view of its responsibility to see that the public receives adequate broadcasting service (although just what constitutes such service is left undefined in law).

Attempts to meet this responsibility appear to have consisted primarily of initiatives intended, first, to promote the development of a nationwide broadcasting system which would make it possible for virtually everyone to receive some type of broadcasting service or, second, to increase state control over the structure and programming of the private broadcast industry. The expansion of state broadcasting (e.g. TRM) into areas not profitable for the private industry and the extensive use of private stations to broadcast public service messages (e.g., the use of official time) indicate some success in using broadcasting to meet overarching social goals. I have also noted, however, that content regulations intended to ensure program quality have been unevenly applied and enforced. Similarly, the state has not countered the alleged violence and consumerist messages of commercial programming by greatly expanding its own production and broadcast operations to provide alternative messages.

Conclusions

The answer to whether controls imposed by the Mexican government on the private broadcasting industry achieve the formal goals of broadcasting regulation must be a qualified yes. In general, it seems that the Mexican broadcast media are relatively free to produce and broadcast the programming they choose despite the existence of a formal apparatus for strict state control. This can be explained in part by reference to the economic strength and potential political power of the leaders of the private industry. The private broadcast industry supplies service (either television, radio, or both) to most parts of the country, while state broadcasting either does not or cannot. This has resulted in broadcasting's being an economically sound business. The Mexican government traditionally does little to compete with or otherwise destabilize successful private industries.[42] Related to this is the strong position of Televisa as the largest single actor in the private broadcast industry. Its high ranking officers are members of economically strong families who are also well connected politically.[43] As a result, it may be assumed that these individuals have rather direct access to ranking government officials who deal with broadcasting policy and regulation.

There is another aspect of the industry—state relationship which is less frequently noted, but which helps to account for the fact that the state does not exercise all the power at its disposal. Given the limited coverage of the state broadcasting system at the present time, the Mexican government effectively depends on private broadcasting media to disseminate its messages to the Mexican people. Not only do the private broadcasting media disseminate government messages, but they provide what is probably the main source of entertainment for the majority of citizens. Any move which disrupted the flow of entertainment would be likely to cause a great deal of public discontent. At the present time the state does not have the technical capacity to expand its services to the scale offered by the private industry. In the absence of a state-owned substitute for what commercial broadcasting now provides, it is unlikely that the state would impose controls which unduly disrupt the supply of broadcasting service to the public.

If this is the case, what purpose do the various controls serve? First, they create a formal communications system between the broadcasting industry and the state. At the very least this serves as an excellent public relations mechanism for both parties. Second, and perhaps more important, the controls discussed are part of a framework for legitimate state action to control the broadcasting industry should that become necessary. While the Mexican government has not enforced the controls on broadcasters which have been established, and, indeed, seems unlikely to, it does possess the power to do so. This alone serves to keep the industry aware of the limits of government tolerance and within the bounds of acceptable action. Ultimately, however, the way in which controls on broadcast media are exercised serves to perpetuate a status quo in the industry—state relationship which appears to benefit both parties. Broadcasting remains a lucrative private-sector industry; the state is able to invest scarce resources elsewhere in the economy while maintaining a critical posture vis-à-vis the private broadcasting industry.

NOTES

1. See Marvin Alisky, "Governmental Mechanism of Mass Media Control in Mexico," in *Mass Media In/On Cuba and the Caribbean Area: The Role of Television, Radio, and the Free Press*, ed. Jan Herd (n.p.: Northwestern Pennsylvania Institute for Latin American Studies, 1979), pp. 63—77; and Robert N. Pierce, *Keeping the Flame: Media and Government in Latin America* (New York: Hastings House, 1979).

2. Susan Kaufman Purcell, *The Mexican Profit-Sharing Decision: Politics in an Authoritarian Regime* (Berkeley: University of California Press, 1975), pp. 3—5, 12.

3. Benno Schmidt, "Pluralistic Programming and Regulatory Policy," in *Communications for Tomorrow*, ed. Glen O. Robinson (New York: Praeger, 1978), p. 193.

4. Fátima Fernández Christlieb, "El derecho a la información y los medios de difusión masiva," in *México Hoy*, ed. Pablo González Casanova and Enrique Florescano (Mexico City: Siglo Veintiuno, 1979), pp. 342—343; and "Audiencia pública sobre derecho a la información: Constante violación a la Ley de Imprenta, denunció Gerardo Medina," *Unomásuno*, 17 July 1980.

5. Pierce, pp. 98, 104.

6. Glen Dealy, "The Tradition of Monistic Democracy in Latin America," in *Politics and Social Change in Latin America: The Distinct Tradition*, ed. Howard J. Wiarda (Amherst: University of Massachusetts Press, 1974), p. 89.

7. Herbert Gans, *Deciding What's News* (New York: Random House, 1980), is a study of how news is reported in the United States. Alisky and Pierce allude to self censorship among Mexican mass media practitioners.

8. William L. Rivers, "Another Government: The News Media," in *Mass Media Issues*, ed. Leonard L. Sellers and William L. Rivers (Englewood Cliffs, N.J.: Prentice Hall, 1977), pp. 17—25, discusses this phenomenon in the United States. Alisky notes the same situation in Mexico.

9. Cámara Nacional de la Industria de Radio y Televisión, *Directorio CIRT 1981—1982*, p. 7.

10. Luis Antonio de Noriega and Frances Leach, *Broadcasting in Mexico* (London: Routlege and Kegan Paul in association with the Institute of International Communications, 1979), p. 37. Richard R. Cole, "The Mass Media of Mexico: Ownership and Control," (Ph.D. dissertation, University of Minnesota, 1972), reached this conclusion with regard to Mexican mass media in general and noted that ownership concentration was increasing. By 1981, Televisa had 114 repeater stations throughout the country in addition to its four channels in Mexico City, a television system which reaches a potential audience of 50 million. The state-owned Channel 13, by contrast, has only twenty-seven repeaters throughout the country.

11. Government purchases of time on Televisa channels account for 18% of that conglomerate's advertising revenues. See Alberto Montoya, "Los condicionantes nacionales y transnacionales de la información en México," in *Aportes de Comunicación Social* (México: Coordinación General de Comunicación Social de la Presidencia de la República, 1981). Time purchased by the state is used to disseminate public service messages which take up more time than the thirty minutes daily which the state receives free on each privately owned station.

12. Legislation which affects Mexican broadcasters is discussed in Mary Elizabeth Mahan, "Commercial Broadcast Regulation: Structures and Processes in Mexico and the United States," (Ph.D. dissertation, University of Texas at Austin, 1982), chapter 4.

13. The ministries with formal jurisdiction over aspects of private commercial broadcasting

are Gobernación, Comunicaciones y Transportes, Educación Pública, Salubridad y Asistencia, Comercio, Patrimonio y Fomento Industrial, Trabajo y Previsión Social, Hacienda y Crédito Public, and Programación y Presupuesto.

14. This was most evident in the language of the decree which established the legal identity of the television industry. "Decreto que fija las normas y que se sujetarán en su instalación y funcionamiento las estaciones radiodifusoras de televisión," *Diario Oficial*, 11 February 1950.

15. See Pierce.

16. The existence of a monitoring division within RTC was confirmed by Oscar Márquez, the Subdirector de la División de Radio of RTC, during an interview in his office on October 28, 1981, and by Jesús Castillo Ruiz during an interview at the offices of the Cámara Nacional de la Industria de Radio y Television on November 4, 1981. Neither, however, identified the monitoring division by a specific name. The "Decreto por el que se reforma y adiciona la Ley Federal de Radio y Televisión" was published in the *Diario Oficial*, 31 December 1974, and updated the sections of the radio and television law which dealt with sanctions.

17. The results of an analysis of television programming during the week of March 7–13, 1973, showed that of 440 hours of programming, 94 or approximately 21% were devoted to U.S. originated series. See "La penetración cultural alcanza en México proporciones alarmantes," *El Día*, 27 April 1973. Noriega and Leach, p. 85, report that foreign productions accounted for 39.1% of Televisa programming in 1976–77. There is need for additional analysis of the content of Mexican television programming to determine if the apparent trend to increase the amount of foreign programming has continued.

18. Miguel Sabido Ruiz Sánchez, Vicepresidente de Investigaciones de Televisa, speech at the 30th Annual Conference of the International Communication Association, Acapulco, Mexico, 23 May 1980. This arrangement was also announced in "La UNAM y Televisa, S.A. se iniciarán la Universidad del Aire," *El Día*, 21 December 1975.

19. Specific productions which have resulted from this cooperation are noted in Sabido's speech before the ICA and in the column "De Medios y Mensajes" by Juan Garibay Mora, *Excelsior*, 21 September 1981.

20. Sabido speech.

21. Sabido speech. This is what is meant by his statement "nos sometemos gustosamente a la supervisión que de los programas hace la Secretaría de Gobernación. . . ."

22. This was explained to me by a source at Televisa who asked not to be identified.

23. Some argue that Channel 11 is not really a state channel since the license is held by the Instituto Politécnico Nacional, a public institution of higher learning, and not by an agency of the federal government. See, for example, Raúl Cremoux, *Televisión o prisión electrónica* (Mexico: Fondo de Cultura Económica, 1974), p. 17. Castillo Ruiz of CIRT agreed with this view, but pointed out that, although Channel 11 is not technically a state channel, it does receive a subsidy from the federal government (Interview, November 4, 1981).

24. The number 27 was cited by Enrique González Pedrero, "Televisión pública y sociedad," *Nueva Política* 1 (July-Sept. 1976), 191. My count of Channel 13 repeaters (including those in the process of being licensed) as listed in the *Directorio CIRT 1981–1982*, yielded a total of twenty-six.

25. These figures for radio stations are derived from the list of licensees of cultural stations in the *Directorio CIRT 1981–1982*, pp. 108, 110. I have included in the category "state broadcasting" those which are licensed to an agency of the federal government or to a state government.

26. The first state broadcast station was XE, a radio station licensed to the Partido Nacional Revolucionario, a precursor of the PRI, in 1931. During the 1930s SEP was also a broadcaster and licensee of station CTE. Station EX was a commercial station whose primary purpose was to supply political information. The station continued under the call letters EXUZ and XEFO as an official organ of the Partido de la Revolución Mexicana (as the PNR was renamed in 1937) and of the PRI (as the PRM was renamed in 1946). Shortly after the establishment of the PRI, however, the radio station stopped transmitting and official state broadcasting lapsed until the formation of state television with the establishment of Channel 11 in 1959.

27. *Excelsior*, 6 December 1975, reporting on talks on Mexican television given by two sociologists at the III Congreso Latinoamericano de Analisis de Conducto, headlined its article: "En México, la TV privada fomenta el consumismo y la violencia; la Oficial 'solo nos idiotiza menos.' "

28. México, Secretaría de Comunicaciones y Transportes, Subsecretaría de Radiodifusión, *Memoria 1970–1976*, p. 253. For the period covered by this *Memoria*, only about 6% of programming was taken from private channels (p. 266).

29. For example, because Televisión Cultural de México (as TRM was then called) was formally created in the first month of fiscal 1973 (e.g., July 1972), it was too late to provide it with a budget adequate to meet its responsibilities: to produce or acquire programming to fill an 18½ hour broadcast day (8:00 A.M. until 12:30 A.M.), it was given only 50,000 pesos per month, roughly $4,000 (Subsecretaría de Radiodifusión, *Memoria*, p. 42). Similarly, from 1972 (when it was acquired by the State) through October 1981, Channel 13 amassed a 278 million peso debt (approximately $11,120,000). See "Se transmitirá el Mundial de Futbol conjuntamente con Televisa: Farías," *Unomásuno*, 14 October 1981.

30. Fernández Christlieb, pp. 336–337.

31. Noriega and Leach, p. 15.

32. Events surrounding two such attempts—the fiscal time issue and the right to information case—are discussed in Mahan, chapter 7.

33. CIRT by-laws are published in the *Directorio CIRT 1980*.

34. "Se fijaron los objectivos del nuevo reglamento de radio y televisión," *El Heraldo*, 26 April 1973.

35. Castillo Ruiz interview.

36. Cámara Nacional de la Industria de Radio y Televisión, *Boletines de Prensa* for the 1981 Semana de la Industria de Radio y Televisión.

37. "Elevado nivel de conciencia ha manifestado la industria de la radiodifusion: Gálvez B.," *El Nacional*, 2 July 1976.

38. "La programación radiodifundida debe seguir siendo congruente con necesidades del país," *El Nacional*, 23 April 1981.

39. México, *Diario Oficial*, July 1, 1969, "Acuerdo por el que se autoriza a la Secretaría de Hacienda y Crédito Público a recibir de los concesionarios de estaciones comerciales de radio y televisión, el pago del impuesto que se indica, con algunas modalidades."

40. Pamela Eoff, "Television South of the Border," *Public Telecommunications Review* 6: 1 (1978), 51, 53.

41. The journal *Nueva Política* 1 (July-Sept 1976) is devoted to the question of television. Articles therein present a number of different views of the relationship between the State, society, and the mass media.

42. Jorge Schnitman, "State Protectionism and Film Industry Development: A Comparative View of Argentina and Mexico," paper presented at the Conference on World Communications: Decisions for the Eighties, Annenberg School of Communications, University of Pennsylvania, Philadelphia, May 12–14, 1980.

43. The political and economic connections of Televisa's owners are discussed in Mahan, chapter 5.

National Policies and Cultural Patrimony

3. The Organization of American States and the Protection of Latin America's Cultural Patrimony

Roberto Etchepareborda

Pan American Union Period, 1889–1938

Soon after it was formed, the Pan American Union began to seek ways of preventing the continued deterioration and pillaging of the Americas' cultural, archaeological, and historical patrimony. The first codified protective measures dealing with archaeological artifacts have influenced relevant legislation in the member states to the present day. For example, the recommendation approved by the Second International American Conference (Mexico, October 1901– January 1902) created an International Archaeological Commission responsible for exploration, conservation, and the installation of museums at historic sites. An International American Museum, at a site selected by the majority of the member countries, would be the center of research and interpretation. Years later, at the Fifth Conference (Santiago de Chile, March–May 1923), the Resolution on Protection of Archaeological Documents was approved. It recommended the founding of two archaeological institutes at the sites most suitable in terms of pre-Columbian cultural ascent—Mexico, Central America, Ecuador, and Peru. It also suggested a variety of legislative and protective measures that expanded its concern to include the protection of a broadened range of cultural artifacts.

The Seventh Conference (Montevideo, December 1933) addressed the issues of monuments and movable pieces. The term monument was extended to include those associated with the independence period and national formation and to sites of artistic value as well as to the protection of nature, indispensable for the study of flora and geology. With reference to the movable pieces, the Conference resolution resulted in the drafting of a treaty that was subscribed to in 1935–1936 by Chile, Ecuador, El Salvador, Guatemala, Nicaragua, Panama, and Uruguay and later ratified by Chile, El Salvador, Guatemala, and Nicaragua. The treaty incorporates for the first time: (1) the need to require a permit to export; (2) the need to present that permit to make the importation legal; (3) the understanding that the private ownership of an object declared to be a national treasure only extends to its enjoyment and use. It is worth adding that the definition with respect to "movable piece" was broad and adequate for

31

its time. This precursory resolution has been decisive in fighting the advance of illicit traffic. The provision for inspection and permits is indispensable for preventing the clandestine export of cultural objects. It would be desirable to incorporate it into the international agreements, which it has been in some cases. It should also be a fundamental part of national legislation in order to improve international cooperation.

The Conference in Lima, December 1938, also sanctioned a recommendation on the conservation of natural regions and historic places, insisting that the archaeological and historic patrimony is inalienable. It recommended that a comparative study be prepared on existing legal dispositions in the countries, to take advantage of and implement those which it considered pertinent. It further explained the advantage of a provision which instructs that the country and place of origin of art objects exhibited in American institutions must be indicated. In addition, the so-called Roerich Pact[1] provides that cultural treasures are to be protected in any time of danger. These are the principal provisions which we might call the prehistory of protective legislation, approved during the first half of the century, by which the American states incorporated the duty of protecting the cultural and artistic heritage of the American nations into the juridical provisions of the regional system.

The Protection of the Cultural Heritage in the Seventies

The Declaration of the Presidents of America (Chapter 5: "Multinational Efforts," paragraph D) establishes the worthy objective of defending the cultural heritage shared by the peoples and countries of the Americas (Punta del Este, Uruguay, 1967). Subsequently ratified in the Charter of the O.A.S., as amended by the Protocol of Buenos Aires which came into force in 1970, it initiated the present approach of the inter-American protective system.

One of the first steps was Resolution 19/68 on the Protection and Use of Cultural Heritage adopted as a result of the report submitted by the Group of Experts on Operation and Use of Monuments and Places of Historic and Artistic Interest, which met in Quito, Ecuador in 1967 to study ways of complying with the mandates of the Presidents of America declaration on cultural matters.

The "Quito standards" state that the absence of protection requires both national and international measures, and concludes that the efficacy of these measures will depend upon their being formulated within a plan to emphasize the contribution of the cultural heritage to economic and social development. The document establishes the concept and nature of the national monument, examines the condition of the monumental heritage to date, discusses its economic worth and emphasizes its value. It also characterizes the situation of cultural tourism, and concludes that the coordination of cultural and economic efforts is required in order to utilize it properly. This meeting was of exceptional importance as a decisive step toward the achievement of goals that, until then, had seemed beyond the reach of our regional organization.

It is true that prior to this general agreement on technical standards, other specialized meetings of the inter-American system had considered the problems of the protection of the countries' heritage. But it is no less true that the recommendations made on those occasions failed to obtain either national or international response. They were merely theoretical statements and the time was not yet propitious for those theories to be carried out. In order for the transition from theory to practice to take place, several steps had to be taken.

The defense and preservation of the cultural heritage of the Americas was set forth in an economic perspective for the first time, and given the same importance as the suitable exploitation of natural resources. Great progress was made at the First Meeting of the Inter-American Council for Education, Science, and Culture (Viña del Mar, Chile, September 1970) with the adoption of Resolution CIECC-38/70, which confirms the need to suscribe to a multilateral convention for the protection of the archaeological, historical, and cultural heritage.

A result of this concern was the study prepared by the Interamerican Committee on Culture (CIDEC) and the General Secretariat of the O.A.S. on the prevailing situation regarding the cultural heritage. This recommended advising the approval of a legal instrument of inter-American scope, which would determine the legal means by which treasures illegally transported to a member state could be retrieved. Doubts were sustained as to whether the dispositions established by the Convention and approved by the Sixteenth International Conference of UNESCO (1970) were sufficiently extensive to accomplish the basic objective of protection.

The definitions contained in the above-mentioned Convention are not objectionable, but they are not comprehensive enough. They do not envisage absolute retrieval because they only advocate the restitution of *stolen* objects, not those which had been exported illegally.

The following steps, taken between 1971 and 1975, were the product of the close collaboration of the General Secretariat, the advisory organs of the CIDEC and the inter-American juridical committee, numerous experts, and a wealth of opinions offered by the member states themselves.

The long evolution from 1970 finally culminated in 1976 with the adoption of two resolutions by regular organs of the O.A.S.: Resolution 275/76, adopted by the Seventh Meeting of the CIECC, held in San Salvador, which submitted to the General Assembly the draft Convention on the Defense of Archeological, Historical, and Artistic Heritage of the American Nations and Resolution

210/76, agreed to by the General Assembly in its sixth session, which adopted the Convention.

The aim of the Convention is to identify, record, protect, and watch over the goods which make up the cultural heritage of the American countries, in order to avoid their illicit trade, export, and import and to promote cooperation among the member states for the mutual knowledge of their cultural assets. The system of ownership of cultural patrimony will be governed by internal legislation and various measures for avoiding illicit trade are established. Each state shall be responsible for the identification, recording, protection, conservation, and supervision of its cultural heritage.

The Convention also charges the General Secretariat with handling various activities. I will only mention a few: (1) promote collective measures aimed at the protection of cultural assets; (2) establish an Inter-American Register of Cultural Assets, movable and fixed, which have special value; (3) promote the harmonization of national legislation on the subject; (4) disseminate information and promote the exchange of cultural goods.

The San Salvador Convention has entered into force among the countries that have ratified it, at present Costa Rica, Ecuador, El Salvador, Guatemala, Nicaragua, Panama, and Peru. Bolivia, Chile, and Haiti have also signed the treaty. In compliance with a CIDEC recommendation, the O.A.S. National Offices are taking steps to obtain those signatures still pending.

Inter-American Inventory of Goods of Cultural Value

At its fourth meeting in 1974, the CIECC agreed that it was necessary to be aware of the different international agreements and resolutions which insist on the protection of the cultural heritage. The Council agreed to take an inventory of the historical-artistic heritage under the uniform standards established by the O.A.S., UNESCO, and other national and private organizations. The multiple card inventory was adopted according to the model plan agreed to at a previous meeting held in Santa Fe, New Mexico, in 1972. It also resolved to create an Inter-American Registry of Goods of Cultural Value (Resolution CIECC-185/74).

Given the importance and magnitude of the work commissioned to the Department of Cultural Affairs, it was considered best to form a center for the purpose of making an inventory and carrying out the related activities. At the suggestion of the CIDEC, it was later decided to create an Inter-American Center for the Historical and Artistic Heritage. Following an offer by the Colombian government, the center should have been located in that member state. The center is not yet operational, but will begin functioning as soon as resources can be allocated by the Regional Cultural Development Program and the relevant agreement is signed between the O.A.S. and the host country. It should be added that the Convention of San Salvador also charges the O.A.S. with preparing an inventory, although this would be more selective, dealing only with cultural assets "of special value." This is being fulfilled by the Department of Cultural Affairs, but once the Inter-American Center becomes operational, it is intended that the assignment be carried out there.

The Inter-American Seminar on the Experience in Preservation and Restoration of Monuments Heritage of the Colonial and Republican Periods was held in December 1974 in Santo Domingo, Dominican Republic. The conclusions formed the "Santo Domingo Resolution." This resolution was later approved by the CIECC (Resolution 185/74) as "complementary to the Quito standards" on the protection of the cultural heritage. Specific tasks have been proposed for the Inter-American Historical and Artistic Heritage Center: to compile documentation from Spain and Portugal, and take an inventory of important monuments.

Preparation of a Model National Legislation

The Eleventh CIECC (Bogotá, July 1980), approved Resolution 498/80, "Prospects for Cultural Development in the Decade of the Eighties," which states, "It is essential that the Governments through their specialized agencies, adopt internally consistent measures that provide the national instruments with certain overall policy guidelines, among which the following warrant particular attention: The protection, preservation, increase, inventory, and diffusion of the archaeological, historic, artistic, scientific and environmental heritage."

The Resolution also recommends that the General Secretariat "Prepare realistic model legislation that clearly sets forth the concepts of cultural heritage and distinguishes the particular characteristics of movable and fixed property, by separating them into goods of historic, artistic and scientific value."

It is evident that a draft of a law is needed to serve as a model and frame of reference in view of the diversity of legislative procedures that exists today.

There is no concensus in the definition of which properties constitute a given cultural patrimony. In many cases folkloric, ethnic, or picturesque elements are omitted. Coincidental factors and differences exist in relation to various aspects, such as protective measures against destruction, modification, restoration, transfer, and export of objects; exchange with foreign institutions; and limitations set to private property, registry, and discovery of objects.

There are no specific provisions for the restriction of the illicit importing of cultural properties from other countries in order to eliminate illicit trading, even if this occurs through other treaties to which the countries subscribe, as is the case of the UNESCO Convention. On the contrary, in some countries, the importation of artistic objects is viewed favorably and duty-free imports have been privileged. This recommendation has been acted upon accordingly by the Department of Cultural Affairs. A draft prepared by the Department will be submitted for the consideration of CIDEC at its next meeting.

A realistic model of effective legislation has already been drafted. It defines the concept of patrimony as "that which is culturally significant." It also distinguishes between fixed and movable cultural assets according to their characteristics, and according to their significance as cultural goods of historical, archaeological, artistic, and scientific interest. It does not include goods of folkloric significance. The model establishes the following parameters: (1) national ownership as a general principle; (2) limitation to the absolute, natural right of property; (3) mechanisms to ensure that protection is guaranteed by proper authority in the registry; (4) mandatory declaration of cultural property and specimens of exceptional value which cannot be sold or transferred without appropriate authorization; (5) the obligation to declare all archaeological or paleontological discoveries—archaeological research, explorations, and excavations can only be conducted by proper authority, by institutions, or by professionally accredited individuals who have prestige, previous authorization, and who exercise care of such authority; (6) cultural property cannot be exported without proper authorization. Unique pieces, or those of exceptional value, may not be exported in any manner, excepting the case of temporary exchange between the member states.

Other Activities Related to the Protection of the National Heritage

Following the same mandate, the Department of Cultural Affairs, together with the National Trust for Historic Preservation of the United States, the Instituto de Patrimonio Cultural of Ecuador, and with the generous help of the Tinker Foundation held the First New World Conference on Rescue Archaeology in Quito, 11–15 May 1981.

In this conference the problems addressed were thoroughly analyzed, particularly the illicit traffic in Ecuadorian antiquities, a growing national problem that not only seems to defy solution, but also extends throughout the continent.

One of the discussants noted that in many of the papers presented it appeared that laws represent not much more than the interests of a group of influential people. He stressed the need for all legislation to clearly show the popular feeling, be efficiently backed by appropriate regulations, and provide the necessary resources to facilitate their execution.

He concluded that the concept of a national cultural heritage is doomed to failure unless the educated middle-class citizen understands and supports it. Some declarations were finally adopted by the general discussions of the

Conference, among them that the importance of our cultural heritage be responsibly and assiduously communicated to the public by every means possible; that concern for an understanding of our cultural heritage be incorporated into education at all levels through formal courses, exhibitions, and extra-curricular activities; that all governments cooperate closely to combat illicit traffic in cultural property by concluding bilateral agreements that cover artifacts as well as monumental antiquities and, by ratifying the UNESCO Convention, adopted by the General Conference on 14 November 1976, and the San Salvador Convention, adopted under the auspices of the O.A.S. in 1976, as means of prohibiting and preventing the illicit import, export, and transfer of ownership of cultural property.

Special resolutions were also adopted with regard to the illicit traffic of Peruvian and Ecuadorian antiquities to the United States and Italy, respectively. The former problem is being resolved through a bilateral agreement between the two governments, and the latter is still pending in the Italian courts.

National Legislation Protecting the Latin American Patrimony

In preparing this paper, I have relied on the data gathered by the Technical Unit of Protection and Conservation of the National Heritage of the O.A.S. Department of Cultural Affairs, for the purpose of elaborating the model legislation previously mentioned. Consequently, I was able to go through the regulations of twenty member states of Iberian origin, and of Puerto Rico, in a general manner.

Considering all these data, we should recognize the early awareness these countries had of the plunder of their heritage. In 1894, Guatemala prohibited the export of its antiquities, followed by El Salvador in 1903 with regulations that forbade both the excavation and the removal from its territory of archaeological antiquities and artifacts. As a result of the first meetings of learned Americanist societies, Bolivia declared the ruins of Tiahuanaco and Lake Titicaca and all those from the Inca period national property in 1906, prohibiting their export. In 1909 another decree forbade all types of excavation. Argentina, a country apparently without a similar archaeological wealth, established the absolute protection of its archaeological heritage and prohibited the removal of artifacts from its territory in 1908.

In the first years of the twentieth century many of the countries legislated on the subject, but it is not until the 1920s and 1930s that we see the beginning of a more integrated legal system: Chile's Decree-Law of 1925; Colombia's Laws 47 and 48 of 1918–1920; Mexico, 1933. Argentina's Law 12665 of 1938 protects all the different aspects of the national patrimony. It is still in force, with a few modifications. Despite these early advances, it was only by the

1960s, particularly due to UNESCO's brainstorming activities, that a renovated legislative trend took shape, forming the characteristics of the present
Latin American protective system. These include, particularly in regard to
national ownership, compulsory registration, prohibition of exports, and wide
and generalized protection of documents, artifacts, and objets d'art. This
legislative process is parallel to the already mentioned preoccupation with the
necessity of establishing an inter-American legal system for this purpose.

Since the beginning of the 1970s, many countries have renovated their
protective legislation, as in the case of Chile (1970), Honduras (1973), Dominican Republic (1973), Panama (1974), Mexico (1975–1978), and Nicaragua
(1979). That of Ecuador (1979) is one of the most thoughtful and complete. I
will only point out some principal characteristics of the regulations in force,
which illustrate the Latin American approach to this important issue. I have
selected some critical aspects, principally with regard to ownership, registration, and the export-import trade.

1. *Ownership*: The prevalent trend is national or state property. Formally
expressed by the laws of Bolivia, Brazil, Panama, Paraguay, and Peru. Also in
the case of Honduras, but extending it to the territorial sea lanes and the
continental shelf.

In Panama, the state will expropriate those in private hands; in Bolivia, the
law establishes a temporary ban on private ownership; in Honduras, national
patrimony in private possession is under the protection of the state. It cannot be
sold, exchanged, or donated, subject to expropriation and other penalties; in
Peru, the law states that private ownership is under legal restraints.

Under state control, but limited to certain goods: In Brazil, national
property of the subsoil; in Colombia, pre-Columbian objects, colonial-period
artifacts, meteoric remains; in Costa Rica, archaeological remains (in the
ground); in Ecuador, exclusive state rights of archaeological possession; in
Uruguay, archaeological artifacts "extracted" from the ground; in Venezuela,
archaeological and artistic objects.

Partial limitations to personal property: Compulsory communication of
tenure: Argentina, Bolivia (the owner must present an inventory), Dominican
Republic, Haiti, Nicaragua, Panama, and Paraguay. Obligation to communicate any property transfer or sale, donation, or inheritance: Argentina, Brazil,
Dominican Republic, Ecuador, Guatemala, and Haiti. Report a possible sale,
giving the state the option to buy: Costa Rica, Chile, Peru, Uruguay, and
Guatemala.

2. *Inventory*: Compulsory registration: Argentina, Bolivia, Brazil,
Colombia, Chile, Dominican Republic, Ecuador, Haiti, Mexico, Nicaragua,
Panama, Peru, and Uruguay.

3. *Imports*: In Argentina, duty-free art objects; in Ecuador, free imports of
all mobile patrimonial assets.

4. *Exports*: Totally prohibited: Bolivia, Ecuador, Guatemala (where it is considered a crime), Haiti, Panama, Paraguay, Peru (only allowed for exhibit), Puerto Rico (if discovered will be expropriated). Only with a special permit: Colombia, Costa Rica, Chile, Honduras (only allowed in case of exchange or temporary loan to museums), Dominican Republic (short-term exhibits), Mexico (only if temporary), Nicaragua, and Uruguay (only if temporary). Sectorial permit limitations: Argentina, limited to art objects and documents. Total prohibition, particular situations: Argentina (archaeological artifacts); Brazil (ancient books, bibliographical collections—in general, all those prior to 1889 and of the Portuguese colonial period); Dominican Republic (archaeological, ethnographic); Mexico ("original" documents related to the history of the country, and those books whose "rarity" makes them difficult to be replaced); Uruguay (manuscripts and "rare" objects).

5. *Excavation*: Its prohibition: Argentina (since 1908); Bolivia (since 1909—severe limitations. Supreme-Decree 07234 (1964) established the need for a permit.); Colombia, Costa Rica, and Chile (require a permit); Ecuador (severe penalties if done without authorization). Totally forbidden: Guatemala, Honduras, Mexico, Paraguay, and Peru.

Conclusions

This general overview of the most important legislation confirms the urgent need to unify the protection of the cultural patrimony. The CIECC mandate to the General Secretariat to prepare a draft of a model law, to be considered by the member countries of the O.A.S., seems an appropriate step in that direction.

Some questions are still awaiting an adequate response, according to certain critiques of the San Salvador Convention. The need remains to involve those countries outside the inter-American system whose cooperation is vital to making it truly effective. Consequently, a global approach is necessary.

A more precise assessment should be made of which cultural assets are to be effectively protected in order to lighten the administrative burdens of the regional customs services of the importing countries. The establishment of national legislation whose regulations could be practicably fulfilled and that is simple in its content and precise in its guidelines is vital for the protection of the cultural patrimony of Latin America.

NOTE

1. Signed by representatives of twenty-one member states in Washington, D.C., on April 15, 1935, and ratified by Brazil, Chile, Colombia, Cuba, the Dominican Republic, El Salvador, Guatemala, Mexico, the United States, and Venezuela.

4. Preservation of Latin American Cultural Patrimony: A View from Central America and Costa Rica

Frederick W. Lange

The topic I have been asked to address is a complex one. The aspects of the archaeological patrimony that I will discuss here are derived from the background of my research in Central America since 1966, participation in the first conference on defense of the cultural patrimony of Central America in San José, Costa Rica in 1975, and full-time employment with the National Museum of Costa Rica from 1976–1979. As such, some of my generalizations represent personal opinions, and may not be universally applicable. Our focus, as archaeologists, is on the preservation of the data base we need in order to pursue our careers. My broader concern, as a social scientist, is that the preservation of that data base often conflicts with the need for economic and social development.

The Preservation of Context

The preservation of the original context in which cultural remains were deposited is the primary need of the archaeologist. Context is of paramount importance whether we are analyzing a micro-setting within a site, comparing different sectors of a total site, or carrying out regional studies of patterns involving a large number of sites. Each research level has its own contextual requirements, but whatever the level, derivation of data from context is the basis for all anthropological comparative and interpretive statements.

Most cultural patrimony legislation deals with the movement of *objects*, while for the archaeologist it is the prevention of destruction of *context* that is most critical. The movement of objects stripped of their original contexts is of little concern to most archaeologists. What then is the status of, and what are the prospects for, the preservation of context in Latin America?

The Status of the Preservation of Context

The problem of preservation of cultural context does not arise solely in Latin America, but exists worldwide, wherever remains of earlier human occupations are found. Furthermore, cultural preservation within Latin America is not a homogeneous problem, but one that is heterogeneous, country by country. The principal variables affecting preservation of contexts in different countries seem to be (1) size of the country, (2) economic conditions, (3) level of pre-Columbian development, and (4) historical tradition. We find in many countries that destruction of context was begun in prehistoric times, was sometimes aggravated by the Spanish, and has usually reached major proportions in the last century.

The two principal influences on the archaeological cultural patrimony are socioeconomic and developmental. We can further divide each of these into two main sources of impact: (1) the impact of the general population, and of the professional exploiters of the patrimony; and (2) the impact of national governments and government-stimulated development, and the impact of internationally stimulated development. Let us look first at the impact of the general population.

The General Population

Within the general population, the majority have only casual encounters with archaeological resources, usually as they are digging ditches for irrigation or sanitary facilities, or plowing their fields for cultivation. The expansion of population into almost every habitable corner of Latin America has been a significant factor in this century, especially since modern populations tend to favor the same locations for settlement that prehistoric peoples did. Moreover, the vast majority of these people tend not to view archaeological materials as their cultural patrimony, but as an exploitable natural resource. These, unfortunately, are the people we have to depend upon most for voluntary cooperation in protection of the cultural patrimony.

Huaqueros or Pothunters

A second major group of nongovernment persons who have an impact on cultural resources are pothunters, or *huaqueros*. Again, their impact varies markedly from country to country, and even regionally within individual countries. We can also distinguish between what we might call the "casual" and the "full-time" huaquero.

The casual huaquero, whom we might also refer to as a "hobbyist," has an infrequent and relatively minor impact on cultural resources. Another casual pothunter, the subsistence huaquero, is responding to much different stimuli than the hobbyist, and his motivation merits more careful consideration. These are people who do not see cultural remains as patrimony, but as natural resources. Digging often takes place only as a last economic alternative, after a failed crop or other unexpected economic pressures. In this case, the cultural patrimony is the buffer between these people and severe economic deprivation.

Full-time huaqueros, on the other hand, are professional exploiters of the cultural patrimony. They are often subsidized by private collectors and commercial antiquity dealers, and frequently utilize highly destructive power equipment in their digging. Among the population at large, these persons are the most serious threat to the cultural patrimony because they provide the link between the source, through the middlemen, or dealers, to the international market and its economic rewards.

It is also worthwhile to take a brief look at "huaqueroing" as a regular means of economic employment. It really is not profitable on a steady basis. As with wild-cat oil drilling or mining, only the infrequent spectacular successes are recounted; the much more frequent failures go largely unmentioned.

However, in most countries, neither the casual nor professional huaquero poses the level of threat to the cultural patrimony that national governments and international development agencies represent.

The Impact of Governments or
Government-Stimulated Developments

For the past twenty years, and into the indefinite future, the greatest threat to cultural patrimony comes in the guise of government-sponsored and government-stimulated economic development. The construction of highways, ports, impoundments, urbanizations, irrigation systems, and tourism complexes, as well as mining and industrialization have probably directly or indirectly damaged more sites in the past two decades than have all the huaqueros in history. The direct impact comes from actual site loss during construction; the indirect impact occurs when land clearing and highway construction make areas easily available to vandals and exploiters, to which access previously had been very difficult.

The Mexican government has developed an excellent program for attempting to mitigate the effects of development on cultural resources, and Costa Rica has also recently passed a progressive law dealing with the same problem. For the first time, construction on government or government-supported projects in Costa Rica will be required to cease for at least fifteen days if archaeological remains are encountered.[1] More important, funding is guaranteed to the National Museum for carrying out the necessary salvage operation during that two-week period.

These examples demonstrate that the government of a country can be the only source of restraint for major development projects which have an impact upon the cultural patrimony, and the only source or stimulus for funding of the rescue of endangered resources. Salvage research is not always adequate, and not necessarily the best solution to the problem, but it is a significant improvement over past practices.

Just as it is very difficult to pinpoint the economic impact of private multinational corporations on national economies, it is equally difficult to gauge the impact of multinational governmental lending and development agencies on national patrimonies. Neither the World Bank, the International Development Bank, nor the Organization of American States, requires a cultural resource impact statement as a regular part of the process of project development and aid; nor do they provide for the expenses of archaeological research as part of the project package. The destruction of cultural patrimonies by such development projects is much more severe than that from illegal digging, largely because the impact tends to be large scale and regional.

The problems of coordinating cultural resource preservation with national planning activities is again not unique to Latin America, but reflects a general lack of comprehensive cultural resource management in the majority of nations worldwide. This lack of a positive emphasis on cultural resources, especially in areas without monumental architecture, is in turn related to a lack of adequate national training programs for archaeologists. This lack can, in turn, be related to historical patterns of the development of Latin American educational systems, and the dampening effect of European and North American intellectual imperialism during much of the twentieth century.

Problems in Protection of the Context and Content of the Cultural Patrimony

We can, at this point, identify two sets of problems in the protection of the cultural patrimony: the practical and the philosophical.

Practical problems include the fact that cultural resources are broadly distributed through space, and those that remain are concentrated primarily in rural areas. This makes vigilance over these resources extremely difficult. We also see that prehistoric boundaries of culture areas do not necessarily coincide with modern political realities. Thus, one part of a prehistoric area may be well protected, while another is not; the archaeologist must have all sides of the picture to conduct effective research. The Maya culture area, which is incorporated into at least five modern political entities, is an excellent example.

The philosophical problems focus on the placement of cultural resources within a broader scheme of national and regional priorities, relative to health, education, military, and other commitments. In making a case for the importance of cultural resources within national priorities, and reflected in the fact that it is a North American making this case here today, we can see ourselves as imposing a European-derived world view on the peoples and countries of the developing and developed parts of Latin America.

Historically, there has been a direct correlation between either national economic success, the degree of Europeanization, or the size of the monumental architecture, and the national (meaning governmental) commitment to cultural resource preservation. Initially, the importance of almost all Latin American prehistoric cultural remains was defined by persons with European or North American training. During the 1930s, 1940s, and 1950s individuals and small groups of professionals in different Latin American countries began to develop interests and skills in archaeology. Their main professional interaction was still with North Americans and Europeans, however. It is only relatively recently, and Mexico is certainly the best example of this, that national programs of training and research have become fully developed. It is only from this platform that the significance of the regional cultural patrimony can actually be defined.

Whether foreigner or national, it is the educated elite which defines the significance of the cultural resources and expresses concern for their conservation. However, it is the mass of population, again largely rural, which controls its future. Are scientists taking an unrealistic approach to the preservation of cultural resources if they block or impede necessary economic activities? The concept of the value of history is to a large extent an abstract one derived from the educational process; it has very little meaning or value in the milpa (maize field, or clearing) or in pulling water from a well.

An indigenous scientist may have one perspective on where cultural resources fit into a broader cultural scheme (although these ideas may have been tempered by acquired values). However, a foreign scientist must be especially concerned with the scientific and humanistic conflict of placing the significance of researching the past on a higher level than the needs of the present. There is a great deal of value to be learned from the past, but within the context of developing nations, there must be limits to the extent to which it is studied at the expense of the present. Archaeologists who have conducted any research in Latin America, and who have lived among the rural poor, have truly been seduced by the ivory tower if they think the importance of their research comes before the well-being of those people. In the search for a balance, the latter must be the most weighty factor.

Conclusion

Whose responsibility is the protection of the patrimony? It must be placed with the governments who control the terrain where the resources are located. Each government should build a national consensus, and hopefully regional agreements might also emerge, about the priority level of cultural resources within each country and region. The international development agencies must also assign a value to cultural resources within their development plans to ensure that development efforts accommodate national cultural values. If necessary, these agencies should be ready to fund research and personnel.

As a profession, archaeologists should strive to promote the preservation of cultural resources within a realistic framework of Latin American priorities. This means balancing the preservation of the past with the needs of the present and future, and creating a sense of responsibility for cultural remains that transcends modern political boundaries.

The Latin American people themselves must want to preserve any sizeable vestiges of their cultural past. That requires a massive educational effort among largely rural populations who either do not comprehend science, do not care, or who simply have more pressing problems. Scientists, diplomats, educators, and bureaucrats can force the protection of selected elements or areas of the past by creating archaeological preserves, but not the full array of contexts necessary for archaeological research. It is with realism, rather than pessimism, that I conclude that the welfare of the cultural patrimony of Latin America "está en las manos de la gente."[2]

NOTES

1. The constitutionality of the new Costa Rican law protecting the cultural patrimony has been challenged in the Costa Rican Supreme Court. As of this revision, the ultimate fate of the legislation is uncertain.

2. "Is in the hands of the people."

5. Cultural Patrimony Issues in Colombia

Cecilia Isaacs

The aspect of the protection of cultural patrimony that I shall discuss is one that is justly alarming: the "flight" of cultural and historical property. This is a euphemistic phrase which suggests that one should approach the issue with much care and tact, even though it is an ancient and universally known problem, recognized in bilateral and multilateral conventions and addressed in the laws of most countries of our hemisphere.

The malaise that concerns us today is truly ancient. At the beginning of the recorded history of our continent it took the form of plunder and destruction. Each country had its Zamárraga (the bishop who almost erased the pre-Hispanic cultures of Mexico). He burned Aztec and Mayan documents; others melted pre-Columbian gold pieces. It has been said that gold killed Colombian archaeology, and it came close to doing so. The price has certainly been high. Greed of the most abrasive nature has cursed our archaeology.

However, between our early history and the present the reasons and methods have changed. The reasons have certainly experienced a 180 degree turn. While historical works were destroyed as worthless symbols of worthless cultures yesterday, today they are "spirited away" by those who wish to preserve and extract knowledge from them. As to the modern methods, they run the gamut from the local petty smuggler to the international auctioneer on Madison Avenue, New York, or New Bond Street, London.

Setting aside for whom or how it is done, the fact is that historical and cultural treasures continue to leave their countries of origin, and, as a colleague said when I mentioned this problem, "Our countries seem powerless to stop it." This would seem to be the case, but it does not have to be. The existence today of illicit transactions involving national patrimonies is not for want of care on the part of countries like Colombia, Ecuador, Costa Rica or Peru. We have certainly shown our concern. We have enacted well-conceived, and sometimes strict laws to protect our patrimony. Current laws in Latin America describe this issue as being of "social and national interest" and the provisions therein as being of a "public order nature." When analyzing the Colombian law, a lawyer remarked that we consider the right to claim our cultural patrimony "as inalienable and imprescriptible." These are terms and concepts frequently found in the laws of other Latin American nations.

Curiously, Colombia began its efforts to combat the flight of its cultural property by passing legislation against the export of bibliographical material. The 1920 law prohibited the exportation, without the approval of the Colombian government and the advice of the Academies, of any papers, documents or objects belonging to public or private archives, libraries, and museums, if such property was of historical interest or import to the State. This law also dictated that rare and unique books could be borrowed only by making a deposit of double the amount of the estimated value of the book. Since then, restrictions have been relaxed—perhaps unwisely.

Colombia has been refining and redesigning its laws over the years to include the preservation and protection of practically all objects related to Colombian archaeology, history or culture which, because of their uniqueness or importance, deserve to be preserved by the nation. Current laws forbid the export and transfer of these objects without approval from the Instituto de Cultura, and punish illicit transactions with fines and/or imprisonment. The government has the right of first refusal and can request expropriation, provided that the items had previously been declared of public interest.

All this does not seem to suffice, and so some among us have resorted to unorthodox and somewhat Quixotic measures. I once read that the University of San Buenaventura, a Catholic university in Cali, had marked each of its old and important books with the warning: "Property of the University of San Buenaventura. Penalty of excommunication if stolen." I do not know whether this threat deterred any potential thief and I doubt whether his Holiness the Pope knew what was expected of him; but, it certainly shows a desperate attempt to plug the bibliographical drain.

Still, the risk is real and current, and national concern has never waned. Just last September *El Tiempo*, a major Colombian daily, carried a series of articles headlined: "The Unstoppable Bleeding of Our Historical and Cultural Patrimony." It dealt mainly with written material and of the concern of Colombian historians who believe that in a few years Colombian researchers will have to travel abroad to consult the sources of their country's history because very little will remain there. This is a sad prophecy, as in the opinion of many experts, Colombia has one of the most complete colonial archives in Latin America. Complaints are heard from all quarters. Eduardo Mendoza Varela, director of the Instituto de Cultura Hispánica, stated that most of the old books such topics as medicine, military tactics, travel, and geography had left the country.

These are not exaggerated concerns, nor are they based on ancient tales. A few days ago I received the list of the historical documents stolen from our national archives during the period between June 1980 and January 1981. Listed there are seventy-seven different documents from two volumes of the "Historical Sources" collection (called "Fondo Historia"), all of which are more than one-hundred years old. Public libraries are being ransacked and entire private collections and libraries are being sold for export. Such are, then, the discouraging results of our efforts.

A brief historical analysis of the Colombian laws leads us to believe that the country has a good juridical basis from which to deal with this problem. A cursory look at the current laws in our sister republics leads to a similar conclusion. What, then, is missing? Are we less able to retain our cultural patrimony than other, more developed, nations?

I do not think so. We cannot place the blame squarely on either underdevelopment or affluence. The flight of cultural patrimony, unlike other issues that spill over national frontiers, is not—unless we wish it—an economic problem whose solution is a soft or hard loan, or the growth of the GNP. It is true that, as in all law enforcement, these laws require resources in order to be upheld. Most of the tools are at our disposal at no extra cost, however.

Within an international framework, there are two principal means to protect cultural patrimony from crossing frontiers illegally: legislation, both domestic and international, and a program of education designed to form an alert, aware public. Education is always useful, but if we have any experience in this matter, we know that valuable historical and cultural objects are traded by local and international curators, researchers, diplomats and collectors who know all too well the value of the objects they covet and who do not always care about their provenance. As someone at the U.S. customs once remarked: "it is an affluent and cultured elite [that is responsible]." In the area of legislation we can mention first the international conventions and treaties which recognize and identify the problem and suggest procedures to follow, conventions and treaties which have long been drawn up and are still open for adherence by OAS and UNESCO member states. As to domestic laws which could enforce the conventions, we have seen that they are well on the way if not already in force.

However, it is disquieting to see that although the countries recognize the problem and the need to redress it, they do not sign the treaties. Colombia adhered to the first regional and international treaties, but has been slow at signing the 1970 UNESCO and 1976 El Salvador conventions. To the best of my knowledge, the United States has never been a party to any of these conventions. The President signed the UNESCO convention but there has been no congressional ratification.

Most of us are quite skeptical of multilateral agreements, and rightfully so, but I believe there is a lot to be said for the usefulness of such conventions. For one, they do not call for additional expenses on the part of the signatories, a significant benefit today. They could create a climate in which constructive measures can be taken and positive attitudes developed. They could also help create a climate in which it would be a stigma rather than a "coup de prestige" to remove outstanding historical and cultural properties from their countries of origin. This would be a good point of departure, for it is still possible for the former director of one of the most prestigious museums in the world to publish a tantalizing book on shady dealings without anyone questioning the ethics of such transactions.

Multilateral treaties and conventions can facilitate necessary procedures and, most important, demonstrate the willingness of the parties to collaborate, which is the essence of any policy the nations involved might wish to adopt. It is a sine qua non condition without which all efforts are in vain. The treaties recognize this. All stipulate that claims must first be handled through diplomatic channels, which is to say that amicable solutions are preferred over legal ones, although the possibility of resorting to the latter reinforces the former.

An excellent example of what collaboration and amicable solutions can achieve is that for several years Colombia had been trying to recover a letter by Antonio Nariño, which had surfaced at a university in the United States. The language and means employed had been legal, until Colombia decided to use diplomatic channels and appeal to collaboration rather than to the claim of rights. The result was swift and mutually satisfactory. Furthermore, no one was deprived of a research tool. A major point worth considering is that, unlike works in the plastic arts, important and unique bibliographical materials can today be photocopied without diminishing the information they might yield to scholars and researchers. It is not an "impossible dream" to say that there are modern techniques which make possible the return of such items to their countries of origin, without jeopardizing scholarly interests. On the contrary, we would then be recognizing the interdependent relationship of the learned communities of the world.

It is important to emphasize the sense of history demonstrated by the people in this example and their willingness to contribute to the cultural well-being of other nations. Cooperation and attitude are the crucial elements at play, and they do exist. Laws or penalties alone cannot suffice in this issue, so charged is it with abstract and emotional values. I hasten to add that I am not ignoring the value these items have in the market place. Rising prices and growing competition for increasingly scarce pieces inevitably encourage looting and dispersal. However, I trust that most believe strongly that the definition of cultural and historical patrimony means precisely what it says: the unique heritage of a nation, the source and the very fabric of its past, its present and its future. The alternatives to a sincere and sound effort now are less and less access to historical sources and more and more restrictions in the future. It will be a sad world indeed, if we question and cannot be answered, if we doubt and cannot be assured, if the doors to the knowledge of our past are literally locked because we failed to act responsibly today.

6. State Policy Toward the Film Industry in Brazil

Randal Johnson

Much has been written in recent years concerning the role of the public sector in Brazilian economic development, and many studies have referred to the important social role served by public enterprises.[1] Little has been said, however, about the state's relationship to cultural production. The state in Brazil has historically served as a patron, guarantor, regulator, repressor, and, at times, producer of culture.[2] While the state's intervention in the cultural arena can be traced back to the colonial period with the establishment of libraries, educational institutions, and more or less direct patronage of the arts, such intervention—along with similar state intervention in the economy and other areas of Brazilian society—increased rapidly in the twentieth century, especially under Getúlio Vargas's Estado Novo (1937–1945) and more recently since the military coup d'etat of 1964.[3]

In recent years, Brazil's authoritarian government has undertaken a veritable cultural offensive, creating numerous federal bodies designed to regulate certain cultural sectors or to formulate an official policy with regard to national culture.[4] In 1976 the Conselho Federal de Cultura (Federal Council of Culture, created in 1967) formulated an official state policy defining and delimiting legitimate areas of cultural concern and rendering explicit the legal foundations of government action in the cultural arena.[5]

Studies of Brazilian cultural policy are in their infancy. Only recently, for example, have film critics turned their attention away from the film-object and toward the modes of production of Brazilian cinema, in which the state has come to play a crucial role.[6] My purpose is to trace the evolution of state policy toward the Brazilian film industry, focusing primarily on the period from 1964 to the present, in the hope that such an overview will contribute to providing the groundwork for future studies concerning the relationship between the state and cultural production in Brazil.

State intervention in the film industry in Brazil can be traced back to the early 1930s when Getúlio Vargas first implemented what would turn out to be a long series of protectionist measures designed to give the national industry a modicum of stability for future development. Since that time, and especially in the last fifteen years, the role of the state has evolved from that of regulator of market forces to active agent and productive force in the industry. Since 1973 in a form of state capitalism the state has invested in the production of commercial

50

films by private production companies. It has also established a commercially oriented distributor, and more recently has entered the exhibition sector as well.

It was only after 1964, however, that a state policy toward cinema began to cohere with the creation, in 1966, of the Instituto Nacional do Cinema (National Film Institute), a semi-autonomous organization (*autarquia*) subordinated to the Ministry of Education and Culture, and in 1969 of Embrafilme (Empresa Brasileira de Filmes), a mixed-ownership enterprise subordinated, once again, to the Ministry of Education and Culture. In 1975 Embrafilme was reorganized and its powers were expanded. At that time it absorbed the executive functions of the Instituto Nacional do Cinema and its capital was increased from 6 million to 80 million cruzeiros. Under the reorganization the Union has a 99.9 percent control of the enterprise. In 1976 a new policy making body, the Conselho Nacional do Cinema (CONCINE), was created to assume the legislative functions of the now-extinct Instituto. CONCINE thus determines policy which is executed by Embrafilme.[7]

Embrafilme is responsible for many different kinds of activities. It produces and distributes cultural and educational films to schools and other non-profit organizations throughout the country. It supports the production of short-subject films and documentaries. It is involved in the preservation of Brazil's cinematic memory through the restoration of films that were thought to be lost or that are in an advanced stage of deterioration. It cooperates with the efforts of the *cinematecas* of both Rio de Janeiro and São Paulo and is responsible for the recent renovation of the cinemateca in Rio de Janeiro's Museum of Modern Art. It organizes courses for film industry technicians and, in coordination with the Conselho CAPES, provides scholarships for study abroad in the area of film production. It gathers and publishes statistics concerning the film industry as a whole and serves as an industry watchdog, assuring that all theaters throughout the country comply with existing cinematographic legislation. It publishes books on cinema as well as the magazine *Filme Cultura*. Embrafilme is thus involved in both commercial and non-commercial activities.

This discussion will be limited to Embrafilme's activities as they relate to the production, distribution, and exhibition of feature films, for that is the area where the paradoxes and contradictions of the state's role become most apparent. While on the one hand the state, through its coercive apparatus, has maintained a certain adversary relationship with Brazilian cinema (censorship), on the other there has been a convergence of interests and a marriage of convenience between independent producers and Embrafilme. Although Embrafilme may, in one sense, be seen as an example of preemptive co-optation on the part of the military regime, in another it is the result of a long struggle of Brazilian filmmakers for state incentives and protection.[8]

Justifications for state intervention in the film industry fall into two broad

categories, one economic and the other cultural. Economic justifications for
state intervention are largely responses to the domination of the Brazilian film
market by foreign, mostly American, film distributors. It is argued that state
intervention is necessary to curb imports and reduce the outward flow of
currency reserves as well as to stimulate an adequate level of sustained growth
in the national industry (the "infant industry" argument) through the correction
of market imbalances and distortions and through the provision of production
capital in a traditionally under-capitalized industry.

Culturally, the cinema is seen as an instrument of national integration. It
transmits and reinforces cultural and social values which are seen as essential to
national development. It also provides a kind of psychological prestige value.
Filmmaker Gustavo Dahl once remarked, "every great nation has a great
cinema." If we accept Dahl's statement, then cinema can be seen as a somewhat subjective measure of a country's development. The cinema also transmits an image of the nation both at home and abroad. It is, therefore, not
surprising that the state would see it as a legitimate area of concern. Nor is it
surprising that Embrafilme entered both the distribution and production sectors
at a moment when Brazilian cinema was on the verge of being dominated by the
pornochanchada, a kind of film designed to bring a rapid return on investments
based on the exploitation of a vulgar sort of eroticism.[9]

Recent developments in Brazilian cinema and the state role therein are
based, therefore, on two fundamental conflicts: external (Brazilian cinema
versus international cinema for the domestic market) and internal (the "quality" cinema supported by Embrafilme versus the pornochanchada in competition for the reserve market). The internal conflict is in a sense a reflection of the
external, since the pornochanchada is produced largely with capital from the
exhibition sector, which has historically been aligned with foreign interests.[10]
It will be shown later that the state is at least indirectly responsible for the
pornochanchada, but before discussing this and other paradoxes of the state's
role in more detail, I will provide an overview of the development of the
Brazilian film industry and the evolution of the state's role in that industry.

The Development of the Brazilian Film Industry

Cinema has a long history in Brazil. The first film was shown in 1896, a
short six months after Lumière revealed his *cinématographe* in Paris.[11] Within
two years, the first filmmaking equipment was imported. Early filmmakers
were highly successful because of a vertically integrated system of production
and exhibition. It may be recalled that the American film industry developed so
rapidly in the first quarter of the century partially because of a similar vertically
integrated system of film commerce. The fledgling Brazilian film industry
continued to grow and thrive throughout its first decade—producing some 100

films per year in 1908 and 1910—a period which has since been called the Bela Epoca of Brazilian cinema.[12]

By World War I, American cinema had been organized as an international industry, and the takeover of the Brazilian market was easily achieved. The arrival of American distributors in the late teens and early twenties drove a wedge between local production and exhibition, and the domestic market began to be organized for the commercialization of American films. World War I virtually eliminated European competition from the Brazilian market. The crisis for Brazilian cinema was exacerbated as the practice of buying films outright for exhibition was replaced with a rental system in which the exhibitor paid the distributor a percentage of total box-office income. The more highly polished American films, which were already paid for in their home market, could be offered at a lower price than the rougher local product, and the foreign film became the standard by which all films were to be judged.

Brazilian production did not end with the demise of the Bela Epoca, but it did become relegated to a minor place in its own market. Without being able to depend even on its own market for a return on investments, national cinema lacked the capital necessary to develop on an industrial scale. Production became cyclical, often far removed from the country's cultural and economic centers. The only sustained production was that of newsreels and short documentaries about local events. Despite the efforts of some of Brazilian cinema's "pioneers," the situation in 1930 was virtually the same as in 1920: the domestic market did not provide an outlet for whatever local production did indeed exist.

Until the last twenty years or so, the dream of Brazilian producers was to emulate Hollywood and build a national film industry based on large studios with expensive sets and contract stars.[13] The reality of the national industry, however, has been quite different. If studio production is the dream, an atomized, artisan mode of production has been the reality. With the advent of sound in the late 1920s it was felt that foreign "talkies" would be unintelligible to Brazilian audiences and that local studios could finally develop without serious foreign competition. Adhemar Gonzaga founded the Cinédia Studios in Rio de Janeiro in 1930 and was followed in 1933 by Carmen Santos's Brasil Vita Filmes, the first two attempts at concentrated industrialization in the history of Brazilian cinema. Between 1930 and 1945 Cinédia averaged two films per year, reaching a high of five in 1936. Brasil Vita produced only thirteen films between its founding and 1958.[14] The optimism of the Brazilian film industry was short-lived as production dropped from twenty-seven films in 1930 to a mere five in 1935 (two of which were by Cinédia). Foreign cinemas once again strengthened their hold on the domestic market.

Other attempts at concentrated industrialization followed in subsequent years. In 1943 a number of producers founded what would turn out to be the

most successful attempt at continuous production on an industrial scale in the
history of Brazilian cinema: the Atlântida studios of Rio de Janeiro. Atlântida
was particularly successful after its acquisition, in 1947, by Luis Severiano
Ribeiro, owner of the largest exhibition chain in Brazil as well as of a major
distributor. His acquisition of Atlântida provided it with a vertically integrated
system of production, distribution and exhibition, which, as has already been
noted, was responsible for the initial success of the Bela Epoca in the first
decade of the century. Atlântida combined its powerful position in the market
with the production in series of relatively inexpensive but immensely popular
film genres, notably the *chanchada*, or light musical comedy. Between 1943
and 1977 Atlântida produced some eighty-five films. Its heyday was the period
from 1945 to 1960. After that time the chanchada began to lose appeal due to
the growing influence of television. Atlântida fondly recalled its production of
this very popular genre in a 1975 film, *Assim era Atlântida* (That Was
Atlântida), modeled on the American *That's Entertainment*. Atlântida was
successful, in short, not only because of its advantageous position in the
domestic market, but also because its production was geared for and based on
the commercial potential of that market.

In sharp contrast to Atlântida was the founding in 1949 of the Vera Cruz
Studios in São Paulo. Created with capital from the Matarazzo group, Vera
Cruz's studios were modeled on the M.G.M. studios at a time when the studio
system in Hollywood itself was beginning to decline. Although Vera Cruz
improved the technical quality of Brazilian cinema, it made many serious
errors. It set up an expensive and luxurious system with contract stars, technicians, and directors, but without the economic infrastructure on which to base
such a system. Too ambitious, it aimed at conquering the world market before
consolidating the Brazilian market. In order to reach the international market, it
naively left distribution in the hands of Columbia Pictures, an organization
more interested in promoting its own films than in fostering a vital Brazilian
industry. Vera Cruz drove production costs way above the lucrative potential of
the Brazilian market, and was finally forced to resort to temporary, but ultimately suicidal, palliative solutions for its problem of capital shortages: short-
term, high-interest loans. Unable to successfully recoup its investments in the
domestic market—only one of its films, *O cangaceiro*, (The Outlaw) made a
profit—and unable to reach the world market (except with that same film), Vera
Cruz went bankrupt in 1954 after producing eighteen feature films.[15]

Coinciding with the final years of Vera Cruz, however, was the emergence
of a new mentality among some Brazilian producers, rejecting the cloistered
artificiality and expense of the studio system in favor of an independent mode of
production taking Italian neo-realism as its model: the use of non-professional
actors, location shooting, collective production financing and, especially, low
production costs. While independent, artisan production had always been the

reality of Brazilian cinema, this new movement represents the first time such a production strategy was adopted by choice rather than circumstance. In the late 1950s and early 1960s this new mode of production blossomed into the internationally acclaimed Cinema Novo movement. Rather than being concentrated around large studios, production is atomized into many small production companies which may produce only one film per year, if that. In this system directors often produce or at least control their own films, thus guaranteeing thematic, stylistic, and political independence.[16]

This model of film production still prevails in Brazil. In 1977, for example, seventy-three films were produced by sixty-five different production companies.[17] Of that total, twenty-four were co-produced by the state enterprise Embrafilme. The specific shape of the state role vis-à-vis the film industry has to a large extent been determined by this model of film production. Mexico, in contrast, turned early toward a system based on large studios, and this is reflected in the form of state intervention in the Mexican film industry, with the state owning major studios.[18] In Brazil the state has tended to support small, independent producers.

Protectionism and the Film Industry

Faced with American domination of local film markets, European countries have traditionally used two different forms of protectionist measures in their attempts to ensure the development of national film industries: (1) limitations on imports and (2) screen quotas for local films, that is, a guaranteed reserve market for national production.[19] Import limitations can take various forms, ranging from import quotas to increased import tariffs and customs duties. Brazilian authorities have not imposed import quotas, and tariffs and duties have traditionally been light or non-existent for foreign films (but not, paradoxically, for raw film stock). In recent years a number of measures have been taken which increase the cost of foreign films entering the country. Import quotas have not been imposed due to a number of international trade accords (GATT, the General Agreement on Tariffs and Trade, for example) in which Brazil has agreed to the principle of the free flow of motion pictures across national boundaries. Such agreements have remained in effect due, in part, to high-level lobbying by local representatives of the American export cartel, the Motion Pictures Association of America.

Screen quotas, reserving a specified amount of screen time in all movie theaters for the exhibition of national films, have been the backbone of state policy toward the film industry in Brazil. The principle of the screen quota for Brazilian films was established by two laws implemented by Getúlio Vargas in 1932 and 1939.[20] The 1932 decree determined that all programs of foreign films exhibited in the country must include the exhibition of one national short documentary or newsreel. Though fought vigorously by distribution and exhibition groups, the measure did stimulate the production of up to 100 short films per year, guaranteeing at least a modest income for local producers.[21] The effects of the measure were short-lived, however, since in 1937 the government's newly established propaganda agency began producing films which fulfilled the requirements of the law.[22]

In 1939 a decree organized and regulated the activities of the Estado Novo's Departamento da Imprensa e Propaganda (DIP). This decree determined as well that all theatres in the country were obligated to exhibit at least one national feature-length film per year. The Propaganda Department was empowered to determine and pass judgement on the quality of films eligible for compulsory exhibition. This direct relationship between the government's censorship agency and the screen quota remained in effect until 1966 and the creation of the Instituto Nacional do Cinema. Nothing essentially new occurred in state policy toward the film industry from 1939, during the authoritarian Estado Novo, until 1966 during another period of authoritarian rule, when the Instituto Nacional do Cinema inaugurated a new phase of development for Brazilian cinema.

Although the initial quota of one film per year seems like mere tokenism, in fact it was an important measure in that it legally established Brazilian cinema's right to a share of its own market as well as the principle of governmental intervention to protect the still-fledgling national film industry. The immediate effect of this law can be seen in production figures for the period, which increased from a mere seven films in 1939 to thirteen films in 1940 (see table 1). The shortage of raw film stock during World War II erased this increase, and production fell to four films in 1941 and 1942. The screen quota for national films has gradually increased over the years, especially in the sixties and seventies, and now stands at 140 days per year of compulsory exhibition of Brazilian films (see table 1). Under these protectionist measures, Brazilian cinema's share of its own market has grown from less than 2 percent in 1950 to over 30 percent in 1980 (see table 2).[23]

The screen quota for Brazilian films has had a number of effects. While it has guaranteed national production at least a chance to compete among equals for exhibition, it has also limited the indiscriminate importation of foreign films. Since foreign distributors and importers must also compete for a smaller portion of the total market, the tendency is for only the best films (or the most commercial) to be imported, even though the television market tends to undermine this competition. In 1975, 1,329 films were exhibited by Rio de Janeiro television stations. Of that number, only six were Brazilian.[24] Brazil continues to be the second largest importer of films in the world, and a screen quota has not yet been imposed on television. The quota has, however, forced the theatrical exhibitor to be more actively interested in competing for the best

Table 1

FILM PRODUCTION AND THE SCREEN QUOTA FOR NATIONAL FILMS IN BRAZIL, 1930–1980

Year	National Production (Features)	Screen Quota
1930	18	
1931	17	
1932	14	One short for each program of
1933	10	foreign films.
1934	7	
1935	6	
1936	7	
1937	6	
1938	8	
1939	7	One feature per year.
1940	13	
1941	4	
1942	4	
1943	8	
1944	9	
1945	8	
1946	10	Three features per year.
1947	11	
1948	15	
1949	21	
1950	20	
1951	22	One feature for every eight
1952	34	foreign films exhibited.
1953	29	
1954	25	
1955	28	
1956	29	
1957	36	
1958	44	
1959	34	Forty-two days per year,
1960	34	distributed by quarter.
1961	30	
1962	27	
1963	32	Fifty-six days per year.
1964	27	
1965	33	
1966	28	
1967	44	
1968	54	
1969	53	Sixty-three days per year.
1970	83	Seventy-seven days per year.
1971	94	Eighty-four days per year.
1972	70	
1973	58	
1974	77	

Table 1 (continued)
FILM PRODUCTION AND THE SCREEN QUOTA FOR NATIONAL FILMS IN BRAZIL, 1930–1980

Year	National Production (Features)	Screen Quota
1975	85	112 days per year.
1976	84	
1977	72	
1978	101	133 days per year.
1979	96	140 days per year.
1980	102	

Sources: Alcino Teixeira de Melo, *Legislação do Cinema Brasileiro*, 2 vols. (Rio de Janeiro: Embrafilme, 1978). Annual reports, Embrafilme, 1978, 1979, 1980.

Table 2
DIVISION OF BRAZILIAN FILM MARKET BETWEEN NATIONAL AND FOREIGN FILMS, 1971–1978

Year	Brazilian (%)	Foreign (%)
1971	13.8	86.2
1972	16.2	83.8
1973	15.9	84.1
1974	15.2	84.8
1975	17.7	82.3
1976	20.8	79.2
1977	24.5	75.5
1978	29.2	70.8

Source: *Cinejornal*, Departamento de Documentação e Divulgação, Embrafilme, I (July 1980), p. 3.

Brazilian films. Previously this had not occurred since exhibitors often preferred the guaranteed profit offered by foreign films. The screen quota, finally, is a non-discriminatory measure, since any and all Brazilian films may compete for exhibition within the reserve market (that is, all films with proper approval from federal censors).

Paradoxically, protectionist measures are at least indirectly responsible for the creation of the pornochanchada, a genre that the state is combating without resorting to direct censorship. By increasing Brazilian cinema's screen quota and forcing exhibitors to diminish profits earned from the exhibition of foreign films, the state has in a sense encouraged them to produce their own films to fulfill the quota. Such "quota quickies" are made at a very low cost with non-professional actors and are directed at a specific (male) audience. The risk is low and the return is quick.[25] More recently, government censors have contributed to the success of the genre by creating a special classification for "pornographic" films. The law stipulates that the films' advertising must warn the public that the films contain offensive material. The word "pornographic," spread across marquees throughout the country, is used by exhibitors as a promotional gimmick.

While import quotas have not been imposed on foreign films, protectionist measures have been taken with the purpose of rendering them more expensive in the domestic market, thus, ideally, equalizing to some degree the cost to exhibitors of local and foreign products. The most important of these measures, fully implemented by the Instituto Nacional do Cinema only in the mid-1970s, is the compulsory copying of foreign films in national laboratories. Previously, film importers and foreign distributors had been able to import all their copies of a given film, since customs duties and import tariffs have traditionally been light. Compulsory copying not only increases the cost of imports and makes distributors more selective with respect to the films imported, but also provides a needed stimulus for an important infrastructural area of the industry.

It is within the context of protectionism that one must examine the evolution of the state's role from regulator of market forces to active agent and productive force in the film industry. The state has intervened not only in production, but also in the distribution and exhibition sectors in an attempt to overcome the bottlenecks that have traditionally stifled the growth of national production. I will discuss briefly the financial assistance provided the film industry by the Instituto Nacional do Cinema before proceeding to an examination of Embrafilme and state policy toward the film industry in the 1970s.

Financial Assistance to the Film Industry Under I.N.C.

The Instituto Nacional do Cinema (I.N.C.) was created in November of 1966 by the government of Castelo Branco under powers granted by the Second Institutional Act.[26] Attempts to create such an institute had been made since 1951, when Getúlio Vargas asked director Alberto Cavalcânti to form a Comissão Nacional de Cinema with the explicit purpose of formulating a legal project for the institute. The Cavalcânti Commission, as it has since come to be known, proposed not only an Instituto Nacional do Cinema, but also a mixed-ownership film production company in which the state would have a 51 percent interest. Cavalcânti's proposal was approved by the Chamber of Deputies in 1953 but died a slow and anonymous death in the Senate. A new proposal was made in 1957 by the Kubitschek-appointed Comissão Federal de Cinema, and was reexamined in 1958 and 1959 by the newly formed Grupo de Estudos da Indústria Cinematográfica (GEIC). GEIC's proposal was reformulated in subsequent years by the Grupo Executivo da Indústria Cinematográfica (GEICINE), created in 1961 during the fleeting presidency of Jânio Quadros.[27] A modified version of GEICINE's proposed film institute was the one that became law through executive decree in 1966.

The Instituto Nacional do Cinema is thus the result of a long struggle by film directors and producers to have cinema recognized as an industry whose problems can be solved only by governmental action.[28] As an untested hypothesis I would suggest that such an institute became reality only in 1966 because the authoritarian executive was more impervious to the lobbying of foreign distributors than was the legislative branch of government.[29] The I.N.C. was formed by executive decree only after the legislature had been unable to move forward with the project. The patronage factor must also be taken into consideration. The president of GEICINE, which formulated the final proposal for the institute, was critic and filmmaker Flávio Tambellini, who also happened to be the brother-in-law of Planning Minister Roberto Campos. Embrafilme was created three years later, largely as a result of Tambellini's influence with the government.[30]

The Instituto Nacional do Cinema was empowered to formulate and execute government policy relative to the development of the Brazilian film industry and to serve as a regulatory agency vis-à-vis that industry. This includes a wide array of specific functions, but the mainstay of its program of financial assistance to the industry was a subsidy provided to national producers based on the box-office income of films exhibited. The I.N.C.'s subsidy is an extension of a program initiated by the municipal government of São Paulo in 1955 shortly after the bankruptcy of Vera Cruz, and of a similar program initiated in the state of Guanabara by Carlos Lacerda in the mid-1960s. The subsidy program is the first direct federal subvention of the national film industry and has had far-reaching consequences for its development, since it attempts for the first time to equalize the average cost of a film with its average income and to provide producers with an incentive to accelerate production.[31] The subsidy was based on a percentage of the total box-office income of individual films. It was a democratic subsidy in the sense that it was paid to all national films exhibited, without regard to genre, social or cultural relevance, or even technical quality. Since it was based on box-office receipts, the most successful films received the largest subsidies. The I.N.C. thus attempted to promote the production of films with a commercial appeal. At the same time, an additional subsidy was offered to a limited number of films (usually twelve per year) based on their artistic or cultural importance or quality. The films in this category were chosen by a panel of representatives from different sectors of the industry, including critics. The amount of the award was based on the monthly minimum wage, thus freeing it from the dictates of the marketplace. In the nine years of its existence, the I.N.C. paid out some 47 million cruzeiros (unadjusted) in general subsidies and an additional 6 million to the "quality" films.[32]

The subsidy program has continued under the expanded powers of Embrafilme. In 1980 alone, Embrafilme paid out over one and one-half million dollars to national producers.[33]

The subsidy has been an extremely important program, for it guarantees an income to small producers who might not be solvent without it. The amount of the subsidy, as has already been noted, is determined by the marketplace. While the program has been significant for the development of the Brazilian film industry, such subsidies can tend to introduce false economies into the film industry and lead producers to think not in terms of the market itself, but rather in terms of the additional increment guaranteed by the state.[34]

Another form of financial assistance to the film industry initiated by I.N.C. has come in the form of prizes, or cash awards, to the best film, best director, best editor, and so on. Various national festivals which are co-sponsored by state bodies also provide cash awards to members of the industry.

The I.N.C. also set up a program of film production financing. A 1962 profit remittance law had determined that 40 percent of a foreign distributor's income tax on profit derived from the exhibition of foreign films be optionally deposited in the Banco do Brasil for possible use by the distributor in the co-production of national films. Between 1962 and 1966, two films were financed under the law, and neither was distributed commercially. The idea behind the law was that the foreign company would have a vested interest in the film which would lead to its being distributed abroad. This deposit was originally established as an option for foreign distributors to participate financially in the co-production of Brazilian films, and thus represents a certain internationalist mentality within state policy and within the I.N.C. The decree-law that founded the I.N.C. made the deposit mandatory. If the distributors chose not to co-produce national films, the money deposited became part of I.N.C.'s budget. By 1969, thirty-eight films had participated in the program. With the creation of Embrafilme in 1969, the unused portion of the deposit reverted to the enterprise rather than to I.N.C., and from that point on the option to co-produce was eliminated.[35]

While many producers took advantage of this financing program, opposition to it was widespread since it represented a potential bonus for foreign distributors which could result in the internationalization of the national film industry.[36] There was no risk involved for the foreign company, since the money to be used in co-production was owed the Union anyway. Among films co-produced under this program were Carlos Diegues's *Os herdeiros* (The Heirs, 1969), Joaquim Pedro de Andrade's *Macunaíma* (1969), Arnaldo Jabor's *Pindorama* (1971), and Nelson Pereira dos Santos' *Como era gostoso o meu francês* (How Tasty Was My Little Frenchman, 1971–1972), just to mention some films by directors associated with Cinema Novo.

During the existence of the I.N.C., the screen quota for Brazilian films doubled from 56 to 112 days per year. In order to properly oversee the market obligatory use of standardized tickets and box-office reporting sheets and later the obligatory use of I.N.C.-approved and -sold cash registers and entrance gates that register the number of spectators entering individual theaters. These measures have tended to limit box-office fraud and to provide more reliable statistics concerning cinematic commerce in the country. The sale of these items was a major source of income for the I.N.C. and has continued to be so for Embrafilme.

Embrafilme/CONCINE

Embrafilme was created in 1969 by a decree promulgated by the provisional military junta ruling Brazil under powers of the First and Fifth Institutional Acts. A mixed-ownership enterprise subordinated to the Ministry of Education and Culture, Embrafilme was created initially to promote and distribute Brazilian films abroad and to "engage in commercial or industrial activities related to the principal object of its activity."[37] Seventy percent of Embrafilme's stock belonged to the Union, 29.4 percent to the Instituto Nacional do Cinema, and only 0.6 percent to private shareholders.

In a 1972 film industry congress, producers Luis Carlos Barreto, Roberto Farias and others proposed that the I.N.C. be transformed into a Conselho Nacional de Cinema with legislative powers and that Embrafilme be transformed from a mixed-ownership enterprise to a public enterprise with executive functions and administrative and financial autonomy. In 1975 Embrafilme was reorganized, absorbing the executive functions of I.N.C., but it remained, at least in name, a mixed-ownership enterprise.[38] I.N.C.'s share of the enterprise reverted to the Union, giving it 99.9 percent control. Under its expanded powers, Embrafilme was authorized to act in all areas of cinematic commerce. It had already entered the production and distribution sectors (1973). One result of the reorganization was that the enterprise moved into the exhibition sector by acquiring or leasing a number of cinemas with solvency problems. To this date it has not attempted to expand the exhibition sector, although in 1978 then director Roberto Farias proposed the creation of five thousand additional theaters, which would bring the country's total to eight thousand. When correlated with population, eight thousand theaters would place Brazil on the level of Spain with regard to the number of inhabitants served by each theater.[39]

In 1976 the Conselho Nacional de Cinema (CONCINE) was created, again, directly subordinate to the Minister of Education and Culture, in order to serve as a legislative and policy making body in matters concerning the film industry. CONCINE is made up of representatives from the ministries of Education and Culture, Justice, Industry and Commerce, Foreign Affairs, Finance, and Communications. The director of Embrafilme is also a member of the council.

Initially, Embrafilme was not particularly successful in its primary function, that is, the distribution of Brazilian films abroad. More recently, however, its attempts at exporting have begun to bear fruit. In its first nine years of existence, Embrafilme negotiated sales of only U.S.$300 thousand. In 1981 alone, its foreign sales amounted to over U.S.$1 million, and it is projected that the figure will rise to $4.5 to $5 million in 1982. Embrafilme has opened offices in the United States and France, and in 1982 it will open offices in Buenos Aires and Lima in order to expand more effectively in the Latin American market. Packages of Brazilian films have recently been sold to both the Republic of China and the Soviet Union. Concentration remains focused on Latin American markets, where Brazilian films have been out-grossing American blockbusters.[40]

Even before its 1975 reorganization, Embrafilme initiated a number of programs highly relevant to the development of the film industry. In 1973 it began its activity as a distributor. Today, it is the second largest distributor in Brazil, trailing slightly behind the Cinema International Corporation, which includes Metro, Paramount, Walt Disney, and Universal. Embrafilme's distribution income in 1981 was on the order of 800 million cruzeiros. C.I.C.'s income was around 1.1 billion cruzeiros.[41] Embrafilme is the only distributor of national films to be organized nationwide and now accounts for some 30 to 35 percent of all national films distributed in Brazil. The distributor is a purely commercial operation, functioning as do most other distributors in the country and receiving approximately 10 percent of the gross box-office income of the films it distributes.

Since 1973, Embrafilme has engaged in three basic programs of financial assistance and investment in the film industry (besides the subsidy program described earlier): (1) film financing, (2) co-production, and (3) advance on distribution. In the financing program Embrafilme functions as a film bank, granting long-term, low-interest loans to production companies for the making of individual films. More traditional forms of bank financing are impractical due to the high risk and slow return on investment in the film industry. Traditional bank loans speeded the bankruptcy of the Vera Cruz studios in the mid-fifties. This program of financial assistance has come to be the least used of the various financial programs available for the undercapitalized Brazilian film industry. As of January 1981, *Bye Bye Brasil* was the last film to take advantage of this system of financing. Between 1974 and 1979 Embrafilme provided such financing to thirty-nine films in the amount of almost 14 million cruzeiros.

The advance on distribution became available with Embrafilme's creation of its own distributor. The amount provided varies according to the film's stage of production and to its relationship to the enterprise, that is, if a film is co-produced by Embrafilme it may receive up to a certain amount; if not, it falls into another category and receives a different amount. The advance on distribution may be paid the producer at the project stage, at the post-production stage, or when the film is completed and ready for distribution. The amount invested in distribution per se varies according to what are judged to be the commercial potential and the marketing needs of the individual film.

Finally, in 1973 Embrafilme initiated a program of co-production financing in which it enters selected film projects with up to 30 percent of total production costs, receiving in return a 30 percent share of profits. For a number of reasons, this amount has increased in recent years to 100 percent of a film's financing in some cases (*A idade da terra, Eles não usam black-tie*). It is with this program, specifically, that the state becomes a producer of culture. Between 1973 and 1979, Embrafilme signed contracts for the co-production of 114 feature films plus nineteen pilots for television series. These films were or are being made by eighty-nine different production companies. With the co-production, conflicts have arisen between the commercial and cultural objectives of the enterprise. Embrafilme has tended to produce films with some sort of cultural or social significance, which may or may not have great commercial potential. The commercially oriented distributor tends to concentrate on films with a certain box-office appeal, regardless of whether they have been co-produced by the enterprise or not. The result has been that many films co-produced by Embrafilme are relegated to secondary exhibition circuits or to the distributor's dusty shelves.

Embrafilme's funding for these and other programs derives from distribution income, the sale of standardized tickets and box-office reporting sheets to exhibitors, interest on film financing loans, and a tax paid by foreign and domestic producers for the development of the industry. The enterprise also receives 70 percent of the income tax on profit remittances owed by foreign distributors. Around 15 percent of its annual budget comes directly from the Ministry of Education and Culture. It has also taken out loans from the National Development Bank (BNDE) to finance film projects. Its total assets in 1979 were some U.S.$14 million. It has yet to become self-sufficient.

Embrafilme's decision to co-produce a film with independent producers or to grant other forms of financing is made by the enterprise's directorate (the director-general, the administrative director, and the director of non-commercial operations) based on a point system that considers the producer's or director's prior experience and activity in the film industry. While it has financed beginning directors who have worked on film projects with other directors, it has tended to support directors and producers with more experience and success in the industry. The first three items on Embrafilme's list of priorities for co-production and other forms of financing concern the number of prizes won in national and international festivals, including the I.N.C.'s awards for quality.[42]

Decisions to enter a co-production are made at the script level, and Embrafilme interferes on no other level of film production unless asked to render technical assistance. Intervention in the content of films does not occur.[43] Only twice has the state enterprise developed programs designed to foster a certain kind of film. In 1973 it sponsored a contest for films based on literary classics by deceased authors, and in 1977 it sponsored research for some fifteen projects for historical films. Neither of these programs has been fruitful.

Through its financing programs, Embrafilme has tended to reinforce the atomized model of production rather than turning, as did Mexico, to a production model based on large studios. Embrafilme does not own, in this sense, the means of film production. Rather, it makes viable the projects of independent producers, that is, producers who are often directors of the films they produce. Such support has guaranteed Brazilian cinema a wide variety of styles and themes. Combining its distribution and exhibition sectors with the work of independent producers, Embrafilme has created a modified form of vertical integration within the broader context of Brazilian cinema.[44]

What has been the result of the state's increased intervention in the film industry over the last few years? Between 1974 and 1978 the screen quota for Brazilian films increased from eighty-four to 133 days per year, an increase of 58 percent. During the same period, the total number of film spectators doubled from 30 to 60 million. The total income of Brazilian films went from around $13 million in 1974 to over $38 million in 1978, an increase of 288 percent. During the same period the gross income of foreign films increased at the lower rate of 19 percent. Embrafilme has provided needed capital for film production and has stimulated capital accumulation in the private sector. It now accounts for some 35 percent of all national films distributed throughout the country, and most films which would be considered "quality" products are linked to Embrafilme in some way, either through financing, co-production, or distribution.[45]

In summary, Brazilian state policy toward the film industry is based first and foremost on protectionist measures designed to correct an economic imbalance between foreign and national films on the domestic market in order to provide the local industry with at least the partial means of recovering its outlay in film production costs. The mainstay of the policy has been a screen quota, guaranteeing an increasingly large portion of national screen time for the exhibition of Brazilian films. Import quotas have not been implemented, yet massive and unrestricted importation of foreign films has been limited through measures such as the compulsory copying of foreign films in national laboratories and through increased costs for the foreign producer/distributor wishing to place its films on the Brazilian market.

Through its direct financial assistance—subsidies, prizes, loans, co-production financing, and advances on distribution—the state, through Embrafilme, has provided necessary production financing in a traditionally undercapitalized industry. Its support for independent producers has guaranteed the development of an increasingly strong national film industry based on a wide diversity of themes and styles, without imposing direct ideological constraints on directors. The Brazilian state has thus contributed to the creation of the premier cinema in Latin America. Much work remains to be done on the relationship between the state and cultural production in Brazil. It is my hope that this empirical outline of state intervention in the Brazilian film industry will contribute to laying the foundation for future studies.

NOTES

1. See, for example, Thomas J. Trebat, "An Evaluation of the Economic Performance of Public Enterprises in Brazil," Ph.D. dissertation, Vanderbilt University, 1978; Werner Baer, Richard Newfarmer, and Thomas Trebat, "On State Capitalism in Brazil: Some New Issues and Questions," *Inter-American Economic Affairs* 30 (Winter 1977), 69–91.

2. Octávio Ianni, "O Estado e a Organização da Cultura," *Encontros com a Civilização Brasileira* 1 (July 1978), 216–241; Walnice Galvão, *Saco de Gatos* (São Paulo: Duas Cidades, 1976), pp. 40–41; Antônio Cândido, "O escritor e o público," in *Literatura e Sociedade* (São Paulo: Editora Nacional, 1965).

3. See Thomas E. Skidmore, "Politics and Economic Policy Making in Authoritarian Brazil, 1937–71," and Phillipe C. Schmitter, "The 'Portugalization' of Brazil," in Alfred Stepan, ed., *Authoritarian Brazil* (New Haven: Yale University Press, 1973), pp. 3–46 and 179–232, respectively.

4. In "O Estado e a Organização da Cultura," Octávio Ianni lists the following federal organizations linked to different areas of cultural production: Conselho Federal de Cultura, Conselho Federal de Educação, Serviço Nacional de Teatro, Empresa Brasileira de Filmes, Fundação National de Arte, and the Conselho Nacional de Folclore. It is my understanding that the Serviço Nacional de Teatro, which was founded by Getúlio Vargas in 1937, has recently been transformed into an Instituto Nacional de Artes Cênicas. Ianni forgot to mention the Instituto Nacional do Livro which, among its many other functions, subsidizes the publishing industry. If we define the "state" as including a variety of public authorities at the federal, state, and local levels, then state intervention in culture is indeed pervasive.

5. Conselho Federal de Cultura, Ministério de Educação e Cultura, "Política Nacional de Cultura," 1976. See also Ianni, "O Estado e a Organização de Cultura"; and Manuel Diegues, Jr., "A estratégia cultural do governo e a operacionalidade da Política nacional de Cultura," in *Novas Frentes de Promoção de Cultura* (Rio de Janeiro: Fundação Getúlio Vargas, 1977).

6. See Ana Cristina César, *Literatura não é Documento* (Rio de Janeiro: Ministério de Educação e Cultura / FUNARTE, 1980): Jean-Claude Bernardet, *Cinema Brasileiro: Propostas para uma História* (Rio de Janeiro: Paz e Terra, 1979).

7. For legislation concerning these organizations and Brazilian cinema in general, see Alcino Teixeira de Mello, *Legislação do Cinema Brasileiro*, 2 vols. (Rio de Janeiro: Embrafilme, 1978).

8. For a definition and a discussion of co-optation, see Phillipe C. Schmitter, *Interest Conflict and Political Change in Brazil* (Stanford: Stanford University Press, 1971), especially pp. 72–73. Professional associations of filmmakers called for state protection as early as 1932. See *Relatório da Directoria*, Associação Cinematográphica de Productores Brasileiros, Secretary Armando de Moura Carijó (Rio de Janeiro: Typographo do Jornal do Commercio, 1937).

9. For a discussion of the pornochanchada and its modes of production, see Inimá Simões, *O Imaginário da Boca* (São Paulo: Secretaria Municipal de Cultura. Departamento de Informação e Documentação Artística, Centro de Documentação e Informação sobre Arte Brasileira Contemporânea, 1981); also Inimá Simões, "Sou mas quem não é?" in *Sexo e Poder* (São Paulo: Brasiliense, 1979), pp. 85–95.

10. Pornochanchada producer Antônio Polo Galante is quoted by Simões (*O Imaginário da Boca*, p. 28) as saying that 50 percent of his production costs come from exhibitors: "50 percent from the exhibitor; 50 percent is Galante. Who pays for my production is the exhibitor."

11. Information on the historical development of Brazilian cinema taken from Carlos Roberto Rodrigues de Souza, "A Fascinante Aventura do Cinema Brasileiro," 1 and 2, *O Estado de São Paulo*, Suplemento do Centenário, 25 October and 2 November 1975; Alex Viany, *Introdução ao Cinema Brasileiro* (Rio de Janeiro: Instituto Nacional do Livro, 1959); Paulo Emílio Salles Gomes and Adhemar Gonzaga, "Panorama do Cinema Brasileiro," in Gomes, *Cinema: Trajetória no*

Subdesenvolvimento Geral do Cinema Brasileiro (Rio de Janeiro: Borsoi, 1973). See also Randal Johnson and Robert Stam, eds., *Brazilian Cinema* (Rutherford, N.J.: Fairleigh Dickinson University Press, 1982).

12. Vicente de Paula Araújo, *A Bela Epoca do Cinema Brasileiro* (São Paulo: Perspectiva, 1976).

13. In "Re-percussões em Caixa de Eco Ideológica" (mimeograph), Jean-Claude Bernardet and Maria Rita Galvão trace the development of the concepts "national" and "popular" as they relate to the film industry. The study includes the evolution of the industrial ideology of Brazilian cinema until 1960.

14. Araken Campos Pereira Junior, *Cinema Brasileiro, 1908–1978* (Santos: Casa do Cinema Ltda., 1979).

15. For a discussion of Vera Cruz, see Maria Rita Galvão, *Cinema e Burguesia: O Caso Vera Cruz* (Rio de Janeiro: Civilização Brasileira/Embrafilme, 1981); also Maria Rita Galvão, "Vera Cruz: A Brazilian Hollywood," in Johnson and Stam, eds., *Brazilian Cinema*, pp. 170–180.

16. For a discussion of the evolution of such ideas, see Maria Rita Galvão, "O desenvolvimento das idéias sobre cinema independente," *Cinema BR* 1 and 2 (September and December 1977), 15–19 in both numbers; also Glauber Rocha, *Revisão Crítica do Cinema Brasileiro* (Rio de Janeiro: Civilização Brasileira, 1963).

17. Data from Embrafilme.

18. Jorge A. Schnitman, "State Protectionism and Film Industry Development: A Comparative View of Argentina and Mexico." Paper presented at the Conference on World Communications: Decisions for the Eighties, The Annenberg School of Communications, University of Pennsylvania, May 12–14, 1980; also Fernando Contreras y Espinosa, *La producción, sector primario de la industria cinematográfica* (Mexico, D.F.: UNAM, 1973).

19. For a discussion of protectionism in Europe, see Thomas Guback, *The International Film Industry* (Bloomington: Indiana University Press, 1969).

20. The repercussions of the first law are outlined the Associação Cinematográphica de Productores Brasileiros' *Relatorio da Diretoria*: the text of the second law is in Mello, *Legislacão do Cinema*, 139–143.

21. ACPB's *Relatorio da Diretoria.*

22. Carlos Roberto Rodrigues de Souza, "A Fascinante Aventura do Cinema Brasileiro."

23. The 1950 figure is based on data from *Cine Reporter* 20:932 (28 November 1953).

24. *Estatísticas 76*, Cinemateca do Museu de Arte Moderna (Rio de Janeiro), 1977.

25. See Inimá Simões, *O Imaginário da Boca.*

26. The text of decree-law no. 43 (18 November 1966) is in Mello, *Legislacão do Cinema*, 37–53.

27. For an overview of these different organizations, see Geraldo Santos Pereira, *Plano Geral do Cinema Brasileiro.*

28. For an earlier expression of the need for state protection, see Cavalheiro Lima, "Cinema: Problema do Governo," *Revista do Livro* 1:1–2 (June 1956), 58–71.

29. In his testimony before a Comissão Parlamentar de Inquérito convened to examine the situation of Brazilian cinema in 1964, critic Paulo Emílio Salles Gomes pointed out that all existing legislation favored the importation of foreign films. He recommended that the government take advantage of the increased strength of the Executive to change such legislation (this was said after the coup d'etat). Paraphrased by Rogério Costa Rodrigues, "A Indústria Cinematográfica Brasileira e a Conquista do Mercado," *Revista de Informação Legislativa* (Brasília) 9 (1966). Offprint.

30. Geraldo Santos Pereira, *Plano Geral do Cinema*, 252–264.

31. A study done by Dieter Goebel and Carlos Roberto Rodrigues de Souza reveals that very few films actually cover their costs in the first year of exhibition, and only a minority make a profit from the market alone. See Goebel and Souza, "A Economia Cinematográfica Brasileira," São Paulo, 1975 (mimeograph).

32. "Informativo SIP," 1973, 1974, 1975, Instituto Nacional do Cinema.

33. Embrafilme, "Relatório da Diretoria," 1980.

34. Guback, *International Film Industry.*

35. See legislation in Mello, *Legislação do Cinema.*

36. For an early example of a view opposed to this co-production program, see Mauricio

Capovilla, "GEICINE e os Problemas Econômicos do Cinema Brasileiro," *Revista Brasiliense* 44 (November–December 1962); also Geraldo Santos Pereira, *Plano Geral do Cinema*.

37. Decree-law no. 862 (12 September 1969) in Mello, *Legislacão do Cinema*.

38. "Produtores: Queremos Concorrer em Igualdade," *O Globo* (Rio de Janeiro) 29 October 1972.

39. "Lei Básica do Cinema Brasileiro," *Filme Cultura* 33 (May 1979), 114.

40. "A Exportação de Filmes Rende Mais," *Gazeta Mercantil*, 9–11 January 1982.

41. Ibid.

42. "Normas para a Co-produção Cinematográfica," Embrafilme.

43. In a speech before the Federal Chamber of Deputies on 30 May 1979, Embrafilme's Director-General Celso Amorim affirmed that Embrafilme does not "exercise any function or activity directly related with censorship . . . to such an extent that it has co-produced two films that are currently interdicted by censorship." He goes on to say that Embrafilme per se does not produce films, but rather makes film projects by independent producers viable. "Embrafilme does not create projects, it does not have a department that elaborates film scripts, that prepares films. With respect to the projects that are submitted for consideration, Embrafilme is limited to, and should be limited to, verifying the technical and professional capacity of its director and producer . . . but in no way does Embrafilme pass judgment on thematic or formal content." The speech is reprinted in *Cinejornal* (Rio de Janeiro, Embrafilme) 1:1 (July 1980). Discussions I have had with many different people in the Brazilian film industry unanimously confirm Amorim's statements.

44. Satisfaction with Embrafilme is far from universal among Brazilian filmmakers. Some, like Joaquim Pedro de Andrade, call for its democratization with filmmakers taking a more active and direct roll in the decision-making process; others accuse Embrafilme of favoring Rio de Janeiro filmmakers over directors from other parts of the country, especially São Paulo; still others complain of its lack of support for experimental and documentary films. Filmmakers of all persuasions agree, however, that Embrafilme is necessary for the continued development of Brazilian cinema. Only the state, it is felt, has the power to compete against the wealthy and highly organized foreign distributors.

45. All of the films released in the last few years in the United States—*Dona Flor and Her Two Husbands, Bye Bye Brasil, Gaijin, Summer Showers,* and *Pixote*—were made with Embrafilme's support.

7. El Patrimonio Cultural en el Perú: Su Defensa, Conservación y Rescate

Ramiro Matos M.

Esta ponencia se propone en primer lugar, para exponer algunas consideraciones en torno a la necesidad de redefinir, ampliándolos, los alcances del concepto de "patrimonio cultural," de tal manera que comprenda una serie de expresiones sustantivamente valiosas y significativas, pero que hasta ahora, por lo general, han sido dejadas de lado. Por otro lado, y de manera un tanto detallada, nos ocupamos de los problemas y del estado actual de la conservación del patrimonio cultural de un país como el Perú, en donde tanto se hace sentir la necesidad de una política efectiva, fecunda y coherente al respecto, y que en tan dolorosa medida es víctima de un verdadero y generalizado proceso de deterioro y expoliación de ese patrimonio. Terminaremos formulando dos recomendaciones concretas y, a nuestro parecer, urgentes.

El Perú es un país heredero de una extraordinaria cultura indígena, conocida como la cultura andina. Las investigaciones arqueológicas, antropológicas e históricas, descubren cada vez más nuestros hechos y evidencias de acontecimientos notablemente peculiares que singularizan y diferencian a esta cultura, y a la sociedad que la gestó y desarrolló, de las demás otras de su época. Si bien la historia de los pueblos ha seguido en general desarrollos o evoluciones más o menos similares, el caso andino presenta caracteres muy propios y originales, que es de toda justicia relevar.

Políticamente los Andes comprenden siete repúblicas contemporáneas: Venezuela, Colombia, Ecuador, Perú, Bolivia, Chile y Argentina, extensa área, donde se sucedieron diversas formas de desarrollo social-cultural. Dentro de esta región, el Perú actual tiene el privilegio de ocupar la parte medular, conocida como los Andes Centrales. Dentro de este segmento se han dado las siguientes correlaciones: (1) ecológicamente, de los 106 pisos de vida natural que existen en el mundo, de acuerdo a la clasificación de Holdridge, en los Andes Centrales ocurren 100, lo cual les da una fisonomía de contrastes en cortas distancias, desde el litoral del Pacífico hasta las cordilleras con glaciares permanentes y desde los altiplanos hasta la hoya amazónica. Esta diversidad de paisajes, con fauna y flora muy variada, por paradoja, constituye uno de los elementos que caracterizan la unidad de la geografía andina; y (2) culturalmente, el hombre llega a los Andes hace aproximadamente 14 mil años en condiciones emergentes del paleolítico europeo, con economía de caza y recolecta, originando al cabo de algunos miles de años y después de la adaptación a este ambiente, una nueva cultura, que empieza a configurarse hacia los 4,000 A.C., con la domesticación de plantas (alrededor de 100 especies) y animales (tres especies) y se hace sedentaria, fundándose las primeras aldeas y luego construyéndose templos y adoratorios, como parte de un complejo sistema religioso, que durante el Formativo, hacia los 1,000 años A.C. alcanza su esplendor. Después de este período, los pueblos se diferencian unos de los otros. Aparecen las culturas regionales, que después del Formativo presentan un espectro muy variado, coexistiendo jefaturas con reynos y estados, que arqueológicamente son bien diferenciados por la variedad de estilos, tipos y horizonte alfareros, asociados a otros componentes culturales, todo lo cual confiere un carácter de homotaxial a la cultura andina, también por paradoja, esta variedad en el tiempo y el espacio, constituye otra de las características de la unidad y cotradicionalidad de la cultura andina.

Esta cultura pre-hispánica, después de la invasión europea a los Andes, permaneció latente al lado de la extranjera, Después de la llamada "conquista" y el asentamiento de la administración colonial, con la población indígena casi diezmada, la técnica, el arte, la ciencia y sobre todo la ideología andinas, de algún modo subsistieron indestructibles. Los llamados fenómenos de aculturación o transculturación fueron los episodios más crueles para el mundo andino. Sin embargo, a la fecha y seguramente por muchos años todavía quedan más de 4 millones de habitantes que hablan lenguas nativas, practican las costumbres precoloniales como la agricultura y la economía, y conservan su ideología. Las manifestaciones propiamente andinas, que algunas veces se suelen identificar como "el Perú profundo," constituyen componentes singularmente importantes dentro de la sociedad peruana. Por eso, la caracterización de la sociedad moderna del Perú, no puede dejar de lado ese enorme capital cultural y humano.

Todos esos componentes y factores forman parte activa de nuestro proceso histórico, y constituyen la base de nuestra personalidad como nación. Y para hablar de "patrimonio cultural," tenemos que comprender a la sociedad andina en todas sus manifestaciones a través del tiempo y el espacio, es decir, en sus relaciones sincrónicas y diacrónicas. Creo por ello que ha sido un error considerar como patrimonio cultural solamente ciertos restos arqueológicos, algunos edificios, y expresiones de arte como pintura, escultura, etc.

El patrimonio cultural del Perú, es pues mucho más de lo que los organismos internacionales como la UNESCO y la OEA consideran. En el caso del Perú, Bolivia, Ecuador y otros países andinos, debe comprenderse dentro de la misma categoría de "patrimonio cultural," el folklore indígena, diferente al arte vernacular, las lenguas quechua y aymara, que fueron la expresión más elevada de la cultura andina y todo lo que constituye o forma parte de la ideología del mundo andino, como las leyendas, los mitos, cuentos, música, etc. Asímismo, los documentos y evidencias de los siglos XVI—XX, que testimonian o describen a esa sociedad, desde la conquisto hasta la vida republicana.

Patrimonio Cultural y Bienes Culturales

El patrimonio cultural de un país no puede estar al margen del interés del estado. Más aún, es deber ineludible de éste velar por su conservación y su estudio. Ello supone, como es conocido, una planificada labor de investigación, y una igualmente planificada política, basada en aquélla, de preservación, defensa, restauración, e investigación.

Para fines de uniformar criterios y objetivizar el concepto de patrimonio cultural, las diversas reuniones internacionales a cargo de gobiernos, de la OEA y la UNESCO, pueden ser resumidos por el documento de la Convención de San Salvador de 1976 donde se establecen las siguientes categorías:

1. Monumentos, objetos, restos de edificios y material arqueológico, pertenecientes a las culturas, americanas anteriores a los contactos con la cultura europea, así como los restos humanos, y de la fauna y la flora relacionados con los mismos;

2. Monumentos, edificios, objetos artísticos, objetos utilitarios, etnológicos íntegros fragmentados de la época colonial, así como correspondientes al siglo XIX;

3. Bibliotecas y archivos; incunables y manuscritos, libros y otras publicaciones, iconografía, mapas y documentos editados hasta 1850;

4. Todos aquellos bienes de origen posterior a 1850 que los Estados partes tengan registrados como bienes culturales, siempre que hayan notificado tal registro a las demás partes del Tratado;

5. Todos aquellos bienes culturales que cualesquiera de los Estados partes declaren o manifiesten expresamente incluir dentro de los alcances de esa convención.

Aparentemente dentro del llamado patrimonio, solamente se han considerado los bienes de orden material o la cultura materializada. Tal es así, que en caso de los Andes, dentro de tal acepción, no se incluye ninguna de las manifestaciones de la ideología andina, lo que constituye una aberración y tiende a identificar al concepto de patrimonio cultural con los propósitos del turismo. Veamos algunos ejemplos en los acuerdos internacionales.

La famosa Carta de Venecia, utilizada en muchos casos como el breviario cuando se trata de rescate, conservación o restauración de bienes culturales, históricos o artísticos, señala:

La noción de monumentos históricos abarca la creación arquitectónica, aislada, así como el sitio urbano o rural que expresa el testimonio de una civilización determinada, de una evolución significativa o de un acontecimiento histórico. Tal nación comprende no solamente las grandes creaciones, sino también las obras modestas que, con el tiempo, han adquirido un significado cultural.

Sobre la continuidad cultural o la tradición subsistente entre las comunidades que rodean el monumento, nada concreto señala la referida Carta.

La convención de la UNESCO de 1972, recoge las mismas recomendaciones resumidas en el documento de San Salvador y agrega en cada caso, "los lugares; obras del hombre u obras conjuntas del hombre y la naturaleza así como las zonas incluídos los lugares arqueológicos que tengan un valor universal excepcional desde el punto de vista histórico, estético, tecnológico o antropológico."

Igual criterio asumieron los demás certámenes, siendo el último de ellos, el reunido en Quito en 1981, que después de resumir los acuerdos de reuniones anteriores, ratifica y amplia el documento conocido como Normas de Quito de 1967. Fue Alberto Rex Gonzáles, arqueólogo argentino, quien se encargó de presentar el documento central, ampliando la visión rígida de monumento hacia el valor de los documentos.

La reunión de 1967 debería haberse realizado en Lima, de acuerdo a los ofrecimientos del Gobierno del Perú, ante la recomendación de la Cuarta Reunión del Consejo Interamericano de Cultura pero por razones no explicadas, el Gobierno Peruano retiró tal ofrecimiento y, la reunión se trasladó a Quito gracias al apoyo recibido del gobierno del Ecuador.

Los conceptos de patrimonio cultural y de bienes culturales tienen pues un sentido bastante general y recogen puntos de vista y criterios que acaso pueden parecer meramente declarativos. Todo ello se vincula, ciertamente, por un lado con la extendida falta de una verdadera política cultural en muchos países, efectivamente consecuente con la idiosincracia de sus pueblos y su historia; y, por otro, sobre todo en el caso de las naciones del area andina—con un marcado etnocentrismo, que ha limitado, y limita una visión que debería abarcar también, y con igual atención, la historia, el arte, la tecnología etc.

El patrimonio cultural, de acuerdo a nuestra realidad histórica y la evolución socio-política de nuestros países, se puede dividir en cuatro categorías:

1. Los bienes monumentales, en los que van implícitas las ideas de materialidad y espacio, y que por ello reclaman medidas adecuadas para su protección física. Dentro de este rubro figuran todos los items enumerados en las diferentes reuniones de la UNESCO, la OEA, IPGH, Acuerdo de Cartagena, el Pacto Andrés Bello y la Sección de Asuntos Culturales del Pacto Andino. La idea de monumento engloba los testimonios arqueológicos, las obras de arte, cuadros or esculturas, las edificaciones coloniales, principalmente iglesias y casonas de familias de aquella época.

2. Los bienes documentales, cuya existencia presupone la escritura. Fueron y son las fuentes principales de la historia. En caso de los Andes, se hallan dispersas en archivos públicos y privados, desde los llamados archivos

nacionales, que cada país tiene como repositorios en oficinas estatales, hasta los archivos de iglesias rurales que abundan por todos nuestros pueblos del interior, las notarías, las casas-hacienda, las gobernaciones, municipalidades, juzgados, las casas comunales pertenecientes a las llamadas comunidades indígenas, las suprefecturas y prefecturas, conventos, etc. La nueva disciplina conocida como etnohistoria, precisamente tiene como fundamento el uso de esos documentos coloniales junto con las tradiciones orales.

3. Las tradiciones orales que presuponen la pervivencia de los valores culturales indígenas, en regiones como la andina, constituyen un importes renglón lamentablemente subestimado y muchas veces menospreciado. En nuestra sociedad, con tan radical estratificación socio-económica, las costumbres indígenas, los patrones de la cultura tradicional y aún algunas formas de vida rural o campesina, son consideradas como expresiones inferiores, y signo de "retraso." En un informe del Departamento de Asuntos Culturales de la OEA, de 1960, la zona de la sierra central y sur-oriental, donde la tradición cultural andina se presenta con más originalidad y fuerza, fue considerada como "la mancha negra del Perú." El estudio y recopilación de las tradiciones orales, de las que forma parte el folklore, han sido poco desarrollados en esta área. Inclusive, las investigaciones arqueológicas, antropológicas y etnohistóricas han recogido escasa información empírica en este campo, y en muchos casos, no se ha sabido manejar los datos en su dimensión diacrónica. Un repositorio de estas tradiciones, tanto indígenas como coloniales y contemporáneas, constituiría otra forma de conservar el patrimonio cultural andino. En una sociedad en constante cambio y con fenómenos de rápida desaparición de muchos de sus expresiones, esta categoría exige inclusive labores como las que Sol Tax, por un lado, y Lévi-Strauss por otro, plantearon, esto es, declarar en "emergencia" las tradiciones culturales de los países en desarrollo.

4. Las lenguas nativas, que suponen la comunicación social de los pueblos y en el caso andino, la vigencia de dos lenguas, con su propia originalidad y habladas por más de 4 millones de personas en el caso del quechua y un millón en el caso del aymara; situación que exige un tratamiento político por parte de los Estados. Aunque algunos pudieran considerarlas como lenguas muertas, la verdad es que en nuestra área conservan una magnífica vitalidad, aún a pesar de los avances del español y la aculturación indirecta o insidiosa que llevan a cabo medios de comunicación masiva, como la radio. Y ello no obstante que incluso ha habido y hay en muchos centros de enseñanza primaria de la sierra, la prohibición de usar esas lenguas nuestras, y a pesar también de los prejuicios heredados de épocas pasadas. Se conservan, esas lenguas, sin apoyo del estado, e incluso en contra de éste. Son ellas un legado en que se expresa y sintetiza toda una visión original y rica de la vida y del mundo, y se les debe, por tanto, una delicada y reflexiva política de estímulo, estudio y conservación.

Estas cuatro categorías de bienes patrimoniales, de las naciones andinas, presentan caracteres y contextos obviamente diferentes. Por ello, quizá, fue más fácil considerar sólo los dos primeros: los monumentos y los documentos, por cuanto se tratan de bienes materiales o materializados, y como tales más fáciles de registrar en un inventario, catálogo o catastro, y reclamar su defensa, conservación, rescate y hasta restauración.

Mientras tanto, las otras dos categorías, la tradición oral y el lenguaje, que precisamente son las normas más reveladoras del pensamiento y la ideosincracia de los pueblos andinos, no son igualmente consideradas dentro del llamado "patrimonio cultural," o en muchos casos, deliberadamente olvidadas. En el Perú, ningún gobierno ha pretendido rescatar este bagage de valores culturales, como parte de una política cultural genuinamente peruana o andina. Algunos regimenes, por curiosa coincidencia dictaduras militares como las de Castilla, Leguía o Velasco, han tratado de reivindicar ciertos "derechos" de los "indios" y campesinos, pero si bien este importante sector de la población peruana fue beneficiada con algunas leyes sociales, su cumplimiento o la vigencia de las mismas, fue superficial y efímero.

En el campo de las investigaciones antropológicas o arqueológicas, en vez de profundizar los estudios en los Andes, algunos colegas han preferido buscar modelos teóricos en sociedades o culturas ajenas. En este sentido, el avance de las investigaciones en las dos últimas décadas, en lugar de contribuír al conocimiento científico, ha servido para ahondar la confusión, o como dijera Kent Flannery, "imponer la arqueología-ficción sobre la arqueología científica." Por otro lado, éstas dos décadas han sido también las de mayor cambio, "evolución," "progreso" o de "integración" de la sociedad andina, vislumbrándose un futuro cada vez más difícil.

Por eso, dentro de los esfuerzos de conservación y utilización de los patrimonios culturales de cada nación, los Estados tienen la obligación de asumir la responsabilidad de velar por ellos, sin que ello signifique un obstáculo para que cada pueblo o cada grupo se integre a la sociedad moderna occidental, o busque el mejor camino para su progreso. De otro modo, habremos perdido definitivamente ese valioso legado, quedando un vacío en la continuidad del desarrollo cultural desde el período pre-colonial hasta la vida actual.

El Patrimonio Cultural y los Acuerdos Internacionales

Se han realizado muchas reuniones internacionales sobre el patrimonio cultural, de manera directa o indirectamente. Sólo el Proyecto Regional de Patrimonio Cultural (PNUD/UNESCO), ha organizado cinco certámenes para discutir el problema, y ha contribuído a otros tantos en conexión con otros organismos internacionales como la OEA (Departamento de Asuntos Culturales) y el IPGH (Instituto Panamericano de Geografía e Historia), con asistencia de delegados de muchos países. Entre aquéllos, unos son funcionarios de los gobiernos de turno que cumplen tareas burocráticas en el sector cultural

(Instituto Nacional de Cultura) y los otros, generalmente profesionales o científicos calificados, pero que, debido a su posición directriz en diversos organismos (Dirección del Museo Nacional, Dirección o Jefatura de Oficinas encargadas de Bienes Patrimoniales, diversas direcciones de los Ministerios de Educación o de Turismo, etc.), asisten a las reuniones, participan en los debates, llevan ponencias, pero luego, los acuerdos quedan en el escritorio de los asistentes, o cuando más se tramitan para la firma de adhesión del gobierno.

En entrevistas hechas a estudiosos de la cultura nacional desde sus diversos puntos de vista, arqueólogos, historiadores, artistas, literatos, arquitectos, médicos, etc., en su mayoría dedicados tanto a la investigación como a la enseñanza universitaria, hemos constatado con tristeza, que el 98% desconocen el contenido de tales reuniones internacionales, y más aún sus acuerdos y conclusiones. Las únicas informaciones son las difundidas en los medios de comunicación de masas, periódicos y revistas, generalmente como noticias hechos por periodistas. Igual situación ha ocurrido con respecto a los acuerdos a nivel presidencial, como los de Punta del Este, el Convenio Andrés Bello y La Declaración de los Presidentes de América, en los que los jefes de estado, dentro de un compromiso de cooperación andina o americana, han aceptado el reto de enfrentar los problemas que afectan al patrimonio cultural.

De igual manera, organismos dedicados estrictamente a labores técnicas o científicas como las universidades e institutos de investigación aprovechando las reuniones en congresos, symposia y mesas redondas, han discutido el problema en profundidad, especialmente en los tópicos de rescate y conservación, y en menor extensión en los temas de restauración y puesta en valor, que más bien fueron campos deliberadamente tomados por organismos internacionales como la UNESCO y la OEA.

En ambos casos, los avances alcanzados son halagadores, aunque el impacto social, el efecto multiplicador en el pueblo y la difusión de estos conocimientos en las mayorías nacionales han sido muy poco alentados. Magníficas reuniones con excelentes acuerdos, han quedado archivados en algunas oficinas. El Estado, a pesar de haber asumido el compromiso y la responsabilidad al haber firmado tales acuerdos, no los ha incorporado en sus bases de política cultural. Mientras el estado no asuma su responsabilidad a plenitud y empiece a tomar conciencia del valor de estas expresiones culturales, el pueblo en general, tampoco alcanzará a valorarlos debidamente, ni contribuirá a su preservación.

En tal sentido, creo que los organismos internacionales, las diferentes reuniones, tanto de gremios de investigadores como de funcionarios, han cumplido dentro de lo previsto. Existen regulaciones normativas detalladas, pero lo que hace falta es la educación, toma de conciencia, identificación nacional y reformulación de la política del Estado con base en nuestra propia realidad. Por ejemplo, las Normas de Quito de 1967 señalan lo siguiente:

El acelerado proceso de empobrecimiento que viene sufriendo una mayoría de países americanos como consecuencia del estado de abandono e indefensión en que se halla su riqueza monumental y artística, demanda la adopción de medidas de emergencia, tanto a nivel nacional como internacional, pero la eficacia práctica de la misma dependerá, en último término, de su adecuada formulación dentro de un plan sistemático de revaloriza- ción de los bienes patrimoniales en función del desarrollo económico-social.

En otro aspecto, que puede considerarse como el ámbito negativo del problema, es que tantas reuniones y recomendaciones internacionales existen, inclusive en muchos casos en documentos que alcanzan a nivel de tratados bi-nacionales, el tráfico con el patrimonio cultural en sus diversas formas y contenidos, el vandalismo cada vez creciente para destruir los monumentos, documentos, tradiciones orales y las lenguas nativas, son irremediablemente crecientes. A más regulaciones hay más destrucción.

Los países andinos en general, y el Perú en particular son herederos de extraordinarios recursos culturales. Lugares arqueológicos de gran importancia para nuestra historia, alternan con estructuras modernas; a veces aldeas completas de tradición andina están junto a otras de fundación española. Iglesias coloniales con pinturas murales y cuadros de lienzo están rodeados por comunidades rurales que se ve en ellos su herencia ancestral. En todos estos casos, se alternan o se confunden lo indígena con lo colonial, y ambos con lo republicano.

Esos pueblos y lugares, en los últimos veinte años, han sido fuertemente castigados por los traficantes de antiguedades por un lado y por los habilitadores de terrenos para la agricultura o para las urbanizaciones por otro. No sería exagerado sostener que en el Perú se pierde cada día un monumento. Sin embargo, todavía el estado ni la población en su mayoría entienden que estos testimonios culturales no son minas inagotables. Estamos asistiendo a la peor depredación de nuestro patrimonio cultural, en forma cada vez más alentada desde el interior del país y desde el extranjero. Expertos en tráfico ilegal de las aduanas del Perú, han llegado a señalar que, en la actualidad, es difícil decir ''si el tráfico de la cocaína o el de antiguedades es más intenso.'' De todos modos, el Perú es refutado como un gran ''exportador'' de ambos renglones.

El documento aprobado por la Organización de las Naciones Unidas para la Educación, la Ciencia y la Cultura (UNESCO) en su Conferencia General de 1970, con el título de ''Convención sobre las medidas que deben adoptarse para prohibir e impedir la importación, la exportación y la transferencia de la propiedad ilícitas de bienes culturales,'' con 26 artículos, es el documento más detallado sobre este asunto. El Perú, al igual que los demás países de América, es signatario nuestro del acuerdo; sin embargo, esta década ha sido la más desoladora para nuestro patrimonio cultura. ¿Es que los estados signatarios no han adoptado las medidas adecuadas para hacer cumplir tales recomenda- ciones? ¿Es que tales regulaciones tiene solamente el carácter de normativas y no precisamente ejecutivas? ¿Es que el hombre ha perdido total respeto a los valores culturales? Estas y muchas otras interrogantes exigen respuestas medi- tadas y claras.

El Patrimonio Cultural y la Legislación Peruana

En general el Perú tiene una adecuada y buena legislación de protección al patrimonio cultural. La Ley 6634 de 1929, pese a su antigüedad, es aplicable. En años siguientes se han dado una docena de nuevas disposiciones por Leyes, Decretos Leyes y Resoluciones Supremas. En general, todas ellas responden a la necesidad de defensa y tutela de los valores culturales, principalmente en lo que respecta a testimonios arqueológicos, las obras de arte, monumentos históricos, etc. A no dudar, el espíritu de nuestra legislación es bueno.

Sin embargo, los resultados no son óptimos. La aplicación de esos dispositivos es compleja, y las causas pueden ser diversas. El país cuenta con un organismo rector encargado de velar por la cultura nacional. Desde los primeros tiempos de la vida republicana esa tarea fue orientada desde una dependencia del Ministerio de Educación. Hace dos décadas se creó un organismo descentralizado del sector, con el nombre de Casa de la Cultura del Perú, cambiándose posteriormente esta denominación por la de Instituto Nacional de Cultura (INC), que constituye el principal organismo que orienta y se ocupa de la política cultural del Estado peruano. Su actividad dentro y fuera del país, depende de muchos factores, pero principalmente, del interés de la administración política de turno y del presupuesto que la misma le confiere. La labor que cumple el INC, constituye el termómetro para medir el empeño del Estado en este campo, no siempre improductivo, como a veces se suele sugerir, sino más bien altamente rentable, si se recuerda el turismo y sus ventajas para el incremento de divisas.

Por mandato de nuestra Carta Magna vigente y las anteriores, muchos de los bienes culturales son propiedad del Estado con carácter de inalienables e imprescriptibles. Para hacer cumplir esta disposición el Estado ha fijado sanciones, generalmente pecuniarias. La paradoja es que el tope máximo de la sanción es una pequeña parte del valor del monumento destruido. En tal sentido, muchos empresarios, especialmente en centros metropolitanos como Lima, destruyen huacas, pirámides y templos para habilitar tierras para nuevas urbanizaciones, pagan luego la multa, y tienen el camino expedito para levantar nuevos edificios. En otros casos menos escandalosos, estas compañías acuden al INC, para solicitar trabajos de liberación. Es decir que el INC encargue a sus profesionales realizar trabajos de rescate para dejar libre el terreno para nuevos fines.

En cuanto a los monumentos coloniales, no existe un catastro de ellos pueblo por pueblo, ni menos un inventario del contenido, en cada uno dejándose la custodia y manejo de los mismos a los servidores de culto, sacerdotes o priostes. En las comunidades rurales, los campesinos han asumido su cuidado, pero no siempre de modo eficiente debido a su excesiva confianza en la sociedad que los rodea, y su benevolencia tradicional. Quizá en este aspecto, los únicos que respetan a sus monumentos, pre-coloniales y coloniales, conservando sus tradiciones y defendiendo sus costumbres, son los campesinos de raigambre indígena. El hombre urbano, contagiado por los problemas de la sociedad moderna, es con enorme frecuencia destructor de su propio patrimonio cultural hasta el punto de convertirse—y tenemos allí la máxima expresión de esa distorsión—en traficante mercentil de ese legado.

Con relación al manejo del patrimonio arqueológico y de la Arqueología Peruana en general, la "Memoria y Exposición de la Comisión Técnica Calificadora de Proyectos Arqueológicos del Instituto Nacional de Cultura; 1979—80," se ocupa a plenitud del problema, analiza sus causas, así como las dificultades con que tropieza el desarrollo de la Arqueología en el Perú, y, sobre todo, enfoca la acción de Estado con sumo realismo. En su parte introductoria señala:

Es evidente que la arqueología no escapa a una de las graves crisis socio-económicas por las que atraviesa el país. La década que concluímos arroja un balance negativo tanto en el campo de la investigación cuanto en la defensa de los restos arqueológicos, patrimonio monumental de la nación. Si bien reconocemos algunos aportes y esfuerzos en estos campos, de ninguna manera señalan un balance positivo. Simplemente han sido hechos aislados, cuyos logros son mínimos frente a los miles de testimonios que desaparecen a diario sin ningún estudio, menos preocupación por parte del Estado. . . . De esta tragedia somos responsables y los de nuestra generación no puede eximirse de ella. Es tiempo de señalar la dimensión de los cargos y precisar la profundidad de sus causas. El primer responsable del panorama sombrío de la arqueología peruana es el Estado. Después de las conquistas alcanzadas por el esfuerzo personal de Julio C. Tello en las décadas del 20 al 30, el gobierno ha desatendido su misión tutelar con relación al patrimonio cultural prehispánico. Al respecto nunca ha existido una política cultural coherente. Prueba de esto es la ausencia de una legislación adecuada y ordenada, de un presupuesto mínimo para atender a su conservación, establecida por Ley, del indispensable personal calificado, de centros de investigación, de laboratorios, de gabinetes adecuadamente equipados y de instituciones con capacidad y poder de decisión. . . .

Este documento, entregado a las autoridades superiores del Estado y profusamente difundido en los medios de comunicación, causó impacto en la ciudadanía pero, lamentablemente de ninguna manera fue escuchado por el gobierno. Antes bien, en el presupuesto del año siguiente, y en la reestructuración del INC, el Centro de Investigación y Restauración de Bienes Monumentales (CIRBM) ha sido reducido a una modesta dependencia, sin actividad funcional, ni menos capacidad para concretar adecuadamente la misión tutelar del Estado sobre tales bienes. Los firmantes del documento son arqueólogos calificados del Perú, que tuvieron el encargo de ocuparse de la Arqueología Peruana por un año. Como parte de esta labor, fue preparado inclusive, el nuevo Proyecto de Legislación sobre Patrimonio Cultural del Perú en sus diversas formas, desde la definición de "patrimonio cultural," su defensa, conservación, restauración, rescate y reservas culturales, hasta el diseño de las bases de una efectiva política cultural que responda a la realidad y a la vocación nacional del Perú y colabore en la búsqueda de su propio destino.

Este proyecto, fue entregado a la Oficina del Ministerio de Educación para su estudio y sometimiento a discusión parlamentaria, pero, nunca salió de tal dependencia. Mientras tanto, el INC ha sido declarado en re-organización mediante una disposición ordenada, aunque no se ha ejecutado pese a los meses transcurridos. Así mismo, subsisten los vacíos legales, las limitaciones en muchas disposiciones, pero sobre todo, es notorio en los dos últimos años, la minimización de la atención que se pone en esta tarea privativa del Estado. Mientras el Gobierno no asuma su responsabilidad es difícil ordenar y coordinar la participación de la población.

En cuanto a los bienes documentales, como parte de la llamada ''reorganización'' del INC el Archivo Nacional y los archivos provinciales han pasado a formar parte del Ministerio de Justicia. Antes, los archivos al igual que la Biblioteca Nacional eran organismos componentes del INC. Los archivos parroquiales quedan al relativo amparo de las iglesias, y los otros están confiados a la buena voluntad de sus poseedores.

Los museos todavía permanecen dentro del INC, pero cada vez con presupuestos disminuídos, sin personal necesario para cumplir con sus tareas, sin infraestructura adecuada, motivando lo que todos sabemos, la pérdida de los bienes, tanto por cuantiosos robos, como los ocurridos en el Museo Nacional de Antropología y Arqueología, como por acción del clima y las condiciones de los depósitos.

En los demás campos como la etnografía, el folklore y las tradiciones populares, la misión tutelar del Estado es poco o nada perceptible. Existen proyectos de investigación histórica, antropológica, folklórica y otros conducidos por nacionales o extranjeros, sin embargo, no existe un organismo fiscalizador o coordinador de estos esfuerzos, así como tampoco un centro de información sobre las investigaciones sociales e históricas en el Perú. No hay un organismo regulador como el INAH de México. En muchos casos, una misma comunidad indígena es acosada por varios proyectos o varios investigadores, que en casos no menos frecuentes, motivan conflictos entre los miembros de la comunidad. Víctimas del asedio de las investigaciones antropológicas fueron por muchos años las comunidades de los valles del Mantaro, Urubamba, Andahuaylas y Ayacucho aunque los resultados se conozcan muy poco, de acuerdo a la magnitud de las investigaciones. En otros casos, las comunidades sirvieron como centros de experimentación en antropología aplicada, desarrollo comunal, crédito supervisado, estudios de seguimiento, etc.

Finalmente, en vista de la ausencia de una política propia del Estado en materia cultural, las manifestaciones folklóricas, en la danza, la música, la vestimenta y los atavíos, son tratados de acuerdo a las circunstancias. En muchos casos, los empresarios de coliseos o de presentaciones dominicales, han sofisticado o alterado el contenido real, tratando de complacer a los afanes de ''la moda'' del momento. José María Arguedas trató de corregir estas desviaciones, desde su alto cargo como Director de la Casa de la Cultura. Lamentablemente, no alcanzó éxito alguno. Las organizaciones empresariales

que explotan ese legado, tienen mayor poder que los funcionarios bien inten-
cionados del Estado.

El Patrimonio Cultural y el Desarrollo de los
Pueblos

El progreso y el desarrollo traen consigo la multiplicación de obras de
infraestructura, muchas y variadas edificaciones, cada vez más extensas, hori-
zontal como verticalmente. En la noción popular, el progreso implica grandes
edificaciones, carreteras, industrias, y una concentración explosiva de la
población.

Esa forma de "progreso," a su vez acarrea la depredación de los testimonios de la tradición cultural, tanto en monumentos arqueológicos como
históricos, y otros de inestimable valor. En casos menos dramáticos, el desarrollo conlleva la alteración del ambiente, la deformación del paisaje y la
distorsión del entorno de las expresiones del pasado.

Las normas de Quito señalan: "No es exagerado afirmar que el potencial
de riqueza destruída con estos irresponsables actos de vandalismo urbanistico
en numerosas ciudades del Continente, exceden con mucho a los beneficios que
para la economía nacional se derivan de las instalaciones y mejoras de infraestructura con que pretenden justificarse."

Efectivamente, en el perímetro de grandes ciudades, restos que evidencian
la grandeza de la cultura andina, como templos, casas, calles y huacas han sido
afectados por el mal entendido y peor administrado progreso urbano, sufriendo
tales monumentos mutilaciones o degradación de su contexto. En el campo,
especialmente cerca a haciendas, fundos o medianas propiedades, los monumentos sufren similares perjuicios en el afán de habilitar terrenos de cultivo, la
construcción de carreteras, represas y otros proyectos semejantes. En ambos
casos, especialmente cuando las obras se enmarcan en los programas auspici-
ados o realizados por el gobierno, los monumentos arqueológicos o históricos
son objeto de una "destrucción oficial u oficializada." Existen numerosos
ejemplos. Uno actual y de gran envergadura es el que ofrece el "Proyecto
Jequetepeque," donde para construír una represa se está destruyendo alrededor
de 200 sitios arqueológicos.

Mientras se realizan obras de desarrollo en algunos puntos—cabe, por
tanto, designarlos como "núcleos"—la mayor parte del país está sumida en un
acrecentado proceso de pauperización y desintegración. Se promociona y
pondera, con gran estridencia, esos "polos," y los habitantes de pueblos y
provincias sueñan con atraer la atención de los gobernantes, para que sus
respectivos lugares se beneficien con esas obras. Se trazan grandes programas,
se elaboran mapas y diagramas, y se gastan sumas ingentes. Nadie, sin
embargo, o muy pocos, se acuerdan de las consecuencias de esos programas y
obras en el legado cultural que pervive en tales regiones, y menos se acuerdan
de los efectos ecológicos. Olvidan, unos y otros, que el patrimonio cultural,

debidamente resguardado y estudiado, representa en sí un gran valor económico, susceptible de contribuír a un auténtico avance social y a una mayor justicia. Y así, alegremente se destruyen por acción u omisión, inapreciables testimonios culturales, en beneficio de un progreso que acaso traerá más bien mayores desigualdades y distorsiones.

Sin embargo, en países como el Perú, donde la otrora ciudad imperial del Cusco, capital del Tahuantinsuyo y conocida como la "capital arqueológica de América," en las dos últimas décadas soporta una total degradación. La UNESCO tiene varios programas en este lugar en estos mismos años, que preferimos no comentar. La nueva denominación popular de Cusco es "la capital hotelera del mundo." Todas las antiguas casonas, pre-coloniales o coloniales han sido habilitadas como hoteles, restaurants o alojamientos. Mientras los nativos de Cusco han tenido que dejar su ciudad natal, la migración de foráneos se ha acelerado. El ambiente y el contexto del Cusco tradicional, indígena y mestizo, casi está desapareciendo. En pocos años, habrá peridido su contenido cultural, sufriendo mutilaciones, degradaciones o transformaciones en todo orden.

Lejos estamos de cumplir con el informe Weis presentado a la Comisión Cultural y Científica de Europa y hecho suyo por la UNESCO (1963), donde se señala: "Es posible equipar a un país sin desfigurarlo; de preparar y servir el porvenir sin destruír el pasado. La elevación del nivel de vida debe limitarse a la realización de un bienestar material progresivo; debe ser asociado a la creación de un cuadro de vida digno del hombre."

Todo lo contrario, en casos como los ocurridos en el Perú, la atención al patrimonio cultural es lo último que se toma en la planificación de cualquier obra, y esto, sólo si a algún funcionario en especial se le ocurre.

8. Cultural Policy Formulation in Puerto Rico: A Macro Perspective

M. Salem

The emergence from colonialism to partial or full independence (that is, the gain of physical freedom or the departure of colonial armed forces) does not necessarily result in mental freedom. Self-imposed psychological colonialism can prevent a large segment of the citizenry from experiencing true freedom. Long after colonizers depart, a mentality of submission to their ways often continues. This manifestation is frequently a latent inferiority complex, a drive toward imitation, and ultimately a crisis of identity. Cultural and artistic institutions everywhere have been attempting to deal with these demoralizing effects. The question "who am I?" has always preoccupied artists, philosophers, writers, and poets, who have often been in the forefront of movements to establish cultural identity and to cement cultural heritage. But that fact in itself points to the natural struggle between the forces preserving one's own culture on the one hand, and on the other those attributing cultural superiority to a former colonizer or idolized, though foreign, mode of life. Those conflicting forces can be from within (that is, within an individual's own soul) as well as from without (that is, between an individual's perception and that of others).[1]

It is with that overall dilemma that cultural policy formulation is often faced. Even if it is not addressed on a formal level by the makers of cultural policy, it is often fervently addressed by those concerned with culture and even by the average citizen.

Although a small island of only 3.5 million people, Puerto Rico experiences an extraordinary tension with regard to its identity. There is the obvious tension between those who live on the island and those who live in the United States but still consider themselves to be Puerto Ricans, although not exactly considered so by the residents of Puerto Rico. To them, those are "Neoricans." The tension increases when they return permanently to the island. And it is a two-way street.

Annie Bello, born in New York of Puerto Rican parents, came to Puerto Rico a few years ago 'to get in tune with my culture' and married a Puerto Rican.

"As a child of the 1960s," she said, "I was very rebellious. My mother would say, "You're an American." I'd say, "No, I'm Puerto Rican." But now that I'm in Puerto Rico, I've decided, "No, I'm a New Yorker."

In contrast, Bello's husband Samuel Vera, 26, although he has a master's degree from New York University and is a salesman for a company called American Home Products, says, "I feel Latin American. I like the United States, but I think of anything from the U.S. as foreign."

The couple lives in a Levittown condominium where, Bello said, "They think I'm a hippie because I wear Indian blouses and braid my hair." Bello is expecting a baby. "I want to call it Michael or Courtney," she said. "My husband wants Alejandro."[2]

Among Puerto Rico's resident population, there is the tension of bilingualism (English versus Spanish) and that of biculturalism (North American versus Latin American or Hispanic).

Eighty-four years under the American flag or in close association with the United States have not erased 400 years of Hispanic culture in spite of a deliberate attempt to Anglicize schools that endured over a generation. Reflecting on this, Rubin Berrios, president of the Puerto Rican Independence Party says, ". . . for 40 years in the Puerto Rican Public Schools, arithmetic, science and all other subjects were taught in English to a people who did not know then, as they do not know now, English."[3] Remarkably, the island still holds onto its language, its culture, and religion with tenacity and pride. "Puerto Rican poets, musicians, playwrights and painters continue to blossom. Of 84 radio stations, only one has programs in English."[4]

Folk singers such as Lucecita, El Topo, and Tony Croato lead in popularity with songs that stress nationalism, protest, and traditionalist sentiments.[5] A revival of "la música jibara" cannot be missed even by the casual observer, and Puerto Rico comes to life during the Christmas season when "la música navideña" fills the air, a music that is distinctly Puerto Rican.

In spite of this tenacity, the islanders remain torn between their Hispanic traditions and the trends toward the Americanization of Puerto Rican life. "The cultural atmosphere is a welter of contradictions and ambivalence. If politically oriented plays and pop protest songs are gaining in popularity, so are discotheques."[6] The cultural clash has created conflicts involving language, entertainment, education, religion, sexual mores, and family life. The unresolved question is how much Americanization Puerto Rico can take without losing its historic and cultural identity. And, people are asking, "Will it be worth it?"[7]

The Institute of Puerto Rican Culture

Fostering cultural identity, building self-worth and ultimately mobilizing people for progress is an essential concern for cultural and artistic institutions. No wonder the major force in Puerto Rican cultural affairs, The Institute of Puerto Rican Culture, emerged during the administration of Puerto Rico's first native elected governor, Muñoz Marín, and started a decline during the administration of its last statehood-oriented governor, Carlos Romero Barcelo. It is also no wonder that its creation has coincided with Puerto Rico's program for economic development, "Operation Bootstrap."

The Institute was created in 1955 amid passionate debate as to whether its creation was desirable. There were those who feared that it might foster provincialism, chauvinism, and narrow-minded nationalism and others who felt that Puerto Rican culture is essentially a Spanish heritage, and should not be isolated from La Madre Patria (The Mother Country). There were those who felt that after so much association with the United States, Puerto Rican culture is or should be far more oriented toward North America than to Spain or Latin America. And there were those who triumphed, feeling that Puerto Rico has its own distinct cultural heritage containing Indian, African, Spanish, Latin, and North American elements. As such, it is rich, distinct, and has its own unmistakable identity.

It was to foster such an identity that the Institute was created. According to the spiritual father of the Institute, Ricardo E. Alegria:

El establecimiento de este nuevo organismo cultural se fundamentaba en poderosas razones de orden histórico y sociológico. En Puerto Rico se requería contrapesar décadas de ignorancia y de abandono respecto de la conservación y promoción de nuestros valores culturales en el orden educativo; se necesitaba contraponer un cultivo consciente de esos valores a muchos lustros de influencias prejudicales y a veces incluso abiertamente contrarias a los mismos; se precisaba luchas contra un condicionamiento psicológico, fuertemente arraigado en nuestra sociedad colonial, que inducia a muchos puertor-riqueños a despreciar sistematicamente todo lo que fuera o pareciera ser autóctono y a valorizar, fuera de toda proporción, lo que fuera o pareciera ser exótico.[8]

Since its inception, the Institute had two fundamental objectives: (1) to study and conserve Puerto Rico's cultural and historical heritage and (2) to stimulate, encourage, and promote the various manifestations of Puerto Rican culture. The organizational structure of the Institute was designed to achieve those objectives. It centered around many areas, most prominent among them are: cultural promotion; archives and libraries; research; theater; music; museums and parks; monuments and historical zones; plastic arts; popular arts; publications and musical recordings; and modern methods of mass communication.[9]

Because a great deal of the funds with which the Institute carries out its functions is appropriated by the legislature, its activities are the subject of an almost annual battle in which passions are displayed and competing ideologies and political perceptions clash. The proponents and the opponents are often well-known actors in the Puerto Rican political arena, that is to say those who compete for a definition for the Puerto Rican political status. The creation of the Institute and all its activities and successes, while giving a boost to "Puerto Ricanism," did not end the debate over what Puerto Rico's cultural policy should emphasize, and how it should be preserved. In the heart of the matter remains the identity question. The main culprit, of course, is the status issue.

Political Status and Cultural Policy

No one who has lived in Puerto Rico can escape noticing the omnipresent status debate and its impact on every aspect of Puerto Rican life. Cultural policy is no exception. Ruben Berrios expresses the sentiments of many Puerto Ricans and their essential cultural identification when he says, "There may be Puerto Ricans who think of themselves as Americans. They need a psychiatrist."[10] Yet, Puerto Rico's present governor Carlos Romero Barcelo insists that, "We ourselves feel no ambiguity about being both Puerto Ricans and Americans."[11] He also states, "Nothing in the U.S. constitution ever prohibited Puerto Rico from adopting a local flag or anthem to accompany the national flag and anthem, and nothing in the U.S. constitution ever prohibited Puerto Rico from maintaining its local language and culture or adopting a local constitution in consonance with the U.S. constitution."[12]

The chance for trying out this vision in Puerto Rico came in 1979 during the Pan American games.

When Romero tried to insist that the U.S. flag be flown next to the Puerto Rican flag at the opening of the Pan American games in 1979, an island-wide controversy erupted. The Stars and Stripes was not raised, and when the Star Spangled Banner was played before the Puerto Rican anthem, it was drowned out in an earsplitting chorus of air horns, police whistles and boos from the crowd of 35,000.[13]

All segments of Puerto Rico's political spectrum declare their support for a Puerto Rican cultural identity. Even statehooders cannot deny that. In the words of Carlos Romero Barcelo, "We statehooders are committed to forging a society in which, while remaining faithful to our linguistic and cultural traditions, we can make a full and meaningful contribution to building a better America. . . ."[14]

Many segments of the Puerto Rican society vary, however, in their degree of commitment to a Puerto Rican cultural identity. There are those who pay lip service to it and those who declare their readiness to defend it with blood. The Independentistas represent the latter. In the words of Rubin Berrios, "There are thousands of Puerto Ricans determined to impede assimilation by any and all means. . . . Any serious attempt at incorporating Puerto Rico as a state would unquestionably precipitate a wave of violence."[15]

The problem in managing Puerto Rican culture is that those who set cultural policy often have a much smaller commitment than those who perform the various types of cultural and artistic manifestations. It is common knowledge that the independence movement has many adherents among Puerto Rican artists, while many of the bureaucrats who manage Puerto Rican culture are either commonwealthers or statehooders. The two groups are frequently at odds, and the unity of vision, of purpose, and of methods necessary for the formulation of a coherent policy are often missing. Therein lies the major difficulty in the formulation of a coherent Puerto Rican cultural policy. The manifestations are many:

1. The undefined role of the Puerto Rican cultural centers. Even though Puerto Rico is endowed with a cultural center in almost each of its towns, perhaps one of the highest rates of such penetration in the world, such centers are largely unused, or at the very least are underutilized. Often, their role is left to the whims of the local mayor and his political beliefs. The result, so far, has been a paralysis of what might otherwise become a formidable cultural force in the community.

2. The untapped resource available annually in the "fiestas patronales." Such spontaneous celebrations, even though they offer a great opportunity for cultural enhancement, have largely been left untapped by cultural policy makers except for a few instances, such as the annual celebration of African heritage in the town of Loiza Aldea.

3. The constant conflict regarding one of the major cultural events in the island—that of the Pablo Casals Festival. In 1979, with everything planned, the festival was cancelled. "The Puerto Ricans were finding their voice and objecting to a situation where their country was merely a place in the event. In their eyes, the festival should be for them. An impasse developed between the local musicians and the management."[16]

4. The attempt to curtail the influence of the Institute of Puerto Rican Culture. A major act in that regard was removing Puerto Rico's newly created major cultural center Centro de Bellas Artes (Center of Fine Arts) from the jurisdiction of the Institute of Puerto Rican Culture, which conceived it, to that of a new organism called the Administration for the Development of Arts and Culture (ADAC).

This act brought on the wrath of Puerto Ricanists, and a group calling itself the Committee for the Defense of Culture went to court to try to stop the inauguration of the Center. When it opened on 9 April 1981, it did so with a group of about 2,000 demonstrators chanting their dismay along Ponce de Leon Avenue. Harold C. Schonberg of the New York Times described the situation:

When Governor Romero took office last year, he completely changed the composition of the cultural administration, setting up four corporations to deal with the arts in Puerto Rico. Heading this new administrative setup is the Administration for the Development of Arts and Culture (ADAC). Many in the artistic community are outraged. A large number of Puerto Rican artists are left-wingers or believers in an independent Puerto Rico. They, as well as many who want commonwealth status to be maintained, think that Governor Romero will use the cultural center to spearhead an "annexionist" or statehood movement, and they demand that the Center be returned to the Institute of Puerto Rican Culture.

Edwin Reyes, the spokesman for the Committee for the Defense of Culture, said on the telephone that the Romero Administration was pushing for Puerto Rican Statehood. "We think statehood is suicide for Puerto Ricans." He said, "We must fight against those intentions, ADAC is a push toward statehood, controlled by annexionists, and the artists of Puerto Rico are against it."[17]

Clearly, the battle for the control of cultural policy formulation and implementation in Puerto Rico is far from over.

NOTES

1. Jack Condous, Janferie Howlet, and John Skull, eds., *Arts in Cultural Diversity* (Sydney: Holt, Rinehart and Winston, 1980).

2. "Puerto Rico and the U.S.: A Political and Cultural Identity Crisis," *The Washington Post*, June 23, 1981, p. 2.

3. Beatriz Ruiz de la Mata, *The New York Times*, October, 1978, p. 50.

4. "Puerto Rico and the U.S.: A Political and Cultural Identity Crisis." *The Washington Post*, June 23, 1981, p. 2.

5. Ruiz de la Mata, p. 50.

6. Ibid.

7. Ibid.

8. Ricardo E. Alegria. "El Instituto de Cultura Puertorriqueña 1955−73: 18 años contribuyendo a fortalecer nuestra conciencia nacional." San Juan: Instituto de Cultura Puertorriqueña.

9. *Origen, gobierno y propósitos del Instituto de Cultura Puertorriqueña* (San Juan: Unidad de Información Cultural, Instituto de Cultura Puertorriqueña, 1979).

10. Carlos Romero-Barcelo. "Puerto Rico, U.S.A.: The Case for Statehood," *Foreign Affairs* (Fall 1980), 60−81.

11. "Puerto Rico and the U.S.: A Political and Cultural Identity Crisis," *The Washington Post*, June 23, 1981, p. 2.

12. Romero-Barcelo, "Puerto Rico, U.S.A.," pp. 60−81.

13. "Puerto Rico and the U.S.: A Political and Cultural Identity Crisis," *The Washington Post*, June 23, 1981, p. A10.

14. Romero-Barcelo, "Puerto Rico, U.S.A.," pp. 60−81.

15. "Puerto Rico and the U.S.: A Political and Cultural Identity Crisis," *The Washington Post*, June 23, 1981, p. 2.

16. Raymond Ericson, "Music Notes: Casals Festival," *The New York Times*, September 30, 1979, section 2, p. 21.

17. Harold C. Schonberg, "San Juan's Disputed Art Center Opens," *The New York Times*, April 12, 1981, p. 57.

9. Modernization and the Cultural Heritage: Can They Coexist in Brazil?

Claudio de Moura Castro

Brazil has been able to modernize its economy at a very fast pace. Manufacturing growth has been spectacular, despite the complete absence of a previous tradition along such lines. However, this ability to transform values, attitudes and habits has proved to be tragic in terms of its cultural heritage. In this paper I will try to examine both this predicament and recent efforts to prevent the defacement of the landscape, the destruction of old buildings, and the disappearance of manifestations of traditional culture.[1]

Historical Roots of Brazilian Culture

Brazil is a country of western traditions. There, the Portuguese did not set an enclave amidst a local culture, as happened in Asia and Africa. Instead, they populated a territory thinly inhabited by primitive tribes. Whereas the Aztec, Maya, and Inca empires, taken over by the Spanish, were highly developed cultures, the Brazilian Indians were in a stage of paleolithic nomadism.

The colonies founded by the Portuguese progressively absorbed the natives and, later, the African slaves. One often-mentioned feature of Portuguese colonization is its cultural permeability. After being ruled for many years by the darker-skinned Moors, with whom they intermarried widely, the Portuguese have varied ethnic origins. As a result, ideas of ethnic purity or superiority never prevailed among them.

Miscegenation with Negroes began before Brazil was discovered, as a result of an official policy aiming to populate the Cape Verde and Azores Islands. Also, close to 200,000 Jews lost their cultural identity in the sixteenth century. This partly accounts for the relaxed attitudes towards racial purity always displayed by the Portuguese. Indians and Africans have intermarried with the Portuguese colonists throughout Brazilian history resulting in a very blurred distinction between the races. According to the 1980 census, only about half of Brazilians are reported to be pure white or black (based on appearance, not on ancestry).

As the slave trade dwindled, substantial European immigration occurred. In addition to the continuing flow of Portuguese immigrants, Italians, Germans, and Poles settled down in the southern regions. The turn of the century marked the beginning of what was to become the largest concentration of Japanese outside Japan. The result is a complex mixture of races that contrasts with the North American situation in many respects. Racial miscegenation has always been much greater in Brazil, and race is not such an important public issue.

The common link has always been language. The Brazilian border is also the Portuguese-language border—exactly. Brazil is the only South American country in which Portuguese is spoken and, except for German, Japanese, and Polish hinterland enclaves, no other language is spoken in the country. There are no Portuguese dialects, only different accents and regionalisms.

Though expressed in a single language, there is a great deal of cultural variety, the common denominator being Western European tradition. The Indian and African strains were absorbed in a syncretic process; it is not a case of parallel coexistence.[2] The situation bears no similarity to countries such as Iran or India.

Brazil inherited from Portugal British dominance in economic matters. Until the late nineteenth century, Brazil was clearly within the orbit of the British Empire. Surprisingly, France was the undisputed source of inspiration for the cultural elites. The French Mission, which brought to Brazil naturalists, artists and architects early in the nineteenth century, is often mentioned as a landmark in the shift towards French influence. Until World War II, French culture set the tone and fashion for the Brazilian elites. French was the most widely spoken foreign language. Until a few decades ago, French was taught in school before English.

Another determining factor in Brazilian cultural history was the transfer of the Portuguese court and royal family to Rio de Janeiro in the early nineteenth century. After independence in 1822, Brazil remained a monarchy ruled by Pedro I, son of João VI, the king of Portugal. Close to one century of court life, with Orleans and Habsburg rulers, provided a very strong European model for the Brazilian upper classes.

A very clear split between English economic domination and French cultural influence existed until recently. Post-war American influence, however, encompasses both the cultural and the economic spheres. While American art and literature have never been exalted and venerated as were the French, the American imprint on everyday activities such as dress, fast food, drinks, television, and music has been pervasive. On a more positive side, the influx of Anglo-Saxon scientific tradition is a welcome counterbalance to the "softer" science borrowed from France.

Despite the common denominator of Western tradition, the disparities in instruction and technological levels and the complexity and sophistication of mores and social life are extreme. Outside the larger urban centers, life styles have remained almost primitive.

Tools are an intriguing index of social and economic organization. Complex, numerous, and highly specialized tools reflect greater division of labor, more advanced levels of specialization of functions, and a greater time horizon in budgeting time.

My hobby of collecting old tools has led me to compare carpentry tools and techniques of Minas Gerais (where the eighteenth-century gold boom took place) with those of German settlements in southern Brazil and also with old New England tools. Very clearly, the tools and techniques of the Portuguese colonists are very simple and versatile, meaning that one tool does the work of many—although less efficiently.

Although furniture and carving from eighteenth-century Minas Gerais are unsurpassed by anything comparable in southern Brazil or in New England, there is ample evidence that technological sophistication has been much lower in traditional Brazil. To examine this evidence would take us beyond the scope of this paper. Traditional Brazil resembles Portugal: although European roots predominate, both are economically backward and technologically unsophisticated. Brazil differs from Portugal in the sense that it is more culturally permeable by outside influences.

The Vulnerability of Cultural Heritage

It is frequently stated that Brazil has no identity problems. An industrial revolution, capitalism (praxis and doctrine), complex organization, and western civilization seem to be corollaries of a vertiginous increase in material well-being. Japan refused the package until the Meiji Restoration; China remained undecided for a century; India is still struggling with the idea; Iran is turning backwards. Mexico is riddled with identity problems, as are other Latin countries with vigorous indigenous cultures.

The question in Brazil is not whether to deny its roots in order to accept the extant models for development, as those roots are European. It is, rather, a matter of social mobilization within values that do not necessarily deny or challenge past traditions. It means moving from simple to complex organization, from personal to impersonal authority systems. The extremely fast rates of development in the last decades may be used as evidence. Notice that manufacturing has been the leading factor in a development process that finds few other rivals in the world. Northeastern peasants migrate to São Paulo to become accomplished machinists on short notice. They drive automobiles, watch television, wear blue jeans, go to discotheques, and increasingly practice birth control. They are envied by relatives who stayed behind for their higher standard of living.

Although this cultural plasticity may be convenient and enable this economic model to materialize, it is alarming from other perspectives: progress is corroding history and tradition. Brazil runs the risk of wasting a rich and pluralistic culture that is neither antithetical to economic modernization, nor an impediment to its development, as happens elsewhere. It is too vulnerable to the overwhelming thrust of this progress, however. This traditional culture still exists, but is having enormous difficulty in coexisting with the modern styles dictated by television. All aspects of traditional culture are threatened: exquisite regional cuisines, a very sensible vernacular architecture, traditional songs and dances, handicrafts such as methods of weaving, basketmaking, leather-work, and ceramics—everything either tends to disappear or to incorporate ghastly contemporary influences. More obvious are the insults to the landscape and the destruction of buildings and sites of artistic or historical interest. From real estate tycoons to the most humble peasant, there is little reticence in destroying the Brazilian heritage. In Ouro Preto, a town of enormous beauty and historical interest—deservedly protected by extensive legislation—people tear down houses or modify the colonial facades during the weekends, in order to evade city inspectors. City planners tore down a valuable eighteenth-century church in Recife in order to widen a street. After the church was destroyed, plans were changed and the street took another path.

This is not the place to bemoan the endless insults to Brazil's cultural heritage. It may be instructive, however, to examine the German influence in the South. Towns like Joinville and Blumenau were founded by German colonizing corporations before World War II. Even street signs were written in Gothic German. During the war there was much government pressure to integrate, but since then there has been little effort, either subtle or open, to incorporate Germans into the Brazilian mainstream. Nevertheless, this has been happening very quickly. Students at the local colleges still speak with a slight German accent, but they read Goethe and Schiller in Portuguese trans-lation. The very pleasant architecture, which bears strong resemblance to its European origin while incorporating local adaptations, is being demolished, to be replaced with nondescript modern architecture.

The Champions of Conservation: The Intellectuals in Government

Germane to Iberian traditions, Brazilian culture has a clearly authoritarian flavor, in the sense that the flow of communication is vertical. Federal govern-ment is strong, and reliance on state action is pervasive. Accordingly, the first efforts to preserve buildings and historical monuments began in 1937 with the creation of a federal agency to protect historical and artistic heritage, the IPHAN.[3] Its founders were aristocratic intellectuals from Rio de Janeiro, and Rodrigo de Mello Franco, a remarkable person and its mentor from the outset, fits this description well.

Much has been achieved by the founders' initiative. Were it not for their decrees, very little of the best we have in architecture would exist today. Their attitude and style were paternalistic as they waged a holy war against the uncouth and heretical Brazilian populace. The strategy of IPHAN was straight-forward: to prevent destruction by legal action and provide expert labor to reconstruct, repair, and maintain.

Brazil owes much to IPHAN, but the shortcomings of its actions are clear.

It could not go beyond protecting the best examples of architecture and other landmarks. By assuming responsibility for further maintenance, it was bound by its budget. Furthermore, its actions focused on monuments. Other cultural manifestations, such as popular art and music, were not dealt with.

The New Rhetoric: Popular Participation

IPHAN has changed hands, incorporated other related programs, acquired a more flexible legal-administrative structure, and reformulated its rhetoric. (It would be better to say, "acquired one," because it has traditionally maintained a low profile and not been concerned with its popular image or with attempts to back its actions with a fully spelled-out doctrine. This was congruent with its aristocratic leadership.)

Interpreting the current situation is an interesting exercise. Conservation has become everybody's business. Traditions and the cultural heritage belong to the people and are to be preserved by the people for their own edification. Communities are to protect their cultural values. Local groups and associations are watching over their heritage.

Recently refurbished buildings are being officially "returned" to the communities and each occasion is commemorated with popular feasts. Listening to the rhetoric of the persons in charge of programs, a new era seems to have arrived.

The Serviço do Patrimônio Histórico e Artístico Nacional (SPHAN, formerly IPHAN) has been publishing a well-presented newsletter covering the whole period of its new administration, in fifteen issues so far. It represents official work from the administration, a sample of opinions of people connected with conservation, and wide coverage of their activities. All important projects are mentioned, making it an excellent document describing the role of SPHAN.

A careful reading of the newsletter reveals much about community action and popular participation. Fifty-four articles referring to such projects were recorded. This number, in itself, is not very meaningful, because some articles group together several projects, while others refer to projects previously mentioned. There is a clear effort to expand issues of community and popular action, hence one should not expect omission here. Fourteen times, community or popular action were mentioned, suggesting that one-fourth of the projects involve popular participation.

Probing deeper into the nature of this participation reveals a somewhat different situation. Two cases ought to be excluded, as one concerns popular action to reverse the decree that prohibits the tearing down of a church and the other the legal efforts of SPHAN to prevent an individual from demolishing his house. In three cases there is indeed community initiative. The interest, however, is clearly economic. One has to do with legalizing titles of land ownership, the second with reopening a fishing harbor, and the third reflects the interest of former workers in reactivating a railway. There are two cases of individual efforts. In the first, a priest becomes interested in an immigration museum while doing research for an academic paper. In the other, a historian with over twenty books published attempts to protect buildings threatened by real estate developers. In both cases, hardly an initiative from the masses. There is one case in which SPHAN attempted to motivate the people to protect their historical buildings and traditions. In another, the community took the initiative of requesting a party to inaugurate some restoration work. Clearly, again, these are not cases of popular initiative.

This leaves us with four cases. In the first, a small town community organized a museum in a building restored by SPHAN. In the second, a local club organized by Projeto Rondon (the Brazilian equivalent of VISTA) attempts to find a suitable function for a building which was also rebuilt by SPHAN. The last two cases report the activities of local associations to protect their towns. These are, in fact, the only examples of community initiative, rather than passive responses to SPHAN animation.

Petrópolis began as a summer resort for the Emperor. It has grown considerably since then, yet it remains a sophisticated town. A recently founded local association is trying to attract attention and rescue the town from unbridled real estate speculation, which is building high-rises where mansions once stood.

Olinda, once a small sixteenth-century town, has become a suburb of Recife. A very vocal local association is trying to prevent further defacement of the town. The newsletter publishes a photograph of a popular meeting without further caption. What it does not mention is that the speaker standing up in the crowd holds a Ph.D. from the University of Geneva.

What do we learn from the newsletter? (1) There is much prolixity when discussing popular participation. Every small possibility is avidly taken. (2) Truly popular initiatives are motivated by economic reasons, not conservation. (3) There is considerable effort to approach local populations after legal provisions are resolved and buildings restored. (4) Non-governmental initiatives to protect and restore are rare and restricted to the local elites. (5) Local associations like those of Petrópolis and Olinda are recent initiatives of intellectuals.

Lessons?

In the preceding sections I have examined the activities and rhetoric of the new SPHAN administration. Are we to conclude that they are misleading and wrong? Far from that. SPHAN seems to have chosen a shrewd and premeditated strategy. Popular support is sorely needed. It is impossible to battle endlessly against a population unconcerned with the protection of a collective cultural heritage.

Surely, those who are keenly aware of the rapid erosion of the traditional ways and things are the better educated. Bewitched by the glitter of progress, ready to accept the full package rather than select what is required for modernization, the Brazilian people are happy to do away with their history. It is, in fact, quite germane to Brazilian tradition that the need to preserve historical roots and their tangible counterparts will be administered from the top down. This may be a patronizing statement, but at least it is not a hypocritical one.

The elitist IPHAN attempted to conserve. The more alert SPHAN also attempts to teach conservation. Careful reading of their prose reveals that the leaders do not misrepresent or show naïveté. The speeches and press releases are carefully worded. The culture is popular. The object of protection is indeed vernacular in form. Notwithstanding, the political will to conserve has not become popular so far. By emphasizing vernacular roots and getting the people involved, even if ex post facto, they may progressively develop attitudes and circumstances more favorable to their propositions.

The scope of conservation has also broadened. From the attempt to save individual buildings, greater effort is now put into the protection of entire areas or sets of buildings. Also, other forms of cultural manifestation are being contemplated, such as handicrafts and dance.

One very important intermediate step in this direction is the joint ventures in restoration. The larger the number of institutions involved, the wider the audience for their ideas. Returning to the newsletter, some comments are warranted: there are about twenty examples of joint ventures with Federal Government agencies (Tourism, Transportation, Army); close to thirty cases of partnership with state governments (state preservation agencies); and about twenty-five cases of association with municipal government.

Since the same federal agencies are listed again and again, their participation is considerably more intense than any state or municipal agency. As a tentative conclusion, one may state that the flow from the top down is a pattern which also prevails at the institutional level. Parallel to the progressive dissemination from the elites to the lower levels of society, the task of conservation is being undertaken progressively by federal, state and municipal agencies.

NOTES

1. Patricia Zimbres revised the manuscript and offered several useful suggestions although she does not agree with all views expressed. The author is grateful to her.

2. For the purposes of the present discussion the delicate problem with the Indians creates no difficulties. Indian tribes correspond to one-tenth of one percent of the Brazilian population, and live beyond the border of regular territorial occupation.

3. Instituto do Patrimônio Histórico e Artístico Nacional (Institute of the National Historic and Artistic Patrimony).

10. Folklore Protection and National Patrimony: Developments and Dilemmas in the Legal Protection of Folklore

Alan Jabbour

The telephone rings at the Archive of Folk Culture at the Library of Congress, and the caller asks to speak to the Archive's head. A blues researcher, devotee, and promoter, he is calling on behalf of his friend and client, an elderly blues singer from Mississippi. The singer and two friends recorded a blues song in 1928 which attained some popularity among blues audiences of the era. It was subsequently rerecorded by one or two early blues artists; then adapted and arranged in the 1940s by a prominent bluegrass musician from Kentucky; then adapted and arranged by a well-known Chicago rhythm-and-blues musician in the 1950s. From there it "hit the charts" in a big way, being arranged and rerecorded by a prominent rock group from the British Isles in the 1960s; the LP on which the item appears sold over a million copies. Why, the caller wants to know, has his friend and client, the elderly blues singer, not received a cent in royalties? He claims that he is the one who actually "made up" the song, and a copyright notice was filed when the recording was made.

Although it is of course possible that "making it up" in this context means the adaptation of floating blues lyrics and melodies that formed the tradition out of which our Mississippi blues singer created, the cause nevertheless seems worthwhile, and a copyright lawyer is enlisted. He assembles the facts and decides to write strong letters demanding royalty payments to the author-composer from the various record companies involved over the years. Some of the companies come through with a check, others ignore the request, and one company protests that it has already paid royalties for that song to someone else (the holder of the claim for a different song with a similar title). Legally and philosophically considered, the resolution of the problem is messy at best, but it has the practical effect of rewarding our elderly blues singer and helping him during a period of straitened circumstances. Everyone is happy, and the case is closed.

A delegation of Navajo Indians, including a rug weaver, a trading post manager, and a friend, calls for an appointment with the Library's American Folklife Center. On arrival they explain that they are very concerned about the use of Navajo rug patterns by non-Navajos, particularly by overseas factories which reproduce rugs in the Navajo style with cheap materials and cheap labor, thus undercutting the Navajo themselves in the market for their famous rugs.

Why can't the traditional rug patterns be copyrighted, the delegation wonders. Perhaps the Navajo could have a special trademark with official sanction, or a law could be passed prohibiting the import of the imitation rugs. The director of the Folklife Center points out that the Department of the Interior has legal authority to develop a sort of a trademark (or perhaps we should say "tribe-mark"), but that tribal participation in the system has not always been regular or effective for one reason or another. An appointment is arranged with officials in the Department of the Interior, and the delegation leaves, perplexed but moderately pleased that some people in Washington are at least interested in the problem.

A letter arrives at the American Folklife Center from the chairman of the education committee of a Plains tribal council. The writer is agitated about a recent glossy publication that both describes and (in part) transcribes the Sun Dance. The Sun Dance is a sacred and secret ritual, it is pointed out, and it should never be published in a book aimed at general audiences. The participants in the Sun Dance are the only persons who have a right to this information, the writer urges. What, she asks, can be done to stop this publication? And also, what procedures should be used for the tribe to copyright rituals like this so that they cannot be published?

None of these three instances is exactly true, but all of them approximate the day-to-day experiences of a cultural specialist working in Washington. Each instance reflects certain special complications and circumstances, and there may be no single solution to the three problems presented by them. Nevertheless, they all represent an area of widespread anxiety and concern in the United States and around the world—particularly among Third World countries—and underlying them are certain profound legal dilemmas which face all governments in developing laws and policies for the nurture of their indigenous cultural traditions.

The impetus for protecting folklore, both nationally and internationally, is a deep-seated but inchoate concern or anxiety, which does not translate easily into clear-cut issues. Nevertheless, here is a taxonomy of the anxiety, thrown together for the nonce:

The first issue may be termed *authentication*. Concern for authentication of folklore comes in various forms. Native Americans and West Africans unite, for instance, in decrying the replication of their traditional crafts in overseas factories, which mass-produce the items with cheap labor and flood the international market, including local markets in Nigeria and the American Southwest. Such replication constitutes not only an economic but a cultural and psychological threat to the authentic practitioners of traditional arts and to the traditional groups whose values those arts express.

To take another example, the issue of authentication hovers about the frequently expressed complaint that outside researchers study and publish descriptions of traditional cultures and their practices without consulting the people being described. Though it sometimes appears that one person's information is another's misinformation, the worldwide anxiety about cultural misrepresentation is genuine; thus it is that this form of the authentication issue is often associated with calls for consultation.

The second issue I call *expropriation*. The expropriation issue represents an anxiety about the removal of valuable artifacts and documents from their place of origin. For years, the great museums of western civilization have heard the complaint that they have removed irreplaceable national treasures from their homelands. I judge this concern to be still on the rise, but it is not limited to artifacts. I have heard fretting, within the United States and around the world, about photographs, films, sound recordings, and other documentary materials being created, then taken away from the original community, region, or country which is the subject of documentation.

Third is the issue of *compensation*. Even when the national and international circulation of a folk cultural item is a source of local pride, or when it is conceded that such circulation is inevitable and proper, there is widespread resentment of the fact that the individuals and communities whence the item originated are not compensated for their contribution.

Fourth is what I shall call simply *nurture*. Although all the other issues seem to pertain to regulation of the circulation of folk cultural items outside their "native habitat," in fact the worldwide expression of concern about these issues is regularly accompanied by a parallel concern for maintaining the health and vitality of folk culture itself in the face of "modernization" and "internationalization" in the flow of commerce and culture. Protests about the external exploitation of folk cultural items, in short, almost always betoken a harder-to-express fear about the disruption of folk culture itself.

This swirl of issues and anxieties has generated a variety of legal initiatives within various countries of the world. I should like to call special attention today to an initiative developed by the World Intellectual Property Organization, based in Geneva, in collaboration with the Copyright Division of UNESCO. Most of the cultural issues I have delineated focus not on culture as a whole, but on the creative expressions of the various traditional cultures of the world. There may be broader anxieties about the future of cultures as a whole, but the anxieties are crystallized by discussions about the use or abuse of creative expressions such as song, dance, and crafts. Thus, it was inevitable that some legal solutions would be proposed in the sphere of intellectual property law.

As a term, "intellectual property" may require some explanation. It is used as the collective or generic term for that class of law which regulates and encourages the flow of creative contributions to society. Under the rubric of intellectual property come such categories as copyright, trademark, patent, appellation of origin, and the like. Copyright law seemed particularly attractive as a framework within which to deal with the protection of the creative expressions of folklore. A folksong is, after all, a song; songs as individual compositions can be copyrighted, thus asserting the author's claim to control over and compensation for the fruits of his creativity. Why not apply the same principles to folk music, folk art, and other genres of traditional creative expression?

As early as 1967, Bolivia passed a law providing legal protection for its national folklore using a quasi-copyright framework, and some other Third World countries followed suit in the 1970s. At the urging of some of these countries, the World Intellectual Property Organization, in collaboration with UNESCO launched in 1980 an initiative to explore the intellectual property aspects of folklore protection as a legal issue. Its working group of legal and folkloric experts convened in Geneva to examine and comment upon a model law for the protection of folklore devised by the legal experts at the World Intellectual Property Organization. I participated in that working group as the United States representative. After several days of debate regarding the overall philosophy of folklore protection, the proper legal frameworks for such efforts, and the specific provisions of the draft model law, the working group adjourned with the resolution to meet again a year later.

The second meeting took place at UNESCO headquarters in Paris in 1981. The working group was presented with a revised model law which incorporated the deliberations of the first meeting. Further debate ensued, but by the end of the second meeting there was general agreement among members of the working group about the fundamental direction and specific provisions of the model law. This summer, the issue will be brought before a formal meeting of "governmental experts" (that is, official representatives of governments rather than individuals debating in their private capacity). Ultimately, even if it survives the gauntlet of international deliberation, the model law is designed simply as a recommendation to national legislatures. In other words, it is not a matter subject to formal international treaty, but simply a formally endorsed concept which will be presented to national legislatures for their consideration. The World Intellectual Property Organization will presumably print up the model law and commentary on folklore protection, and it will enter the network of current ideas from which nations may elect to choose in devising or revising their statutes.

The scope of this paper does not permit me to analyze in detail the provisions for the model law protecting expressions of folklore. For now, let me try to highlight the fundamental dilemmas presented by efforts to protect folklore through an intellectual property framework.

First, the implication of such a concept is that traditional cultural groups possess intellectual property rights, *as groups*, to the creative expressions created and maintained by the group. Thus, the Sun Dance of our earlier example is felt to be created, maintained, and owned by adherents to the ritual. Copyright law, however it may vary from nation to nation, has as its common denominator a concept of individual property rights arising from individual creativity. It, in effect, carves out a sphere of rights from what otherwise would be the free flow of creative ideas in the larger "public domain." Protecting folklore means, essentially, acknowledging an intermediate sphere of intellectual property rights between individual rights on the one hand, and the national or international public domain on the other. In terms of legal history and legal frameworks, this is a radical idea.

Second, the effort to protect folklore raises fundamental issues about the concepts of folklore and of particular expressions of folklore, which define that which is to be protected. Among some nations and people, there is a tendency to identify "folklore" with a vague tribal or peasant past, and to assume that such expressions have rights because of their origins in an imagined primeval cultural source. For others (amongst whom I number myself) the word "folklore" should be applied to living creative traditions, connected by powerful ties to the past but evolving creatively in the present. In terms of protection, then, it must be decided whether rights being protected proceed from what I shall term "ultimate origin" or "proximate origin." Using our Navajo rug example, we might say that the living creative tradition implies collective intellectual property rights, even though that tradition evolved from earlier borrowings from other tribes, and thence from Mexico, and thence from Spain, and thence from Moorish North Africa. On this issue the draft model law has been oriented by the deliberations of the working group to emphasize the protection of living traditions, rather than the protection of historic or prehistoric creative forms.

Third, legal protection of expressions of folklore raises the question of who will judge. The inclination of most nation-states is to create what lawyers call the "competent authority" as part of the national government, in a ministry of culture or the like. Given the structure of most national governments, that may be the only practical solution, but some of us in the working group struggled to interpose a concept of adjudication or consultation by the group itself. This is conceivable where a traditional culture possesses formal legal sanction, but not so easy when the group lacks such sanction. The Navajo tribe, for example, has legal status in the United States and possesses an official tribal council; but there is no organization of blues singers. The skeptic will perceive the potential for a power grab in the Third World governments' interest in their folklore traditions. Indeed, some of the lawyers representing Third World countries wondered aloud whether this might be the occasion for implementing an old lawyers' dream expressed by the French phrase *domaine publique payant*. When there is no individual author, in other words, we should pay a royalty to the state. Without adequate safeguards to ensure that the source group of an expression of folklore has some say in the matter, the concept of folklore protection is disquieting.

Fourth, all these legal dilemmas about protecting folklore are imbedded within the larger dilemma regarding the relationship of the world's traditional cultures to the nation-states within whose legal frameworks they must exist. The great international issue of the coming decades will be an effort to define and protect the basic human rights of traditional cultures vis-à-vis the national governments under which they exist. Although the issue of folklore protection has sometimes been raised in a rhetorical style suggesting that the enemy and exploiter of folklore traditions is the world of international corporations and developed countries, in fact a thoughtful observer may have reason to fear that the greatest dangers to folklore, and to the cultures from whence that folklore arises, come from national governments, including those of the Third World. Rising concerns in such forums as UNESCO about dealing with "migrant populations" represent but the tip of the iceberg of this worldwide dilemma.

These thoughts are scantily realized, but I hope that in introducing them I can help to clarify the nature of and developments in the subject of folklore protection. It is an important and challenging aspect of the rising international concern for defining, understanding, protecting, and nourishing the world's cultural patrimonies.

Networks and Databases
in Latin America

11. The Effect of MARC on International Networking and the Role of the Library of Congress in the Development of International Data Bases

Henriette Avram

Effect of MARC on International Networking

The development of MARC in the United States was closely followed by the development of national MARC projects by the national bibliographic agencies in countries all over the world. The process is still going on in developing countries. Today many of the western European countries, countries in the Eastern block, and in Latin America, Australia, Canada, Japan, Malaysia, South Africa, and Taiwan have their own national MARC formats and operational or planned MARC systems. In the relatively short time span of thirteen years, many of these systems have become operational and in a number of cases the national agencies are exchanging their bibliographic records in machine-readable form. Thus, an international MARC network has been evolving.[1]

The events of the 1960s and early 1970s increasingly led us closer to the International Federation of Library Associations and Institutions (IFLA) goal of U.B.C. The Paris Principles served as the basis for international standardization in cataloging codes and many nations have already formatted their rules following the Principles. The International Standard Bibliographic Description (ISBD) for different forms of material brought together various national practices for describing and identifying an item into a standardized form. The International Organization for Standardization (I.S.O.) standard format structure for bibliographic information interchange based on the Library of Congress and the American National Standard Institute work in this country provided the facility to exchange bibliographic data in machine-readable form and thus took advantage of the technology and its potential for greater resource sharing than possible in the past. The majority of the many national MARC systems were designed to input, process, and distribute data based on these standards.

In spite of all this progress, however, problems for international exchange of data still remained. The content designators used by the national MARC systems were not standardized. These tags, indicators, and data element identifiers varied among the national formats, partly because of remaining differences in cataloging codes and practices. Consequently, although the national format structures were identical, there was so much variation among the MARC implementations that tailor-made computer programs had to be written by each national agency to process MARC data of every other national agency, thus severely detracting from the advantages created by the Paris Principles and the ISBD. For example, the National Library of Canada has written programs to process UK MARC, US MARC, and the French InterMARC.

In 1972 IFLA created a joint working group charged with the responsibility for investigating the differences in national MARC formats and recommending a standard to be used by national agencies for the international exchange of bibliographic data in machine-readable form, and thus UNIMARC emerged. UNIMARC makes it possible to write and maintain only two conversion programs, one from the national format to UNIMARC and the other from UNIMARC to the national format.

Since completion and publication of the first edition of UNIMARC in 1977 there have been two types of implementation activities. For national formats that were already well established before 1977, new conversion programs were needed so that national data could be distributed internationally in UNIMARC. For agencies recently undertaking the development of a national format (or substantially revising an existing one), UNIMARC could stand as a format model, thus facilitating conversions.

It was recognized that the development of conversion programs would be slow, as in many cases UNIMARC was published at a time when several MARC-producing agencies were involved in a major change of rules for recording data—the implementation of *Anglo-American Cataloguing Rules*, Second Edition (AACR2). This change has had the beneficial effect of extending the use of the ISBD, but it has slowed the implementation of UNIMARC. At this time, however, the Library of Congress is working on conversion programs between US MARC and UNIMARC. Current plans are to be able to offer UNIMARC-formatted records for Library of Congress data by late 1982. The National Library of Australia is also working on conversion programs.

The second principal type of implementation activity involves national agencies developing national formats since 1977. They were in the position of basing them on UNIMARC. Hungary, Japan, Taiwan, and South Africa, among others, now have formats that closely resemble UNIMARC, although they contain slight differences to accommodate special national requirements.

A few years prior to the completion of UNIMARC, an organization which became known as the Conference of Directors of National Libraries (CDNL) was formed and later operated under the auspices of the International Federation of Library Associations and Institutions (IFLA). This conference, in considering the problems of national libraries, gave the highest priority to the evolving international MARC network and formed a steering committee charged with the responsibility to conduct studies regarding technical and policy considerations of data exchange across national boundaries. This committee was responsible for the development of a model agreement to be used between national agencies for the exchange of records for the imprints of their countries, the recommendation through the CDNL to IFLA that an International MARC Office be established, charged with the responsibility for the functions needed for an effective international network, for example, maintenance of UNIMARC, training, and policy issues for exchange.

In the fall and winter of 1980−1981, a study of UNIMARC conversion was carried out under the auspices of the Steering Committee. The participants were national agencies with established MARC formats. Each agency was given the same set of approximately seventy-five title pages for monographs and serials and asked to supply UNIMARC records for each bibliographic entity. The national agency was to derive each UNIMARC record from a national MARC record, simulating machine conversion. If no national MARC record existed, the agency cataloged the item as well as possible based on the title page, converted the data to national MARC and then converted the national MARC to UNIMARC. When the results of the test are available in 1982, IFLA will have data concerning the compatibility of data content among various agencies and the relative completeness of UNIMARC records for possible participants in international data exchange. The test will provide valuable aid to countries that are implementing UNIMARC.

Another major important project for an International MARC Office will be the preparation of a UNIMARC document that includes rules for recording the actual data. UNIMARC has no rules for the actual form of the data except by reference to the ISBD. This is adequate for countries with well-developed cataloging codes, but developing countries may not have an established cataloging code tradition. An ''annotated'' UNIMARC that incorporated basic cataloging rules and essential ISBD instructions, in addition to format specifications, would be a useful handbook for system development in these countries. It would help ensure data compatibility for eventual exchanges—one more step toward the distribution cataloging goal of the IFLA Universal Bibliographic Control program.

In summary, US MARC developed the standards—the sine qua non of networking—which were incorporated in all national systems. In addition, it demonstrated the feasibility and utility of the conversion of bibliographic records to machine-readable form and the exchange of these records nationally and internationally, thus reducing costs, duplication of cataloging, and conversion.

**The Role of the Library of Congress in the
Development of National and International
Data Bases**

In addition to the significant contribution of the Library of Congress (LC) in the area of standardization, LC has also played a major role in the development of national and international data bases. Some of the programs in this area are briefly described below.

In 1966 the National Program for Acquisitions and Cataloging (NPAC) was established in the United States at LC, with the aim of cataloging every scholarly work published in the world and making these records available to the research libraries of the United States. The NPAC effort was followed shortly by LC's MARC Project, which initially concentrated on English-language books. As that project expanded into materials in languages other than English and into other forms of materials, these records also became available in machine-readable form. Today, LC's MARC files, which are the records distributed in the MARC Distribution Service, contain records from over 600 countries in more than 180 languages.

Through the MARC Distribution Service, these data are made available to the national and international subscribers. Internationally, where LC has agreements with other national bibliographic agencies, it exchanges records for U.S. imprints free of charge, but sells the records for non-U.S. imprints. Thus it is possible for the bibliographic agency in any country to purchase LC MARC files representing records for items from that and/or other countries which LC has acquired and cataloged. Since all the other bibliographic agencies make only their own country's imprints available, LC is the only international data base.

To illustrate the international nature of LC's data base, I have gathered the following figures for the areas of particular interest to SALALM. All figures are approximate.

The LC books data base alone contains 60,000 records for items in the Spanish language, of which almost 12,000 items were cataloged in FY 1980 and 7,000 in FY 1981. The number of records of items in the Portuguese language is over 21,000, with almost 4,000 of those cataloged in FY 1980 and 2,200 in FY 1981.

The combined databases for books, serials, maps, and films contain 9,000 records for items published in Mexico and Central America; 41,000 records of items published in South America; 4,000 records of items published in the Caribbean area; 3,000 records of items published in Portugal; and 25,000 records of items published in Spain. All figures are based on the MARC country of publication codes for the countries within each area.

In addition to their international scope, the LC files represent a consistent catalog, in terms of cataloging rules and established forms of headings, among others. Consistency is one of the most important ingredients of building a data base, since it not only reduces the duplication of records within that data base but greatly simplifies use of records from a data base by other agencies. Even if an agency does not follow the practices of that data base, it is easier to convert to national (or local) practices from one consistent file than from multiple files representing different practices.

In addition to cataloging and distributing the records for bibliographic items from around the world, LC has been involved in a number of cooperative projects aimed at developing consistent machine-readable files which will then be made widely available. Various approaches can be used to provide consistency within databases: (1) build the data base in a single computer system with an authority system available; (2) build the data base in two or more systems which are linked and synchronized; and (3) designate one or more agencies responsible for authenticating the contributed records.

In the Name Authority Cooperative Project (NACO), participating libraries contribute name authority records for specialized areas to LC. For example, the University of Texas was selected for its ability to contribute Latin American headings. Staff from libraries participating in NACO are trained at LC. Such LC tools as the National Union Catalog, the printed MARC references, and the LC online files are used by the participants to search for names already established. If one exists, it is used by the participants. If none exists, the name is established by the NACO participant and the record sent to LC for incorporation in LC's authority file and distribution to subscribing libraries via the MARC Distribution Service.

The CONSER Project provides an example of a collaborative effort to build a file of quality machine-readable cataloging records for serials based on cooperative creation and maintenance of the records by the participating institutions, and authentication of the records by appointed national cataloging agencies. CONSER authentication is a candidate for reevaluation at LC. The premise of authoritative review is not at issue so much as is the way in which it is now conducted in this Project.

The notion of decentralized authentication of CONSER records has been introduced, as exemplified by the Government Publication Office's newly expanded role as a center of responsibility for its own CONSER records. This new approach to authentication draws upon the experience of the LC NACO Project training participants sufficiently to make them experts in their own right. It is possible that other CONSER institutions could function in a similar manner, that is, create records which do not require external review in order to be considered authenticated in the CONSER data base.

The WLN/RLG and Library of Congress Linked Systems Project (LSP) are developing specifications for a computer-to-computer connection to allow intersystem searching, file maintenance, and message exchange among the participants. The Name Authority File Service will be the first application of the Linked Systems Project capabilities. The nationwide name authority file will be built at the Research Libraries Information Network (RLIN), the technical manager of the file. LC will be the bibliographic manager of the file, and will have a copy of the file in the LC system.

The Linked Systems Project application's specifications make it possible for participants on the RLIN, WLN, and LC systems to add, change, and delete records on the file.

The Name Authority File Service is to be a service in which an authority file for names, titles, and series will be created and maintained by specially trained persons from a group of selected libraries which are members of different automated systems. Again, for quality control of the file, the emphasis has been placed on proper training of contributors instead of on authentication. Checking of records will only take place for new contributors and on a sampling basis for trained contributors.

LC is cooperating with the Research Libraries Group (RLG) to build a database for Far Eastern materials, the China, Japan, Korea Project. The database will be housed in the Research Libraries Information Network (RLIN) system, and LC and several other research libraries with an interest in Far Eastern materials will contribute to the data base. An authority file will be maintained to permit the consistent building of this data base. The records will be distributed by LC's MARC Distribution Service. It is hoped that tapes of records from MARC projects in Japan, Korea, the People's Republic of China, and Taiwan can be used as part of the CJK file.

A working group on an International Authority System has been established under the auspices of IFLA. This working group is charged with formulating the ISBD for printed authorities as well as the design specifications for the international exchange of authority records, not to include subjects. The working group is made up of staff members of national libraries. LC is participating, as is the National Library of Mexico.

In its cooperative efforts with other agencies, LC has maintained its consistent practices while at the same time broadening its coverage. The library community benefits from this expanded data base while maintaining the advantages of consistency.

NOTES

1. This section draws on an article entitled "UNIMARC REPORT," by Henriette D. Avram and Sally H. McCallum which is to be published in the *IFLA JOURNAL.*

12. Toward a National Information Network in Chile

Juan R. Freudenthal

Bibliographic systems in Chile generally followed European models until the early twentieth century. Dewey interrupted this complacency. The foundation of a library school at the University of Chile in the late 1940s allowed new possibilities for the cataloging, classification, storage, and retrieval of information. The perils of an information explosion in Chile were not easily understood because information was not perceived as one of the significant factors underlying political and social development. But neither Chile nor any other nation of the so-called Third World could escape the global village syndrome made possible by electronic wizardry and satellite connections.

This brought about a disruption of conventional methods in favor of more modern and politically expedient information systems which reflected the technocratic demands of the times. Chile and Latin America as a whole are undergoing severe disruptions of traditional communication patterns and information services. Mexican writer Carlos Fuentes speaks of "the synthetic quality of the ideologies and . . . the sacrifices imposed by the indiscriminate rush toward the dogmatic values of the future and progress . . . the internal tensions within the cultures themselves, between the technocratic, multinational demands of the so-called global village . . . and the assertions of local differences, regionalisms, decentralizations, and subcultures. . . ."[1] An apt description for the 1980s and the tensions they will bring in their wake.

An information revolution (not explosion) is taking place in Chile within this framework of uneasiness and frustration. The need for accurate and prompt high technology information services has resulted in certain misunderstandings about professional responsibilities. The sudden emphasis on specialized information and networks seems to imply that reader-oriented librarianship is on the wane. Because of the nature of Latin American societies, libraries will continue to be considered social systems rather than information systems.

The Emergence of Documentation in Chile

The history and present status of information and documentation in Chile (including several annotated checklists of up-to-date reference materials and compilations in the sciences) have been reviewed in three contributions which appeared in the *Journal of the American Society for Information Science* in

1972, 1977, and 1980.[2] In order to consider the present structure of Chile's information systems we need to look back, for a brief moment, at certain developments of historical importance.

During the 1950s, Chile's scientific community proposed to the State the creation of a commission to be in charge of assessing the national needs for scientific and technological progress, specifically, to obtain new revenues for these purposes beyond those allocated by the universities and national or foreign government-sponsored projects. Foremost among the concerns of this community was Chile's dependence upon foreign resources for its basic and applied research, of which a great proportion was provided by the United States. There was a desperate need for information resources which could support the nation's future scientific and technological commitments. Many university libraries possessed fair holdings and rendered adequate services, yet in the broader context of Chile's bibliographic system, these research centers had not received the attention they deserved.

In 1954, government decree 11, 575 established the National Fund for University Construction and Research. It also created the Council of Rectors of the Chilean Universities which would review and coordinate the educational and scientific activities of the Chilean universities. This Council, in collaboration with the Nation's scientific community, sought to create a national center for information and documentation which would coordinate all the scientific and technical libraries in the country. A succession of experts came from the United States as advisors in the organization of such a center, including consultants from the Stanford Research Institute, the National Academy of Sciences and the International Atomic Energy Agency.

Chile had much to learn from the United States, but little to adopt without making considerable changes. The Chilean experience had to be shaped by its own peculiar growth, for its realities were not those of any other nation, and certainly not those of a highly developed country such as the United States. In Chile's higher education programs, more emphasis had always been placed on the classic humanities curriculum rather than on the encouragement of scientific investigation and applied research. Undoubtedly, the cultural ascendancy of Spain and the nation's slowly expanding economy and industry were responsible for this condition.

This situation finally led to the establishment, in 1963, of CENID (Centro Nacional de Información y Documentación, or National Center for Information and Documentation). CENID became a referral center with emphasis on the coordination of special information and the analysis of the transfer of scientific knowledge at a national level. CENID also provided a documentation center, sponsored and compiled important bibliographies, offered continuing education courses, and represented Chile in international events vital for the formulation of a national information policy. In 1968 the government created the Comisión Nacional de Investigación Científica y Tecnológica, CONICYT,

(National Commission on Scientific and Technological Research). This agency reports directly to the President of the country, acts as a consultant body to the Chilean government, and is administered through the Ministry of Education. In 1969 CENID began operations within the framework of CONICYT. In 1977 CONICYT acquired an IBM 470/148 computer.

A year later, and with the cooperation of the Organization of American States, a pilot project was funded to provide a database of mostly research projects belonging to the Department of Statistics of CONICYT's Dirección de Información y Documentación.[3] Theses and dissertations will be included in this database in the near future. CONICYT has also initiated a project which will result in the automation of its national union catalog of periodical publications, now available only on index or filing cards. The documentation center of CONICYT offers free online and manual reference services. Its staff consists of one computer expert, one librarian, one statistics specialist, and two assistants.

The creation of CENID and CONICYT during the 1960s heralded a greater comprehension among government officials and the scientific community of the need for up-to-date, organized, and easily retrieved information. Chile, along with a few other Latin American nations, has also been able to provide leaders of the first magnitude in the areas of librarianship and informatics. In July 1977, CONICYT, with the support of the Organization of American States, sponsored the First National Seminar on Scientific and Technological Information. During January 12–16, 1981, the Instituto Chileno-Norteamericano (Chilean-North American Institute), in Santiago, sponsored a seminar entitled "Computer Applications in the Field of Information. The Chilean Experience." Finally, the awareness of the need for nationwide and worldwide standardization of cataloging practices, and faster access to all types of information, has led to the automation of library operations (cataloging, acquisitions, circulation, and retrieval) and the use of MARC tapes at the Universidad Católica.

Presently, the National Library is also considering the use of MARC for the automation of its card catalogs. Chilean information professionals have spent a great deal of effort trying to raise consciousness among government officials for a greater commitment toward the formulation of a realistic national science policy. Furthermore, they have sought the full support and contributions of the Chilean scientific community.[4]

The latest and most important achievement in this area, one which may have far reaching consequences for the future of Chile's scientific and technological progress, was the creation by an October 27, 1981 government decree of the Fondo Nacional de Desarrollo Científico y Tecnológico (National Endowment for Scientific and Technological Development). This endowment, administered by the Ministry of Education through CONICYT, consists of three councils: Consejo Nacional (National Council), headed by the Ministers of Education and Finance, and the National Bureau of Planning; Consejo

Superior de Ciencias (Higher Council of Sciences), administered by seven scientists; and the Consejo Superior de Desarrollo Tecnológico (Higher Council for Technological Development), with five scientists.

The National Council's major responsibility will be to obtain funds through the national budget and international economic assistance. The other two councils will work independently. Although the first group of scientists was selected by the President of the Republic, in future its members will propose their own successors. Thus, this new regulatory system of scientific and technological activities in the country will be left in the hands of the scientists themselves. Undoubtedly, this system will not be able to escape some political pressures, but it should give a new thrust to scientific and technological endeavors in Chile.

Contemporary Developments: Networks and Databases in Chile

During the late 1970s Chile saw the slow emergence of a nationwide information network consisting of several semiautonomous and autonomous components. Such a network should not be compared with those existing in highly industrialized societies, for it still lacks their high technological sophistication and wide range of applications.

In Chile, the conversion from manual to automated storage and retrieval systems is a recent phenomenon. It continues to be a slow process, hampered not only by economic and technological restrictions, but also by a certain intransigence and lack of cooperation among institutions, and even among the information managers themselves. Notwithstanding, the widespread use of computers and the introduction of automated information services in the country is a reality and its effects are already being felt in the commercial, banking, industrial, educational, and private sectors.

The following is a brief description of some of the major components of an information and documentation system in Chile and includes national and international producers of bibliographic databases.

The Empresa Nacional de Computación e Informática, ECOM (National Company for Computerization and Informatics) was created on September 5, 1968 to facilitate and modernize information systems in Chile. It serves as the major central processing unit, which provides a clearinghouse and the essential mechanism for the development, distribution, and maintenance of databases in the country. In September of 1981, ECOM became a public communications network with satellite connections between the United States, Europe, Japan and the Chilean cities of Santiago, Valparaíso, and Concepción. There are plans to link ECOM to Arica, Antofagasta, La Serena, Temuco, Puerto Montt, and Punta Arenas. In 1982, ECOM was serving the information needs of industries, banks, government agencies, the educational sector, hospitals, insurance companies, banks, and other, similar institutions. Probably the greatest impact of this new *red pública de transmisión de datos* (public network for the transmission of data) is that it can serve to interface diverse electronic equipment and types of memories and programs, which were incompatible until recently. ECOM receives information from about 500 U.S. data banks, mostly in the areas of sciences and social sciences. It also has been determined that transmission costs of information in and out of the country have been lowered considerably through the use of this company. Finally, ECOM offers expert personnel; storage and retrieval capabilities; analysis, design and programming of information systems; training and continuing education courses, etc. Most online information services in Chile are connected to ECOM in one way or another; exceptions to this rule are the international databases and those generated by Chilean universities, particularly by the University of Chile.

The Servicio de Sistemas de Información, SESI (Information Services System at the University of Chile) became operational in November 1977 and features a computer center, with access to several national and international databases, including COMPENDEX and AGRIS. It has also generated its own information units for the COMPENDEX database, offers SDI, and provides access to most of the research done at the University since 1973, university decrees and laws (available in full text), and online reference, particularly for the faculties of Engineering, Agronomy, and Veterinary Sciences. This documentation center also served until last year as the focal point for the Automated Union Catalog of Periodical Publications at the University of Chile.[5] The query language used by SESI is STAIRS/IBM. Finally, SESI provides training for information managers. For example, between June 8 and August 21, 1981, ten librarians were trained in the use of AGRIS, databases specializing in the agricultural sciences and technology.

The Instituto de Investigaciones Tecnológicas, INTEC (Institute for Technological Research) was founded in 1969 as a research division of the Corporación de Fomento, CORFO (Development Corporation) and as such has offered reference services to the entire Chilean industrial complex. In 1977, it began online information services, including access to the data banks of Lockheed, such as CAB Abstracts (Commonwealth Agricultural Bureau Abstracts), COMPENDEX, ENERGYLINE, NTIS (National Technical Information Service), Excerpta Medica, Biosis Previews, METADEX and CA Search (Chemical Abstracts Search), and to SDC. The Institute for Technological Research has also devised its own data bank, consisting chiefly of technical reports of CORFO and its seven subsidiaries. INTEC's documentation center is staffed by three librarians, one engineer, one administrator, and one assistant. Its collection consists of books, periodicals, technical reports, audio-visual materials, patents, standards, indexes, and abstracts. For a fee it offers online searches, reference services, ILL, compilation of bibliographies and thesauri, and photoduplication services.

The Instituto Nacional de Investigaciones de Recursos Naturales, IREN (National Institute of Natural Resources Research) is another research division of CORFO and began its first program of machine-readable records in 1978. The documentation center staff consists of five subject specialists and two assistants. It offers only information about natural resources in the country. In 1980 this database had incorporated about 12,000 machine-readable records and continues to add about 2,000 more entries each year.[6]

The Ministerio de la Vivienda y Urbanismo, MINVU (Ministry of Housing and Urbanism) has a documentation center within its Technical Division of Housing Development. It provides online (batch mode) information on urban development and planning. Staffed by three professionals and two assistants, the center has a collection of books, serials, magazines, indexes, abstracts, technical reports, legislation, and standards. It offers, free of charge, reference services, ILL, analysis of information, and SDI.

The Academia Superior de Ciencias Pedagógicas de Chile (Chilean Higher Academy of Pedagogical Sciences) became a newly administered body of higher education in 1981. Until the end of 1980 it had been an integral part of the Division of Education of the University of Chile. This academy, with the support of the Ministry of Education, may possibly incorporate the ERIC database into the entire Chilean educational system. Efforts towards creating an educational subsystem started as early as 1965, with the creation of the Centro de Investigación y Desarrollo de la Educación (Center for Educational Research and Development), a Chilean private foundation. During an international meeting held in Montevideo, Uruguay, in March, 1977, the Center proposed the creation of an educational documentation network in Chile and Latin America.[7]

The Dirección de Informaciones para el Comercio Exterior en Chile (Information Directorate for Foreign Commerce in Chile) provides through its documentation center an array of commercial information, including statistics on national trade and foreign markets. The Chilean industry may now request a complete market analysis of a specific product. (This service is believed to be the first of its kind in South America.)

The documentation center belonging to the Comisión Nacional de Energía Nuclear (National Commission of Nuclear Energy) offers SDI services and selective retrospective online searches, and has access to the INIS ATOM-INDEX databases, thanks to an arrangement with the Center for Nuclear Information in Brazil.

Other information subsystems of importance in Chile are those of the Televisión Nacional de Chile (National Television of Chile) which recently implemented an online retrieval system of information contained in videotapes; the documentation of the Empresa Nacional de Petroleo, ENAP (National Oil Company) and the Empresa Nacional de Electricidad, ENDESA (National Electric Company).

Among the international producers of bibliographic databases in Chile, the most prominent ones are the Centro Latinoamericano de Documentación Económica y Social, CLADES (Latin American Center for Economic and Social Documentation), the Centro Latinoamericano de Demografía, CELADE (Latin American Demografic Center), and Instituto Latinoamericano del Fierro y del Acero, ILAFA (Latin American Iron and Steel Institute).

As a subordinate body of the Comision Económica para America Latina, CEPAL (Economic Commission for Latin America), CLADES was founded in 1970. Its primary responsibility is for the indexing and processing of documents generated by CEPAL. Sixteen persons work in the center, including nine documentalists. CIADES offers online services through its nine databases and offers retrospective searches back to 1970. The search system used is ISIS (Integrated Set of Information Systems), based on a United Nations manual, and uses a controlled vocabulary. Services are free for CEPAL personnel and the general public.

The Centro Latinoamericano de Demografía, CELADE (Latin American Demografic Center) was established in 1976 to collect materials on population and related topics in Latin America and the Caribbean. The first two years of operation of this system were supported by grants from the International Development Research of Canada. The documentation system of CELADE is known as DOCPAL, Documentación Sobre la Población en America Latina (Documentation on the Population of Latin America). DOCPAL is staffed by eleven persons, including four documentalists, four full-time librarians, two administrators, and one part-time systems analyst and programmer. The documentation center contains books, journals, magazines, indexes, abstracts, technical reports, etc. It offers, free of charge, online information services (batch mode), and retrospective searches. It also publishes *Resúmenes sobre población en América Latina* (Santiago, Chile: DOCPAL, 1977–).

Finally, there is the Instituto Latinoamericano del Fierro y del Acero, ILAFA (Latin American Iron and Steel Institute), a non-profit association of the iron and steel industries in Latin America. The documentation center provides well over 150,000 references from the world literature of siderurgy, and since 1980 it offers access to online databases. In 1971, several nations agreed to form the Sistema de Información Siderúrgica para América Latina, SISAL (Iron and Steel Information System for Latin America). The information gathered became a database known as Banco de Información Siderúrgica para America Latina, BISAL. This service has been complemented with information processed by the American Society of Metals through its METADEX system of documentation.

Conclusion

I have given an overview of recent developments in the areas of documentation in Chile, including the creation of several information subsystems linking major cities in Chile with international producers of bibliographic and numeric databases. A viable national information network may emerge in the near future. For the time being, new databases, online services, some attempts at resource sharing, and the adoption of MARC tapes for the storage and retrieval of information are being tested and remain the first and most important steps in this direction. There is still a dire need for the construction of thesauri tailored to specific discipline and language requirements. Finally, operating automated information systems in Chile will continue to be expensive as long as these services remain underutilized.

One of the most crucial questions is whether or not sophisticated information systems perfected in the United States, Great Britain, and a few other highly industrialized nations can contribute substantially to the progress of less developed countries. The imposition of these technologies may reduce the technological gap but may not help improve social conditions. Do all societies (or cultures) communicate the same way, or define the concept "information" in a similar fashion? And will this information (which so many countries purchase with alacrity, putting political prestige or self-aggrandizement before economy and common sense) answer the specific needs of those societies? There are no good or extensive research studies which can give us reliable answers to these questions. The 1980s will find the entire region south of the Rio Grande incorporating information resources and systems into more dynamic communication patterns, including the automation of important bibliographic systems and resource sharing at national, regional, and international levels. It is hoped, however, that Chile and other Latin American nations will proceed with caution in their endeavors to build pertinent and self-sufficient information networks that they will adapt, not imitate. To learn from others is praiseworthy; to merely imitate is to fail.

NOTES

1. Carlos Fuentes, "Writing in Time," *Democracy* 2 (January 1982), 61–74.
2. Juan R. Freudenthal, "Information and Documentation in Chile," *Journal of the American Society for Information Science* 23 (July–August 1972), 283–285; Juan R. Freudenthal,

"Information and Documentation in Chile: Progress Report and Bibliography, 1970–1975," *Journal of the American Society for Information Science* 28 (January 1977), 58–60; and Hector Gómez Fuentes, "Information and Documentation in Chile: Progress Report and Bibliography, 1974–1978," *Journal of the American Society for Information Science* 31 (November 1980), 445–448.

3. Many of these documents can also be consulted in the printed version of *Guía Nacional de Proyectos de Investigación en Curso, 1974–1980*, CONICYT/DID, an irregular publication.

4. It is believed that approximately 500 papers of a scientific nature have been published annually in the last few years. Nearly 75 percent are researched in and published by the major Chilean universities, notably the Universidad de Chile and the Universidad Católica.

5. The Catálogo Colectivo Computerizado de Publicaciones Periódicas de la Universidad de Chile (Automated Union Catalog of Periodical Publications at the University of Chile) is a project initiated in the fall of 1978 at the Department of Library Science, University of Chile. This important undertaking was conceived and directed by Professor Alicia Gaete with the collaboration of several library science students. A more comprehensive undertaking (in its initial stage in 1982) will be the automation of the union catalogs of all the universities in the country. This project is sponsored by the Council of Rectors.

6. A printed version, *Bibliografía de recursos naturales*, is also available from IREN. It includes periodical publications, technical reports, and sundry research projects.

7. Gonzalo Gutiérrez, *Diseño preliminar de una red latinoamericana de documentación de la educación* (REDUC) (CIDE, 1978).

Scholarly Communication and Public Policy

13. Summary Report: Scholarly Communication and Public Policy

Charles Fineman

Moderator: Colleen Trujillo, Latin American Center Publications, UCLA
Rapporteur: Charles S. Fineman, Humanities Bibliographer, University Library, University of California, Santa Cruz
Panelists: James Buchanan, U.S. Department of State
Barry Sklar, Foreign Relations Committee, U.S. Senate
K. Larry Storrs, Congressional Research Service, Library of Congress
Commentators: John Hébert, Hispanic Division, Library of Congress
Stephen Kane, Office of the Historian, U.S. Department of State

Ms. Trujillo put the subject of the session in focus by observing that a wealth of information on Latin America exists for the use of academics, scholars, and researchers, but that unreported or unshared information results in progress for no one. The papers and the discussion of the session would examine the availability and the use to which information on Latin America was put by publishers and other information managers. The credibility and reliability of this information generated by the scholarly community would also be studied.

The theme of Mr. Storrs' paper was that, in general, scholarly research competes poorly with other sources of information when public policy on Latin America is made. The time of every member of Congress is limited, and there are votes every day on a large number of issues. Members of Congress are, almost by definition, generalists and not specialists, although some specialization does occur on committees. However, there is no comparison with the specializations encountered in the executive branch. (There is, for example, no El Salvador desk officer in Congress.) Congressional action often tends to be reactive and counterbalancing, a check on the executive branch. Congress is not the main formulator of foreign policy. Finally, congressional attention on specific matters is not, and cannot be, comprehensive or sustained.

Mr. Storrs mentioned the sources members of Congress draw on as they make decisions. Scholarly material ranks low on the list because it is not quickly available. Members of Congress respond to spontaneous letters from constituents, articles and editorials in the media, visits from and to constituents, and information presented orally during hearings. He then described the organization and activities of the Congressional Research Service (CRS) and its staff, which in 1981 handled over 300,000 requests for information. The CRS may provide material (for example, clippings) for hearings, issue briefs (summaries of major issues, bibliography, chronology, all in a standard format), CRS reports (sample subjects: Panama, human rights in Latin America), committee prints (e.g., the Panama Canal treaties), witnesses, tailored bibliographies, packages of citations to recent articles and books tailored to particular needs, oral briefings, and seminars. The requirements are that all such information be timely and up to date, that it directly concern congressional policy issues, that it be directed at a generalist audience (e.g., no foreign language materials or citations), be well documented and objective, and be concise and understandable.

Scholarly research competes poorly when there is a need for up-to-date information—the category into which 60 percent of requests for information fall. Obviously, it takes the results of academic research a long time to appear in journals. The impact of scholarly work is high, however, when background information is needed. When a point of view or an advocacy stance is needed, scholarly information has some impact, but advocacy groups have much more. In conclusion, Mr. Storrs stressed the characteristics of the informational needs of Congress and the consequent need for academics to translate their scholarship into an appropriate form if they wish this scholarship to have some bearing on the workings of Congress in a foreign policy area.

Mr. Buchanan spoke of the Department of State and its interaction with academic research in general, with both publishers and individual scholars. He began with a description of the library of the Department of State, its book officers, and other library channels the department uses to obtain printed information. He mentioned the scholar-diplomat program, one funded by scholars themselves, in which desk officers and similar personnel get to know scholars in their field of interest and exchange ideas and information. Another method of gathering information is the department's Bureau of Intelligence and Research, which mirrors the department's organization of policy officers. It is the bureau's job to provide the Secretary of State with unbiased views of issues; however, it is not responsible for the ultimate formulation of policy. It is an important liaison with the national intelligence community and, as such, maintains contact with the scholarly community and helps information from that quarter enter into the policy-making machinery.

"XR," external research, a branch of the Department of State now called Long-Range Research and Assessments, contracts with outside researchers and arranges for brief, concentrated conferences in Washington on subjects which have immediate, direct, and clear relevance to national policy in specific areas. Such mini-conferences are frequently organized when a new ambassador is about to assume duties, and revolve around one country or one policy or one area of the world. Academics are frequently called upon to participate in these meetings, where no formal papers are presented; instead, oral expertise is rapidly and most efficiently disseminated to those who have a need for it.

Mr. Sklar summarized the nature of informational needs on the Senate Foreign Relations Committee. When called for, information needs to be absolutely up to date, relevant, and provided as quickly as possible. In addition, it needs to be policy oriented and timely. Speaking as a former staff member of the Congressional Research Service, Mr. Sklar observed that, in theory, the Senate Foreign Relations Committee has access to the contents of all libraries in the Washington area, but time acts as the most severe limitation on the collection of information for the committee. As a result, the Washington academic community lends much assistance as a human resource. Members of that community can act as witnesses and have credibility before Congress. Sklar reiterated that the needs of Congress are always for material that is specifically policy oriented, clear, concise, and very much to the point.

As the first commentator, Mr. Kane identified three characteristics of academic research which often prevent it from entering the mainstream of information used in public policy decisions: (1) it is often amorphous in form, and therefore frequently fails to meet the criteria for policy makers; its flow is irregular; (2) it tends not to be uniform over a variety of subjects, concentrating on antiquarian problems at a time when the need for information relating to a crisis is acute; and (3) it tends not to be projective; much academic research tends to offer retrospective analyses of problems and does not predict or offer guidance in future problems. Kane identified two other broad areas of concern. First, there are various channels through which information can flow as it becomes part of the decision-making process. Informal contacts, the personal contact, frequently offer the best possibility for interaction, and the scholarly community's interests are served if such contacts increase in the future. The final area of concern was about what happens to research once it gets into policy-making institutions or offices. Kane stated that research is neutral. It is the obligation of the policy maker to *select* from the information available before putting it to a particular use. Mr. Kane believes the utility of academic research could be increased if the scholarly community took proper cognizance of these facts.

Mr. Hébert, as second commentator, reflected on the role an organization such as SALALM can play to make scholarly materials more available to policy-making bodies, given the fact that there is apt to be little variation in the way researchers conduct their investigations in the future. Even after raw data are collected, analyzed, and written up, the fact remains that the results of academic research then leave the academic who compiled them and are transmitted to a person or an office which, in turn, extracts facts or points of view relevant to a particular decision or policy. He stated that it is very much the concern of SALALM and like organizations to discover and present the most accurate, objective, and current information on Latin America and to preserve this information. It is similarly the function of institutions such as the Library of Congress, with their long histories of collecting, to collect for both posterity and for today. Hébert's final concern was with the question: How is information used once it has been synthesized?

There was a brief discussion among the panelists and the commentators on information gathering and policy making. Mr. Sklar noted that the ultimate responsibility for policy making still rests with members of Congress. Mr. Buchanan noted increasing concern among policy makers for tailored information. Mr. Storrs noted that the objectivity of the Congressional Research Service is its greatest strength. By being unaware of the orientation of its information requesters, the CRS provides balanced views and pros and cons. Mr. Kane advised that information providers need to perceive the needs of policy makers they assist so that their needs can be satisfied as well as possible, although all policy makers reserve the right not to use some of the information they are given.

Peter Johnson (Princeton University) wished to learn from Mr. Storrs the value of machine-readable data files, given the immense backlogs of uncataloged materials in libraries through which a researcher might have to wade. Mr. Storrs acknowledged that this is sometimes a problem, but that there are ways around it. The CRS can obtain information from the executive branch or from foreign embassies, for example. He stressed that with limited time, limited staff, and a responsibility to all members of Congress, emphasis is always on U.S. policy, and access to that type of information is unhindered.

Frederick Fisher (F. W. Faxon Company) asked about information in Department of State briefings which later turned out to be incorrect. Mr. Buchanan replied that a response was difficult because, given the complexity of the information-gathering and policy-making process, it is often impossible to know the precise source of a piece of information. Every effort is always made to obtain the best and most accurate facts. Mr. Storrs alluded to the verity that different people see different things in the same fact and observed further that, in the work of the CRS, an attempt is always made to provide a diversity of *balanced* information, well-established facts and areas of controversy being clearly labeled.

Barbara Robinson (University of California, Riverside) asked the panel members to comment on the irregular flow of scholarly research and the lack of research on areas or in fields which have become the objects of public policy. Mr. Kane stated that he does not have a solution to the problem, alluding to the system of academic grant giving and the methods by which scholars in our society choose the topics of their research. He expressed the belief that it is difficult to prescribe such matters to academic scholars.

The Role of Quantitative
Data in the Formulation
of Public Policy

14. Summary Report: Quantitative Data and Public Policy

Sonia M. Merubia

Moderator: Peter T. Johnson, Bibliographer for Latin America, Spain and Portugal, Princeton University Library

Rapporteur: Sonia M. Merubia, Serial Records and Acquisition Librarian, Benson Latin American Collection, The University of Texas at Austin

Panelists: Peter T. Johnson

James W. Wilkie, University of California, Los Angeles

Leobardo Estrada, University of California, Los Angeles

Michael J. Moran, Inter-American Institute for Cooperation on Agriculture

John Beresford, Data Use and Access Labs, Washington, D.C.

Moderator Peter Johnson opened the session and proceeded to present his paper. The early 1960s saw the beginning of national and regional planning, however, the data used for these plans were rather minimal. By 1981 there was greater sophistication in this area and a recognition of the value of statistics as a planning tool. The presentation then concentrated on data collection, data processing by electronic means and data access. This compilation was the result of interviews conducted for five months with government officials in Mexico, Brazil, Chile and Peru.

Most data used in planning are drawn largely from the following sources: Population censuses, surveys of business and industry, surveys of agriculture, and statistics which are the by-products of the administrative process. Several basic considerations exist with regard to data collection. The first concerns standardization. Frequently, data do not support higher sophisticated research and their sensitivity and quality suffer at the point of collection. For example, many sectors in Peru lack monthly statistics rendering it impossible to measure fluctuations. Currently, an effort is being made by intergovernmental agencies (FAO, UN, WHO) to monitor governments in this area through advising and consulting. Other major considerations relate to the levels of collection, the level of detail desired, timeliness of the material and, finally, there is the question of confidentiality and privacy, something which has not been largely explored in Latin America. CELADE, the organization which attempts to resolve and meet some of the problems created by these factors, concentrates on services which relate to data processing by electronic means.

The problems related to data processing are varied because so many more procedures are now feasible. Frequently, the data do not support sophisticated levels of analysis. Also, the lack of qualified personnel affects most countries. CELADE does provide continuing education and training. In the technical sphere, the infrastructure for supporting the necessary hardware is often lacking in Latin America, or is inadequate. Because the main frames are expensive to purchase or rent and to maintain, more countries are turning to microcomputers. Presently, there are no standard formats for microcomputers and one can find different systems within each country. Mexico imports almost all of its equipment while Brazil opted in the other direction, sacrificing the latest technology for a Brazilian developed microcomputer. Solutions center around the promotion of standardization of equipment and the utilization of time sharing as well as the balancing of the sales demands of various transnational corporations. Since, in addition to being expensive, this causes money to flow out of the country, the tendency has been to consolidate statistical processes within Latin America. Today, only Haiti has all its data processed abroad.

Questions of software again involve compatibility. Different agencies in a given country have different machines, making program transferability impossible. Obtaining software designed by transnational corporations is fairly easy and it is one of the most active types of contraband.

In general, though, there is much resistance to change since statistical institutes remain dominated by bureaucrats, who are reluctant to give statistics or data processing the importance they require. Also, since many countries lack researchers with interest in many sectors of activity, the potential of the computer is not being realized.

Much difficulty also exists in matters of access. Often, special studies or print-outs are not available. Governments frequently manipulate data for political objectives. In Chile many definitions and methods were changed over time by the Instituto Nacional de Estadística, but these were not indicated publicly. Also in 1976, for Chile, a great deal of technically incorrect information was found in the basic time series. The political structure can also prohibit ready access. The Mexican agricultural survey which was taken two years ago is still not generally accessible because, as Mexicans who work with the data suggest, it would reveal the government's near total failure in this sector for employment and production. Another factor inhibiting access is outright censorship, which continues to be a practice with printed as well as machine readable data. In 1973 the Brazilians falsified a price index, which is another example of control.

Other limitations on access are more technical. The documentation which accompanies machine readable data requires standardization so that it can be quickly utilized. Fiscal constraints also serve to limit access because of the high initial and continuing costs as well as the high cost of producing a full range of detailed analyses. In some cases agencies lack the legal right to bring pressure to correct data from other agencies. Contrasting with this are super-agencies like Mexico's Secretaría de Programación y Presupuesto which has the authority to use data for anything it chooses.

Data archives supply an answer to the problem of access and are assuming the place of traditional libraries. They save a great deal of effort, since they eliminate the time needed for material to be published. In the United States the Inter-University Consortium for Political and Social Research (Ann Arbor, Michigan) actively collects various data files and makes them available to institutions. The Princeton University library has published a bibliography which lists 87 pages of machine readable files.

In summary, data statistics are just one of the various elements used in the formulation of public policy. Inter-governmental agencies are becoming increasingly important as coordinators between national plans even though available data remain quite limited. The focus for planners should not be on the immediate issue but on long-range policies. Although technical facilities are improving rapidly, these improvements are not reaching Latin America quickly enough and are limited by the previously mentioned considerations. Also, the need for more education and training of personnel cannot be overstated. Finally, the planners must be in positions where they can formulate and oversee public policy. In many cases central statistical offices are engaged only in data collections and demographic analysis and are not involved in the planning process itself. In order that goals may be meshed accurately and consistently, personnel in positions of power must recognize the value and quality of data.

Mr. Estrada, who described himself as a demographically trained social scientist, made his presentation next. He stated that he had just survived the process of compiling the 1980 census for the United States. The most amazing aspect of it was that it was completed at all. The prohibitive costs and the types of pressures generated by the process indicate that the limits of this particular methodology have been reached and the census will probably never be done in this fashion again. He looked forward to the development of new methods and hoped that new ideas would result from studying the way Latin American countries take their censuses.

Although he specializes in studying the Hispanic population in the U.S., he conceded this could not be done without investigating the immigration experience. He then gave a short historical overview of racial and ethnic statistics in the United States. Article 2, Section 1 of the U.S. Constitution requires statistics by race as part of the two-thirds compromise in which Negroes were counted as two-thirds of a white person for purposes of congressional representation. Thus, the first census of 1790 used race and ethnic statistics for purposes of public policy. Racial items in each census have been extended over the years. American Indians first began to be counted in the 1860s, while oriental races do not appear until the 1920s. In 1930 the Mexican category was included as a racial item. It became difficult to get measurements because the question of national origin was confused with that of race. Questions of race, color and nationality were grouped together because they were significant categories in this society. Ethnicity, which refers to a national, cultural, or language grouping, has become so important that most Hispanics will distinguish among themselves and white Anglos, thus raising ethnicity to the level of race. In contrast, Latin American statistics make no mention of race and ethnicity because it means little if anything in these countries. For the 1980 census two separate questions were developed: one for race and one for ethnicity. The result is a very strange conglomeration of data which makes research on Hispanics very difficult. Certain concepts used to measure the Hispanic population (Spanish mother tongue, Spanish language, Spanish heritage, etc.), which were not available in the 1950 or 1960 censuses, were eliminated. This makes interpretation more difficult.

The Hispanic population has several distinguishing characteristics. One major factor is its youth. The average Hispanic is eight years younger than the average non-Hispanic and, accordingly, there is higher fertility. Twenty percent of the growth of the Hispanic population is due solely to migration from Latin American countries. Therefore, it is not surprising that Spanish language usage continues to be the highest non-English language use in the United States. In addition, most Hispanics are urban dwellers.

These characteristics relate directly to public policy issues. For instance, the important issues at the moment are adult issues—career development, medical costs, retirement. The more youthful Hispanic population, though, is concerned with children, schools, delinquency, etc. Likewise, current trends in suburbanization mean that businesses and jobs are moving out from the central city while Hispanics remain in the cities.

In conclusion, though public policy resolutions are not usually affected by social researchers or academics, it is possible to enter the public policy debate process by getting policy makers to focus on the right questions.

Mr. Jack Beresford followed with his presentation. He described an AID project with which he had been involved that concerned the censuses of all developing countries. Its purpose was to assess computer and technical capabilities for census processing, review the necessary software, maintain a roster of consultants, and illustrate the utility of the census in the policy framework. Ultimately, it was created to satisfy the goals of the Jersey Amendment to the Foreign Aid Bill which affirms the importance of women in development and indicates the need to create statistical resources to measure this. This concentration on the female population results from a knowledge that in developing countries women are responsible for much of the commercial and marketing activities. Census information would supply the data to illustrate these activities.

From the outset, it was understood that individuals within these countries would have to demonstrate an interest in preparing these reports. It was hoped that these persons would also have some connection with the policy making and executing groups of their governments so that this information might be fully utilized. Each AID mission was advised of this project and a request went out for volunteers. Out of sixty missions there were three responses. The informal network was more successful and, finally, resulted in offers from: Peru, Costa Rica, Indonesia, the Philippines, Bangladesh, Panama, Kenya, Togo, Mauritania and Ghana. The project is still continuing and could use more volunteers.

The following procedures were recommended for the completion of the reports. The authors were asked to identify their audience before they developed what they wanted to accomplish and to meet with the persons who would be utilizing the reports in order to tie-in census data with national goals. They were requested to use graphics rather than tables in communicating to those bureaucrats and planners who hold positions of power, but who do not understand statistics. Finally, they were asked to focus solely on a few main issues.

The result for the Latin American countries has been that when the author has had statistical and demographic preparation, as in the case of Costa Rica, he has not had the influence to cause his report to be employed in the policy planning process. Conversely, those authors who have this influence had not proved to have much knowledge of or interest in statistics.

In conclusion, to get data to become a part of the policy making process is not a statistical problem, nor a demographic or rational problem, but an emotional one which involves sociological or political principles. The exact nature of these problems is difficult to determine and a sociologist would probably only be able to outline them in the abstract.

The next speaker was Michael J. Moran who represented the Inter-American Institute for Cooperation on Agriculture. After describing the work of the center, he stated that its basic purpose was to strengthen agricultural development plans and increase their effectiveness. In conjunction with this, the Institute plans to increase the efficiency of the institutional system in implementing agricultural policy objectives.

Mr. Moran then presented two transparencies which aided in conceptualizing the agri-policy formulation process by showing agricultural planning as a continuing policy producing process conditioned by the political position of the governments and the problems arising out of the socio-economic realities. He further pointed out that one of the key problems planners face is that they deal with a formulation process without looking at the implementation and control processes, thus generating plans without looking at the operational aspect. It should be conceptualized as a national management system within the field of agriculture, as a dynamic relationship rather than a static one.

Mr. Moran proceeded to report on the findings of a study which his institute conducted on agricultural planning systems in Latin America and the Caribbean. One of the critical problems which all indicated was a lack of contact with the political administrative system. This type of contact was something which all desired. But, when talking to planners, it became apparent that many considered entering the political arena as unacceptable to their profession. In addition to this linkage breakdown, there was very little relationship in terms of information sharing between the agricultural planning unit and the entire planning system. These units often utilized non-conventional sources of information, such as the central banks and the national statistics institutes. Interestingly, these key agricultural planning units did not perceive financial restraint as a major problem, but pointed to physical deficiencies such as data processing and the lack of library materials as major stumbling blocks.

In the area of human resources, excluding Argentina and Colombia, there were 1,250 technicians in 1978 or, roughly, 60 per country. If Brazil and Mexico are excluded, the number of planners drops to 38 per country. Thirty percent of these specialize in agronomy, twenty-nine percent in economics, and ten percent in business administration. Less than one percent had doctoral degrees and only nine percent had master's degrees. In most cases, the preferred type of training was in-service. Of lesser importance were seminars and external advisory services because when utilizing external resources, the tendency is to depend on international organizations.

Clearly, when dealing with new technologies, the absorptive capacity of the institution must be considered. Often, when an effort is made to apply new analytical procedures, an examination of the data base makes it impossible. For example, in the case of agro-climatic systems, although the information and data exist, it is collected on a yearly basis. Planting decisions, though, must be made within a minimum of ten days. Thus, the information must be restructured in order to be useful.

Mr. Moran concluded by stating that he would like students to research the problem of getting useful information from the Latin American Studies Centers in the United States to farmers, politicians and planners in Latin America. He believed that this information would be valuable for the policy formulation process.

The final speaker was James Wilkie, who stated that the session which had begun on an optimistic note was becoming more pessimistic in tone. He considered the title of his talk to be the possible misuse and misunderstanding of quantitative data in the formulation of public policy. He stressed the need to refine concepts so that one has clear definitions of what is being measured. One of his negative examples was Mexico, which under José López Portillo developed a series of national plans. Since these required the conversion to a new data bank, the rich source of time series which went back to 1910 was destroyed. Also, the 1980 census was not linked to previous censuses. In the

United States seriously inaccurate estimates with regard to the buildup of inventory were made for 1973−1974. Since planners could not project correctly and businessmen did not know what they should be producing, the recession for this period was prolonged. Also, this country has suffered a variety of "crises" ending with the current "defense crisis." The real crisis in the United States, though, centers around the fact that the infrastructure is wearing out and, without a viable road system, any type of defense will be impossible.

Another problem centers around how to incorporate conceptual matters into computers. It usually takes an academic idea seven years to be implemented by policy makers. For example, devaluation of the Mexican peso was the result of a mistake. The President and his advisors, operating under old information, tried to remedy a social situation by causing the country to stop investing in the economic structure. They did not realize that it was this economic structure that was creating the jobs and making opportunity possible. In fact, over a long period of time a larger number of people have had access to a better life. But, because Mexican officials trained in superficial values wrote superficial programs for their computers, they developed an economic model which was a disaster for Mexico and had serious consequences for the United States. The role of the historian, then, is to remind us that we need to be a little more humble and employ rigorous testing of all data.

Another great misconception, concerned the widening gap between the GNPs of developed and underdeveloped countries. Actually, it is not widening but rapidly narrowing. No area in the world has improved socially at the rate at which Latin America has. Also one must remember to distinguish between a social and an economic gap. Another example is the case of the Alliance for Progress. Everyone agrees that it failed. But although its goals were not reached, it did generate a great number of very accessible social statistics which are no longer available. Mr. Wilkie said that this affected him gravely as editor of the *Statistical Abstract of Latin America*. Finally, this lack of social data is reflected in the fact that current policy is being based solely on economic and human rights statistics.

Mr. Johnson closed the session with an admonition to all listeners to be very critical of all statistics appearing in newspapers and on television.

15. Management and Mismanagement of National and International Statistical Resources in the Americas

James W. Wilkie

If the 1960s brought with the Alliance for Progress a consensus among policy-makers about generally accepted guidelines for management of statistics needed to measure comparative change in Latin America, by the end of the 1970s that consensus had evaporated. At the onset of the 1980s, there are policymakers who see little use in retaining older data resources, and others who have misplaced faith that data banks can resolve the qualitative problems of statistics. And some even question the very usefulness of statistical series. Such contradictory views are represented in the analysis here of the management and mismanagement of statistical resources on Latin America by the U.S. government, the Mexican government, and the Organization of American States.

U.S. Government

During the halcyon days of John F. Kennedy's presidency there appeared to be no limits on state policy. Even the troublesome matter of inflation seemed to have been bested and all that remained was some fine tuning of the economy in order to establish lasting and meaningful change. To this end, the Kennedy administration decreed that funds would be forthcoming for the development of Latin America, once wasteful duplication of efforts within the countries was replaced by rational planning. State planning in Latin America, which has never existed in the United States, was to be based on statistical goals, thus requiring that statistical agencies be given the funds and necessary researchers to eliminate Latin America's social and economic poverty in the ten years following the establishment of the Alliance for Progress in 1961. Although the Alliance could not have eliminated poverty in ten years, its "failure" has had a devastating long-term impact on the politics of data gathering in the United States and Latin America.[1] As I have written elsewhere:

If we can marvel at the official naïveté in the 1960s that could see the possibility of solving Latin America's problems in only 10 years, it is appropriate, then, to marvel at the notion that the Alliance could be seen in the 1970s to have failed. Not only does the persistence of the latter concept suggest that observers still maintain the faith that initiated

134

the Alliance, but it involves a serious misreading of history. If the Alliance were to follow the Marshall Plan meaningfully, not only should external funding for Latin America have been double what it has been since 1946 but it would have had to be concentrated in one-sixth of the time span to date. Moreover, the Marshall Plan had mainly to rebuild factories destroyed by war, not build them in the first instance, let alone educate the manpower necessary to run them. In short, whereas the Marshall Plan was based upon tradition, the Alliance's job was to break old traditions in order to forge (or at least reinforce) new ones.[2]

The point missed by most observers is that the Alliance for Progress successfully fostered the collection of statistics to measure "progress." After nearly twenty years of generating statistics and organizing them in such a way that it is possible to begin to assess long-term social and economic change, however, we are confronted by a decline in interest in statistics on the part of U.S. and OAS policymakers and, ironically, a rise in interest in Mexico. The data-gathering function of the Agency for International Development (US/AID) has been severely crippled, the Inter-American Statistical Institute as a resource base for statistics has been dismantled, and Mexico, in contrast, has expanded its statistical program, through the creation of a misorganized Mexican statistical agency.

Loss of interest in data by many U.S. and OAS policymakers probably began when the statistics of measurement could not be made to show that the goals of the Alliance for Progress had been achieved. Too, the misuse of "body-count" statistics by the U.S. government during the Vietnam War tended to call into question the use of statistics. Finally, the shift from analysis of social data to obviously erroneous political data by observers of the guerrilla war in El Salvador since 1980 has continued to cause statistical data to be viewed as less than useful. (Some observers point out similarities between the war in Vietnam and that in El Salvador, but the only connection is in the misuse of body-counts—by the right in the former case and by the left in the latter.)

In the United States, government budgetary reductions in offices such as US/AID paralleled the declining importance of social policy during the 1970s as the socially oriented Alliance for Progress passed into history.[3] Only economic statistics remained of major interest to U.S. policymakers, but the generation of such economic data was left to international agencies.[4] While no longer gathering and publishing data on social matters, US/AID also saw its research on Latin American economic change (which had proved "easier" to measure than social phenomena) go into eclipse along with financial analysis of its own expenditures. US/AID economic data had provided a useful alternative to international agency reporting in that US/AID worked with figures supplied by U.S. embassies after consultation with host country officials had led to insightful adjustment of the data.

If the loss of US/AID-sponsored data publications were not serious enough, the routine destruction by US/AID of its own records has meant the loss of valuable manuscript materials. These manuscripts (including US/AID Reports) are needed to understand the contemporary history of international relations of developing countries wherein the political, social, and economic impact of U.S. policy has become crucial.

It is imperative that internationally oriented U.S. government agencies such as US/AID establish a Historical Office with a statistical division in order to expand research into the development process. Specific justification for a US/AID Historical Office includes the following points:

1. US/AID records contain major documents and data about U.S. social and economic assistance and funding of countries around the world. Without careful attention to archival, these records may be lost to posterity and hence we will not be able to fully understand the nature of U.S. foreign aid programs as they affect either U.S. policy or the course of events in foreign countries.

2. Unlike the Department of State, US/AID does not have a Historical Office staffed with professional scholars; and US/AID records are quite as important as State Department records.

3. Although US/AID does permit the National Archives to access documents upon request, this activity is inadequate because:

   a. The National Archives cannot always know what to acquire when its staff is not fully involved in reviewing US/AID documents—often of a subtle nature—on a daily basis.

   b. In the meantime many US/AID records are unavailable to researchers owing to the fact that they are classified and their declassification tends to be conducted on an unsystematic basis.

   c. Although scholars outside of US/AID currently can gain access to even classified material if they closely know what they seek, US/AID does not have professionally trained researchers conducting the detailed inventory with priorities necessary to encourage full use of US/AID's records.

   d. If scholars outside of US/AID have not requested that documents be declassified, they may be destroyed within a specified time period after earlier review only by staff members in the Office of Records Management, staff who do not possess a well-cultivated "sense of history."

   e. The Office of Records Management tends to be more concerned with destruction of records than with their retention.

   f. The history of US/AID itself is not being written in any systematic or professional manner.

   g. At present there is no consistent way in which US/AID contract reports/documents are received in US/AID Washington for archival and research.

4. Although US/AID is to be commended for attempting to develop an Office

of Development Information and Utilization, this function should logically be a responsibility of a Historical Office because:

a. The development of a "memory" to show the results of thousands of US/AID-sponsored programs requires the employment of professionally trained historians who have specialized in economic, social, and political matters especially as they concern policy analysis over time.

b. Documents needed for US/AID's "memory" must do more than show us what can be learned from past programs and thus build upon lessons and mistakes. The "memory should also be constructed to allow scholars":

    (1) To assess the history of US/AID programs and interactions of US/AID staff within and between its own and other bureaucracies as US/AID has attempted to wield influence as well as protect funds slated for world development.

    (2) To interpret the history of the U.S. impact on foreign countries over time.

    (3) To study the history of foreign countries which, because of massive infusion of U.S. funds and ideas administered by US/AID, cannot be understood as having purely national histories.

    (4) To use US/AID-gathered data on the history of change in the world, including psychological, social, economic, and political change.

5. The establishment of a US/AID Historical Office should allow for consultation with scholarly associations concerned with the preservation and utilization of historical records as they relate to disciplines and world regions.

In short, US/AID records constitute a major national and international resource. Only a part of this resource is currently being saved or utilized. Vision is needed to assure that these records are as fully protected as possible. And only an appropriately staffed US/AID Historical Office can assess materials and make them available to the public in a coherent way.

Organization of American States

In early 1982 the Organization of American States (OAS) ceased supporting the Inter-American Statistical Institute (IASI) Focal Point Library in Washington, D.C. An extremely valuable collection of statistics on development in the Americas, the library had served as the single repository for statistical publications from OAS-member nations. The IASI staff, in coordination with the OAS, used these publications to assemble statistical series and organize them in comparative form for publication under the title *América en Cifras* issued at regular intervals (1961, 1963, 1965, 1967, 1970, 1972, 1974, 1977).

In addition to its publishing function,[5] IASI archived the statistical sources received in the Focal Point Library, where materials on OAS-member countries date to the 1930s.

Plagued by financial problems in the early 1980s, the OAS chose to sacrifice its data-gathering operation in Washington, D.C. The organization abandoned its statistical research with the IASI on development in Latin America and ceased publishing *América en Cifras*. Lacking OAS funding, the IASI stripped mainly methodological works from the Focal Point Library and, without bothering to remove the titles of the books from the library card catalog, shipped the works to the farthest corner of the hemisphere—Santiago.[6] The IASI Focal Point Library of statistical data was thus closed, the basic volumes of historical data remaining with an incomplete card catalog.

In light of these circumstances, the Latin Americanist community must move decisively to save and consolidate the IASI collection of research materials. Specific reasons for this propsal are as follows:

1. Detailed benchmark statistical data need to be preserved on a continuing basis to quantitatively assess social and economic change in the Americas.
   a. Generation of such data was stimulated by provisions of the Alliance for Progress that quantitative targets be set as part of national planning efforts to achieve "social and economic progress."
   b. Although the Alliance targets were often unrealistic, the data generated since the early 1960s is absolutely necessary for realistic planning and providing criteria for international aid as well as for permitting basic scholarly assessment of the changing social and economic situation in the Americas.
2. Benchmark statistics (mainly since the 1960s), until recently brought together in the IASI Focal Point Library in the OAS Office Building in Washington, D.C., are no longer being assembled in one place. A valuable collection of statistical yearbooks, population censuses, public health, housing, and agricultural data, for example, still remains at the IASI Focal Point Library but the collection is closed. Without a staff, with incomplete records of holdings, and with no plans to centralize new data now being generated by the IASI Program of the 1980s Census of the Americas, a major resource base is deteriorating.
3. Pre-1960 historical statistics for the Americas are held in the OAS Library in the headquarters building. These historical statistics need to be fully cataloged and gaps in holdings completed in order to provide a link between long-term data and benchmark statistics in the IASI Focal Point Library.
4. It is proposed here that the OAS and IASI collections be consolidated and cataloged in an OAS Statistical Reference Library. With a full-time staff of as few as three persons, and at relatively little cost, the Statistical

Reference Library could be maintained and expanded to cover the 1980s and future decades as well as linked to historical data needed by scholars interested in assessing long-term change.

   a. The now closed IASI Focal Point Library could be transferred to the control of the proposed new OAS Statistical Reference Library.

   b. The OAS Library collection of historical statistics could be transferred to the control of the proposed new OAS Statistical Reference Library.

   c. The proposed OAS Statistical Reference Library could be housed in the OAS office building where the IASI collection is still located.

5. Although the IASI was originally established in 1940 as an independent professional organization coordinated with the Pan American Union (after 1948, the OAS), and it may have made sense to develop statistical collections at both the IASI and the OAS, the IASI never had significant funding outside of the OAS. Even if the two organizations did not face an era of financial stringency, it makes better sense to bring all OAS/IASI statistics together in one place.

There is time to consolidate the OAS and IASI data collections because the avalanche of 1980 statistics scheduled for generation by the most recent population, housing, and agricultural censuses of the Americas will not be available for centralized collection until after the mid-1980s, by which time the proposed OAS Statistical Reference Library could be formed. The schedule for conducting the 1980s censuses is given in table 1. The earliest scheduled censuses for the decade were conducted in 1980 and the latest in 1985, in politically troubled El Salvador. For some countries no schedule was available because of social and economic turmoil (Nicaragua, for example) or because the 1970s censuses did not take place early in the decade, thus postponing the scheduling of 1980s censuses (Bolivia and Uruguay, for example).[7]

Mexican Government

Contrary to the trend elsewhere away from emphasis on, and confidence in, the statistical basis for assessing past development and planning for the future, the Mexican government since the mid-1970s has placed increased faith in statistics. Ironically, so much faith was placed in data and in the idea that all could be stored in one comprehensive computer bank that Mexico severely crippled its ability to assess change or plan for the future.

During the presidency of José López Portillo (1976–1982), Mexican policymakers decided to convert the typeset statistical yearbook published by the Dirección General Estadística (DGE) to a volume printed directly from the new computer bank. At the same time, the DGE was transferred from the Secretariat of Commerce and Industry to a new Secretariat of Planning and Budget, charged with responsibility for reorganizing all official data-gathering

Table 1
CENSUS DATES IN THE COUNTRIES THAT WILL PARTICIPATE IN THE PROGRAM OF THE 1980
CENSUS OF AMERICA
(As of September 1981)

Country	Population	Housing	Agriculture
A. ARGENTINA	22-X-1980	22-X-1980	1982
B. BOLIVIA	~	~	~
C. BRAZIL	1-IX-1980	1-IX-1980	1-1981
D. CHILE	IV-1982	IV-1982	~
E. COLOMBIA	~	~	~
F. COSTA RICA	IV or V-1983	IV or V-1983	IV or V-1983
G. CUBA	1981	1981	~
H. DOMINICAN REP.	XII-12-13-1981	XII-12-13-1981	~
I. ECUADOR	VI-1982	VI-1982	1984 or 1985
J. EL SALVADOR	~	~	~
K. GUATEMALA	23-III-1981	23-III-1981	IV-1979
L. HAITI	VIII-1982	VIII-1982	IV-1983
M. HONDURAS	1984−85	1984−85	1984−85
N. MEXICO	4-VI-1980	4-VI-1980	1-IV-31-V-1981
O. NICARAGUA	1982	1982	~
P. PANAMA	11-V-1980	11-V-1980	V-1981
Q. PARAGUAY	VII-1982	VII-1982	VII-1981
R. PERU	VII-1981	VII-1981	1982
S. URUGUAY	~	~	~
T. VENEZUELA	19-X-20-XI-1981	19-X-20-XI-1981	1981
UNITED STATES	1-IV-1980	1-IV-1980	1978

Source: IASI Document #7729a-9/24/81-20 and U.N. Demographic and Social Statistics
Branch.

functions into one ministry with one efficient data bank that could at the push of
a button reveal the daily status of Mexico's position on the road to development. Last but not least, planning began for conducting the 1980 population,
housing, and agricultural censuses by disbanding the prestigious advisory
board comprised of former census directors and others cognizant of the problems in gathering, processing, and making data available. This three-pronged
attack on the well-established Mexican statistical system (certainly one of the
best in Latin America and in some ways more efficient than the U.S. system)
upset Mexico's ability to understand from whence the country is coming and
where it is going.

First, the yearly statistics necessary to gauge Mexico's near-term development could not be made available in the country's statistical yearbook because
inept reorganization of the DGE meant that the process of gathering regular

series was completely disrupted—indeed the yearbook could not be published until 1978, more than two years later than scheduled. In the meantime, planners, scholars, and observers had little data upon which to base investigation of the trajectory of affairs in relation to many dozens of historical time series. Worse, when the statistical yearbook finally did adopt a computer-printed format in 1980, only 154 series were included, compared to the 458 in the typeset volume—a 66% reduction in available series. The decline in production of data has continued.

Second, the elimination of a number of series seems to have been made on political grounds. Witness the suppression of the wholesale price index compiled by the DGE from 1899 to 1976. Apparently because the DGE index showed greater inflation than the Bank of Mexico wholesale price index, the former was discontinued to emphasize the more favorable Bank view. (Theoretically the Bank of Mexico index is more complete but that hardly compensates for the time-series value of the DGE index.) The idea that there should only be one index of wholesale prices so as not to "confuse the public" is specious and counterproductive for thoughtful analysis of the Mexican scene.

Third, by revising the population census of 1980 without reference to Mexico's historical experience in taking censuses, and by omitting many important historical time series revealing the welfare of the Mexican population, Mexican officials gravely harmed our ability to assess long-term change in Mexico. Data on food consumption and the wearing of shoes, for example, was omitted in the 1980 population census. The 1980 census questionnaire was prepared by persons who, if they had sought to "reinvent the wheel," would not have asked whether or not wheels ought to be round.

Regardless of decline in quantity and quality of data, the Secretariat of Planning and Budget drew up the most exhaustive series of plans in Mexican history, filling many rooms with volumes of detailed projections. It is doubtful, however, that they will be read or understood. Such a problem might not have mattered in the past when each new president of Mexico discarded plans of his predecessor and started anew. But Miguel de la Madrid, who will take office in December 1982, was the minister of planning and budget who drew up the plans during the López Portillo regime. For the first time in Mexican history, then, plans that take too many years to conceive to be carried out under one president now will stand a good chance of being implemented. If the plans were based on the former quality and quantity of the Mexican statistical system and upon the realization that the government had overextended its ability to effectively accomplish even half of what it intends to do, then the new use of data would be welcome. In reality, though, the Mexican government has neither foreseen all of the problems that hinder planning and budgeting nor, in many cases, based its plans on a consistent statistical view of the past.

Conclusion

The United States, particularly since 1981,[8] and the OAS/IASI have unjustifiably deemphasized the statistical basis for research and planning, while Mexico has placed too great a focus on limited statistics. If balance is to be found between these extremes, adequate emphasis must be given to gathering and maintaining many historical series in published form. We must not, in the name of "clarification" or "data banking," permit the suppression of alternative data, especially time series figures needed to measure what happens to societies and economies. The computer data bank is useful particularly if alternative series are included, but the methodological notes necessary to make sense of the statistics may not fit into the computer format. The creation of a historical office in US/AID and the establishment of an OAS Statistical Reference Library would constitute positive steps toward improved management of national and international data. As for Mexico, perhaps it is not too late to propose that planning there be undertaken on the basis of long-term, historical data series. Dependence upon limited data now available to the Mexican government has resulted in the elaboration of grandiose plans unrealistic in scope and detail.

Clearly, there are obstacles in the road toward the judicious management of national and international statistical resources in the Americas. Overcoming them requires institutional and governmental vision and cooperation if we are to make progress toward assessing change in Latin American societies and economies in the decades ahead.[9]

NOTES

1. In "The Alliance for Progress and Latin American Development," *Statistics and National Policy* (Los Angeles: UCLA Latin American Center Publications, 1974), James W. Wilkie tests statistically major goals of the Alliance.

2. Ibid., p. 428.

3. US/AID last published its *Summary of Economic and Social Indicators: 18 Latin American Countries* for the period 1960–1971 (Washington, D.C.: Office of Development Programs, Bureau for Latin America) in 1972; a draft volume in computer format (1973) was never published.

4. Thus US/AID ceased publication of its *Gross National Product: Trends by Region and Country* (Washington, D.C.: US/AID-OSR), the 1975 edition summarizing data from 1950 to 1974.

5. The IASI coordinated statistical data-gathering in the hemisphere and published analyses of the quantity and quality of data for each country; see the IASI series *Actividades Estadísticas de las Naciones Americanas*, published by the OAS for each country beginning in the 1950s.

6. The Economic Commission for Latin America, headquartered in Santiago, had published twice yearly *Boletín Económico de América Latina* (1964–1972) which in 1973 became the ECLA *Anuario Estadística de América Latina*. These works did not compete with *América en cifras* in coverage or detail.

7. Although note that Bolivia has yet to undertake an agricultural census since its first in 1950.

8. President Ronald Reagan, more than any other post-Lyndon B. Johnson president, has

severely damaged the U.S. bases for statistical research. His budgetary cuts have incorporated the following orders: cancellation of surveys (e.g., on multiple job holding), reduction of frequency of observation (e.g., of health and nutrition), reduction of sample size (e.g., for income tax data), delay of revisions in sample surveys (e.g., to reflect changes in the population that occurred between 1970 and 1980), abandonment of plans to collect data crucial to interpretation of survey results (e.g., transcript and admission test data), delay in revision of critical time series (e.g., export and import price indexes), delay of schedules for publication of data (e.g., 1980 census of population and housing), curtailment of publication programs (e.g., publications of the U.S. Department of Agriculture Economic Research Service), involuntary reductions in staff (e.g., at the Bureau of Census), the involuntary furloughs of staff (e.g., at the Bureau of Labor Statistics). See the Social Science Research Council's *Items*, June 1982, pp. 12–13.

9. This article was first published in *Statistical Abstract of Latin America*, vol. 22 (Los Angeles: UCLA Latin American Center Publications, University of California, 1983), pp. 655–660.

A National Plan for Latin American Library Collections in the United States

16. The Implementation of a National Plan for Latin American Library Collections in the United States

Carl W. Deal and William E. Carter

The idea of a national plan for Latin American library collections is not a new one. It has its antecedents in the not too distant past when members of the Association of Research Libraries (ARL) participated in the Farmington Plan,[1] and more recently in the recommendations of the Task Force on Library and Information Resources of the American Council on Education and the President's Commission on Foreign Language and International Studies. As this interest continues, the Research Libraries Group is developing a Latin American conspectus for its bibliographic data base, RLIN, and the Seminar on the Acquisition of Latin American Library Materials (SALALM) is organizing a national network along the lines of the Farmington Plan to again assure that at least one research library is committed to collecting extensively from each Latin American country.[2] Finally, ARL is sufficiently concerned about foreign acquisitions and national needs to have formed a short-term Task Force on Collection Development to "review the commitment of ARL as an association to problems in foreign acquisitions" as its first charge.[3]

In the face of such broad and commonly held interests, it appears that a national plan for foreign area collections is a legitimate goal and that the library community is moving closer to that goal. That movement, albeit unofficial in nature, is taking place as a result of new library technology leading to better bibliographic control, closer cooperation between libraries in sharing resources, and organized efforts by the various area library associations, which have improved both the coverage of their areas of collection responsibility as well as access to those collections. However, what is seemingly taking place naturally and out of necessity needs to be hastened and given a life of its own with realistic goals tied to a properly financed and adequately implemented national plan.

It is the purpose of this paper to focus specifically on the needs for and problems of a national plan for Latin American collections. This in turn might serve as a model or point of departure for similar considerations for other world areas. The issues to be covered in this paper are common to other world areas and are in line with the recommendations of the American Council of Education task force and the president's commission. In the pages which follow, a historical perspective on a national plan for collection development for Latin American materials will be provided. From this perspective, we solicit a response from the panelists, representing government, the foundations, and the library world, with their advice on how such a high goal can be achieved.

Historical Perspective

The first extensive effort to establish a national plan for collecting foreign area materials was the Farmington Plan, developed by the Association of Research Libraries in 1948 following World War II. Initially designed to ensure that copies of European materials of value in research would be acquired and rapidly cataloged, the plan was extended to Latin America by including Mexico in 1949, and all of Latin America in 1959. It was phased out in 1972.

The Farmington Plan had great impact upon U.S. research collections, and its success was influential in the establishment of the Latin American Cooperative Acquisition Project (LACAP), which was undertaken by the New York book firm Stechert-Hafner.[4] From 1960 to 1972, LACAP first prospered and then failed, to the dismay of some forty participating research libraries. Both the Farmington Plan and LACAP contributed enormously to the reasonably good coverage of Latin American materials which was maintained by so many research libraries during those affluent years. The fact that both projects coexisted for more than a decade also contributed to a sense of cooperation and ongoing commitment to Latin American studies which is still maintained today by many research libraries.

One specific proposal for a national acquisitions plan for Latin American materials was conceived during this period of affluence and growing cooperation. Designed by Stanley L. West, director of the University of Florida Libraries and consultant to the Library of Congress, and funded by the Library of Congress and the Ford Foundation, the proposal called for a five-year plan based on the participation of approximately twenty U.S. institutions. West recommended that costs be equally borne, one-third each by the Library of Congress, the participating institutions, and outside private support. He furthermore proposed that the plan should also serve as a pilot effort to provide data and experience upon which similar projects for other world areas might be based.[5] Although the plan (which was discussed at a special meeting at the Library of Congress in 1965) did not become operational, it would have dealt with problems and needs of that time which are still present today.

In the absence of such a plan, some of these problems and needs have been served by the National Program for Acquisition and Cataloging (NPAC) of the Library of Congress. Since 1966 NPAC has been highly acclaimed for its contributions to foreign area research collections in this country. Building upon the Library of Congress Public Law 480 program, by which trade deficits in the Middle East and Southeast Asia were exchanged for library materials from certain countries in those areas, NPAC added the feature of shared cataloging in cooperation with the producers of foreign national bibliographies to speed entry of these foreign materials into circulation. The nearest thing to NPAC for Latin America has been the establishment of a Library of Congress overseas acquisition office in Brazil. Brazil was a crucial country, highly productive, and impossible for any single library to cover comprehensively.[6] Since its establishment, the Brazil office has led to a wider knowledge of research materials from that country and has greatly enriched the Library of Congress holdings.

The accomplishments of these programs have been nationwide in their impact. They have involved a substantial amount of national, and sometimes international, coordination and planning, and have gained national and international recognition, yet they represent only a portion of our efforts for national cooperation to deal with the vast bibliographic, political, and economic problems associated with foreign acquisitions.

The ACE Task Force on Library and Information Resources

In May 1972 a group of scholars and government officials with major interests in international education were assembled by the Assistant Secretary of Educational and Cultural Affairs of the Department of State to explore the means by which the interaction between the academic community and government agencies might be improved on a broad range of issues in the international field. The recommendations of a small follow-up committee led to the establishment in 1973 of the International Education Project of the American Council of Education with five special task forces set up under a Government/ Academic Interface Committee. Financial support for the International Education Project was secured from the Bureau of Educational and Cultural Affairs of the U.S. Department of State, the Ford Foundation, the Council on Library Resources, the National Science Foundation, and the Longview Foundation.

The Association of Research Libraries accepted responsibility for forming an appropriate task force to study the problems related to library resources and to produce a task force report.[7] The lengthy report of the ACE Task Force on Library and Information Resources, which reviews the status and national needs of research collections in all world areas, was produced after extensive study by library area specialists, scholars in various disciplines, library directors of several ARL institutions, and staff members of the Library of Congress and the Association of Research Libraries.

The recommendations contained in the report are important for several reasons. First, they came from a wide group of practitioners and library administrators and focus on national needs. Second, input was sought from representatives of the various world areas and was included whenever appropriate. Third, a formalized national plan and policy is proposed that, if implemented, could meet national needs.

The ACE report undoubtedly was the single most influential and authoritative document on library resources upon which the president's commission could draw in formulating its own recommendations regarding libraries and library resources. Many of the statements on the needs of libraries made by other individuals and groups to the commission were derived from or duplicated in this report. Because the ACE and the commission reports are so compatible, and because the ACE report is much more detailed, the ACE document could be said to constitute a more complete guide to library needs in foreign languages and international studies from a global point of view.

The first recommendation of the task force was for "the creation of an organization in the form of a permanent Secretariat, charged with planning and coordinating a national scheme capable of providing adequate library support for area study programs throughout the country."[8] This secretariat would receive continued support from participating institutions and the federal government, and it was proposed that the Association of Research Libraries, with the backing of the National Commission on Libraries and Information Science, should take the initiative in forming this organization.

A second recommendation was for the development of a given number of large multi-purpose regional centers, along with smaller specialized centers, to provide coverage of materials for individual countries and disciplines. The ACE group recognized that there existed complex intellectual and political problems in the selection of these centers, which are analogous to those faced in the selection of NDEA Title VI Foreign Language and Area Centers.

Some requirements of the national system proposed by the task force would be: "1. a more precise definition of the resources needed for present and future scholarly endeavor; 2. a systematic and comprehensive approach to acquiring such resources; 3. an organization to index these resources under uniform bibliographic authority and conventions; 4. a coordinated approach for allocation of these resources with a central record of the location of each title; 5. a communication system to transmit requests and exchange messages promptly . . .; and 6. a faster, more dependable delivery system than now available through our traditional interlibrary loan operation."[9] In addition, special projects, ranging from the improvement of bibliographic control to the movement of people to resources, could be selected for study and implementation. The priorities among representatives of the various area studies groups would vary, however.

Further recommendations relating to funding and organization were found in the overall final report of the Government/Academic Interface Committee— the parent body of the ACE Task Force on Library and Information Resources.

Two major ones were that specialized libraries and other services should receive five percent of the total dollar amount of all government contracts or grants made to universities and colleges, and that a national library system for international education should be formed with a permanent secretariat created with the assistance of the Library of Congress. The report further recommended that research library support be made available to institutions as part of the necessary overhead of grants and contracts, that the NPAC program be funded at a higher level, and that the MARC project be given higher priority. Overall, the Government/Academic Interface Committee report shares the concerns and also endorses virtually all of the recommendations of the Task Force on Library and Information Resources. Prophetically, it calls for the establishment of a Presidential Commission on Foreign Language Training "charged with the conduct of a systematic inquiry into the scope, adequacy, quality and effectiveness of foreign language training and resources in the United States. . . ."[10]

The ACE report does not specify for whom those recommendations ultimately were intended, but they presumably were directed at the sponsoring agencies. The report emphasized the need to better educate citizens and public officials in global issues.[11] The ACE report was not alone in voicing the concern of foundations, colleges, universities, federal agencies, and individual scholars. Long before the establishment of the President's Commission on Foreign Language and International Studies, the Lambert report had raised considerable discussion in academic and official circles and is probably the most quoted (and sometimes misquoted) authoritative study of the field ever undertaken.[12] The creation of the President's Commission on Foreign Language and International Studies brought new hope to the international education community that, once again after the country's needs were assessed, there might result new ideas, a broader and more responsive constituency, and greater financial support for foreign language and international studies.

The President's Commission on Foreign Language and International Studies

There is little need to dwell at great length on why the commission came into existence. Its activities and recommendations were highly publicized in the media, and while its recommendations have not been funded extensively under specially designed programs, some of them have been implemented under presently existing ones. Its recommendations will probably continue to be taken seriously by federal agencies and foundations because of their participation in formulating them and their need for guidelines for developing future funding policies which are more closely connected with national needs.

It would be instructive to review some of the documents which were especially commissioned or undertaken for the benefit of the commission. In almost every case, these documents point to the precarious financial conditions of our libraries' foreign area collections. They emphasize the need to share resources on a larger national scale, and they provide warnings that it is beyond the budgetary capabilities of more and more institutions to maintain and service these collections at previous levels of excellence.

A special report of the Rand Corporation, prepared for the Commission with NEH funding, cites the loss of Ford Foundation support and the rise in processing costs as serious problems which could affect the quality of students and faculty.[13] Rising costs also constitute a major concern of a report on foreign languages and related areas by the U.S. General Accounting Office, issued about the time the President's Commission was formed.[14] Reflecting a similar concern, a third report, the International Studies Review, prepared by staff of the National Endowment for the Humanities and the Ford Foundation, concluded that existing funding problems would be exacerbated by the termination of the availability of Public Law 480 funds. Noting that national proposals are pending for a division of labor with regard to acquisitions and cataloging, the Review concludes pessimistically that the "International Studies librarian is unsure of the direction these will take,"[15] and urges national financial support of certain designated research collections.[16] In a subsequent article, "The Preservation of the Cosmopolitan Research University," the authors of the Review cite library resources as one of four factors upon which the stability of international studies in universities hinges.[17]

Two other special reports—the proceedings and recommendations of the Wingspread conference sponsored by the Consortium of Latin American Studies Programs and the Latin American Studies Association,[18] and the analysis prepared by Louis Wolf Goodman and distributed by the Latin American Program of the Wilson Center—placed high priority on establishing a network of regionally based centers and libraries.[19]

While none of these numerous reports and analyses appear in the Background Papers and Studies of the President's Commission, they do agree with recommendations of other documents which are included. The three that fall into this category are those prepared by Roger Paget, Robert E. Ward, and William E. Carter.[20] All support the concept of a national-level network. Paget suggests that "twenty to twenty-five national resource centers would be chosen, principally according to magnitude and quality of research holdings on one or more global regions, and, very secondarily, according to suitability of physical plant and domestic geographic distribution."[21] Commission member Robert Ward supports the designation and funding of sixty-five to eighty-five National Centers, budgeted at $50,000 annually for library needs, and the provision of funding for five hundred mini-grants to bring scholars to these regionally located collections. While some libraries and users would view with apprehension his caveat that "a reasonable fee" be charged for services, there would be general support for his observation that a "substantial measure of rationalization and systematic inter-library cooperation on a regional and national basis is essential'' and that the ''best and most economic policy is to build and utilize existing strengths.'' His proposition of ''building upon the relatively small number of major research libraries in the country that with few exceptions are located on the same campuses that would house the NCs, and, second, adding thereto on a regional and national scale an apparatus of bibliographic control, rationalized acquisition policies, improved access for external users, and more efficient inter-library loan mechanisms,'' implies that a national network would be constructed.[22]

The single essay specifically addressed to research library needs in the *Background Papers* is that prepared by William Carter. It synthesizes most of the needs already outlined and makes a number of specific suggestions, some of which recapitulate those contained in the earlier ACE Task Force Report.[23] Carter's paper supports the establishment of a national secretariat which, he suggests, for financial and political reasons should be located outside of government, possibly within ACE or ARL, and should be funded through competitive bidding for federal support on a five-year, renewable basis. He reminds the Commission of the model for regional repository libraries recommended by SALALM in a letter to the Commission and specifying that each repository have a base of 150,000 volumes and an acquisitions budget of at least $50,000.[24] And Carter proposes that designated repositories accept responsibility for materials from a given country, or in the case of small countries, a group of countries; that there be shared cataloging responsibilities and bibliographic control; and there be an expansion of NPAC centers.

Based on a large amount of public testimony garnered through regional hearings, documents both solicited and unsolicited from the broadest imaginable educational constituency (reaching from K–12 throughout the entire higher education establishment), and in a national political climate characterized by financial uncertainty, the president's commission made its final recommendations. Those which relate to research libraries appear in a single paragraph which follows:

The steeply rising costs of area studies library collections calls for more inter-library cooperation, the rapid introduction of new technologies, an expansion of the Library of Congress' National Program for Acquisition and Cataloguing and the establishment by the Library of Congress of a National Center for Foreign Area Bibliography. National international studies centers should receive annual federal grants of an average of $50,000 each toward library costs. NEH should finance a program of 500 ''mini-grants'' annually at an average of $300 each to facilitate access to national centers' collections of faculty and graduate students at other institutions.[25]

The success of presently functioning cooperative library activities would seem to indicate that the goal of a national network for foreign area collections is both logical and reasonable. Obvious examples of national cooperation feeding into a national network include such well-known programs as interlibrary loans, regional and national bibliographic networks, cataloging data bases, and special services provided by the Library of Congress and the Center for Research Libraries.

It is through special programs at the Library of Congress and the Center for Research Libraries that the various foreign areas are particularly well served. Among the area studies programs maintained by CRL, it seems that the Asian studies librarians are especially well organized and directed as evidenced by the new special project designed to expand East Asian acquisitions by the Center with support from the Ford Foundation.[26] The project committee is developing a statement for CRL's International Studies Committee which will deal with the imminent national decline of South Asian and Southeast Asian materials soon to result from the termination of the Special Currency Program supporting the Library of Congress field operations in those areas. This gives CRL's international studies activities a strong focus on Africa and Asia, in terms of financial commitment, although the Latin American Microforms Project (LAMP), organized by SALALM in 1975, is at this moment perhaps the most dynamic of the center's cooperative area studies acquisitions programs.

The special library organizations serving the various area studies associations obviously have similar goals. Although contact between them is minimal, their executive officers collectively presented a signed document urging the commission to give special attention to library needs and to contact their library associations for further assistance.

While not directly representing the various area studies library groups, a special conference committee, representing several world areas at the 1980 meeting of Title VI Center Directors in Washington, recommended that a special conference be called to deal with the recommendations of the president's commission and the ACE task force. The committee proposed that the conference take place at the Library of Congress and include appropriate representatives of the library community, foundations, and government. Further conversations with the directors of area studies programs at the Library of Congress encouraged members of the committee to formalize its request for such a conference through a letter from the SALALM Executive Board to the Librarian of Congress. The Librarian's response was to take the matter under serious consideration while the Research Libraries Group and the Center for Research Libraries were examining some of the same key issues that the proposed conference sought to address.

The Formalization of a National Plan

Several alternative approaches could be taken in developing a viable, national-level network of area studies research libraries. The most ideal would perhaps be the establishment of a central secretariat that could coordinate efforts, help clarify and resolve differences of opinion, lobby appropriate funding agencies, suggest the initiation of new approaches, and encourage multi-institutional activities. The model for such an office was set out in the ACE report on area studies libraries. Progress in solving the problems we face would undoubtedly be more rapid if such an office could be established. However, given the threat of reductions in federal funds available for international education, and the general disinterest of major foundations in anything demanding long-term commitment, the creation of such an office may be, for the moment, an unrealistic hope. What, then, might be the alternatives?

Although universities tend no longer to be expanding their commitment to international education, many allow for at least annual inflationary increases. Together with the Library of Congress, these universities still provide the major sources of support for the development of foreign research collections in the United States. That support continues to be quite massive. If one were to take the top fifteen or twenty Latin American collections in the country and add together all the resources they absorb annually, the total would probably reach into the millions.

Rather than simple scarcity of resources, then, our problem would seem to lie elsewhere. Accounting for it in large part is the continuance of duplication of both materials and effort. Compounding it is a chronic neglect of fugitive and/or poorly formatted materials that, in spite of their often excellent research content, can all too easily be dismissed as ephemera. Few librarians or scholars would object to the need to collect all the production of major presses, as long as that production falls within a library's declared scope. Yet the content of such publications may be patently inferior to the content of mimeographed pieces from obscure research organizations. Although we are all collecting the major press works, probably none of us is doing the job that needs to be done with the poorly formatted materials.

Even within the constraints of existing resources, and in spite of the failure of the Farmington Plan, some sort of cooperative acquisitions plan can be developed, with or without a central secretariat. A beginning was made during the 1981 meeting of SALALM, when representatives of various major Latin American collections indicated the willingness of their institutions to take on primary responsibility for collecting materials from given countries. But not all were willing to take the next logical step and commit their institutions to cataloging those materials. For that, they still were looking mainly to the Library of Congress, to OCLC, and to other cataloging data bases.

The economics of collection-building are such that the expenses involved in the exchange or purchase of research material represent only a fraction of the cost of getting it under bibliographic control and on the shelf. For success to come to any national-level division of labor with regard to foreign acquisitions, participating institutions must assume responsibility for processing as well as for collection.

Although computerized cataloging makes the sharing of processing information much easier than it was in the past, it does not solve the knotty problem of quality control. Should there be a national secretariat for foreign language collections development, that office could spearhead such an endeavor. In its absence, a committee with the true power of sanction would seem to be one of the few viable alternatives. Such a committee could be composed of representatives of participating institutions, appointed on a rotating basis, with its operational costs underwritten by the participating institutions themselves.

A third approach to cooperative development for the nation's foreign language research collections could be for the Library of Congress's overseas offices to increase activity in the acquisition of multiple copies of materials and in their distribution to libraries that have taken on the commitment to house and service such materials. The viability of this approach would be immediately limited by the fact that the Library of Congress has offices only in a few countries where bibliographic control is especially poor, namely Indonesia, India, Pakistan, Kenya, Egypt, and Brazil. There is every indication that such offices are on the decline: the Library's office in Spain was closed several years ago, and its office in Japan is being phased out this year.

In order to develop national-level cooperation in collection development either new resources will have to be found, or existing resources reallocated. Given the present political and economic climate, the latter would seem more realistic than the former. Even reallocation will not occur, however, unless research institutions are willing to question the egocentric a priori principles that have undergirded their operations for years, and this would be a painful task. In the end, we all stand to gain from such introspection. Before we initiate it we should realize that it will probably force us into the uncomfortable situation of challenging vested interests with the fact that no institution, not even ours, can do everything, and that most can do only a very few things truly well. If we, as a corporate body, succeed, it will be due in no small degree to our ability to endure just such discomfort and to pose just such a challenge.

NOTES

1. For a full description of the plan, see *Farmington Plan Handbook* (Bloomington, Ind.: Association of Research Libraries, 1953). The Cooperative Acquisitions Project for Wartime Publications (CAPWP), established through the Library of Congress, functioned from 1945 to 1948 and served as a forerunner of the Farmington Plan, as noted by Robert D. Stueart in "Mass Buying Programs in the Development Process" in *Collection Development in Libraries: A Treatise* (Greenwich, Conn.: JAI Press Inc., 1980) edited by Robert D. Stueart and George B. Miller, Jr., pp. 204–205. For a review of the Farmington Plan accomplishments in Latin America, see Robert K. Johnson, ed., *The Acquisition of Latin Americana in ARL Libraries* . . . (Tucson: ARL Latin American Farmington Plan Subcommittee, 1972).

2. Commitments for collection responsibilities made before and during the annual SALALM conference in April 1981 are under review by the responsible libraries to include a responsibility

also for cataloging priority. The SALALM Ad hoc Subcommittee on the Status of Latin American Acquisitions in U.S. Libraries is investigating the formation of parallel RLIN and OCLC cataloging groups.

3. Association of Research Libraries, *Staff Report on the ARL Committees on Foreign Acquisitions* (Washington, D.C.: ARL, Jan. 1981).

4. A full study of LACAP prepared at the height of its success may be found in M. J. Savary, *The Latin American Cooperative Acquisitions Program . . . : An Imaginative Venture* (New York: Hafner Publishing Co., Inc., 1968).

5. Stanley L. West, *A Proposed Cooperative Acquisition Plan for United States Institutions with Latin American Interests* (Gainesville, Fla., 1965).

6. The extraordinary range of research publications produced commercially and by official agencies at the municipal, state, and national levels can be reviewed in U.S. Library of Congress, Library of Congress Office, Brazil, *Accessions List, Brazil*, vol. 1–. Jan. 1975–.

7. American Council on Education, *Library Resources for International Education: A Report Submitted by the Task Force on Library and Information Resources to the Government/Academic Interface Committee*, Occasional Paper No. 1 (Washington, D.C.: ACE International Education Project, 1975), pp. iv–vi.

8. Ibid., p. 74.

9. Stanley McElderry, "Cooperative Arrangements for Access to South Asian Materials: Problems and Prospects" (Paper presented at Conference on South Asian Library Resources, Boston, April 4–6, 1974). Cited in ibid., p. 76. The pattern of national library cooperation recommended by the ACE task force for foreign area collections is compatible with recommendations for a national library network in a study commissioned by the National Commission for Libraries and Information Science. See Vernon E. Palmour, *Resources and Bibliographic Support for a Nationwide Library Program* (Rockville, Md.: Westat, Inc., 1974).

10. American Council on Education, *Education for Global Interdependence: A Report with Recommendations to the Government/Academic Interface Committee* (Washington, D.C.: ACE International Education Project, 1975), p. 42.

11. Ibid., p. 14.

12. Richard D. Lambert, *Language and Area Studies Review*, Monograph 17 (Philadelphia: The Academy of Political and Social Science, 1973). While this study gives slight mention to library problems, it specifically notes the vulnerability of library programs to cuts in funding. Lambert, in his role as the Director of the Language and Area Studies Review conducted for the Social Sciences Research Council, showed considerable frustration and alarm over the dearth of information on national library strengths and weaknesses, selection processes, use, etc. This is reported in a talk he gave to an unspecified meeting of area specialists entitled "Area Studies and the Library: A Plea for Data," date unknown.

13. Sue E. Berryman et al., *Foreign Language and International Specialists: The Marketplace and National Policy* (Santa Monica: Rand Corporation, September, 1979), p. 172. The report also calls for "a more clearly defined division of interest among university libraries, permitting the concentration of resources by region, field, or function in one or several suitable places" (pp. 68–69).

14. U.S. General Accounting Office, *Report to the Congress by the Comptroller General of the U.S.: Study of Foreign Languages and Related Areas—Federal Support—Administrative Need* (Washington, D.C.: USGPO, Sept. 13, 1978).

15. Elinor G. Barber and Warren Ilchman, *International Studies Review: A Staff Study*, Sept. 1979, p. 40.

16. Ibid., pp. 123–124.

17. Elinor G. Barber and Warren Ilchman, *The Preservation of the Cosmopolitan Research University in the United States*. Reprinted from *The Annals of the American Academy of Political and Social Science*, May 1980, p. 14.

18. Donald R. Shea and Maureen J. Smith, eds., *New Directions in Language and Area Studies: Priorities for the 1980's*. CLASP Publ. No. 9 (Urbana, Ill.: Consortium of Latin American Studies Programs, 1979), pp. 14–15.

19. Louis Wolf Goodman, *Latin American Studies in the United States: National Needs and Opportunities*, Working Papers No. 37 (Washington, D.C.: Latin American Program, The Wilson Center, 1979), p. 16.

20. William E. Carter, "International Studies and Research Library Needs;" Roger Paget, "Graduate Foreign Language and International Studies;" and Robert E. Ward, "Statement on Advanced Training and Research in International Studies," in *President's Commission on Foreign Language and International Studies: Background Papers and Studies* (Washington, D.C.: GPO, November 1979).

21. Ibid., p. 132.

22. Ibid., pp. 150−155.

23. Ibid., pp. 157−186.

24. Other political questions regarding selection and responsibilities of repositories also were addressed in the SALALM letter.

25. *Strength Through Wisdom, A Critique of U.S. Capability: A Report to the President from the President's Commission on Foreign Language and International Studies* (Washington, D.C.: GPO, Nov. 1979), pp. 19−20.

26. "Center to Target Expansion of East Asian Holdings," *Focus on the Center for Research Libraries* 1, (May−June, 1981), 4. It is in Asian Studies that perhaps the most planning has been undertaken for a national network. See American Council of Learned Societies, Steering Committee for a Study of the Problems of East Asian Libraries, *East Asian Libraries: Problems and Prospects* (n.p., 1977).

17. The Library of Congress and a National Plan for Latin American Collection Development

John Finzi

In considering various thoughts and ideas for this paper, I was confronted with several alternatives and at least one question. The alternatives were easily disposed of. I would not present lists of figures, statistics, and activities, nor would I give a historical review of the Library of Congress' role in Latin American Studies as a background to current and future prospects. I would simply stay with those thoughts, considerations, ideas, and questions which form the framework of the topic of collection development. The "question" I had, however, could not be so easily disposed of, and in reading between the lines of this paper, you will probably realize that I have not answered it.

I asked myself, at the very outset, whether one can talk solely of a "National Plan for Latin American Collection Development" outside of and without reference to a "National Plan for Collection Development" of which the first can only be a subset. While I have avoided an explicit answer to this question, much of what I have to say could be extended by inference to a wider context. Even had I wanted to, in all likelihood I could not have done otherwise, since the demands of my task at the Library of Congress have obliged me, during the past eighteen years, to think in terms of global coverage. I have tried, however, to stay within my appointed topic and what I have to say will, I hope, be pertinent.

The historical commitment of the Library of Congress to the development and maintenance of comprehensive research collections in the area of Latin American studies is, I think, well known. Prescinding from certain specialized topics or certain types of publications, the Library of Congress still has, and will continue to have, the most extensive collections of Latin American materials in this country, whether they be newspapers, official gazettes, government publications, or monographic materials. The collections are a national asset and a national resource to be counted on both for their retrospective depth and for their future potential. Why, then, should we at the Library of Congress look toward the development of a national plan not only with favor but with supportive and strong expectations for practical implementation? The answer is obvious.

Whether we consider the area of acquisition, the area of bibliographic control, or ultimately, that of preservation of these materials, it becomes quite plain that no single library, no matter how well endowed, can do the job alone. Nor, for that matter, should it. The sharing of responsibilities within a national configuration is, in this respect, not only a necessity born of need, but a positive and creative development. Each research library has a set of individual requirements and imperatives and will, for this reason, develop best those areas that meet their requirements, making possible a rich pattern of specialization that no single institution could duplicate.

Through the past several decades, the idea of national plans for the development of American research collections has been repeatedly discussed, moving by degrees from purely theoretical and often pious statements to a practical thrust for its realization. We have passed, I would say, from a purely intellectual belief in the idea to a state of psychological readiness and to a new willingness to see it done. National planning for the sharing of resources and responsibilities is now in the process of being translated into reality. The intensified activities in this area of the Research Libraries Group and of the Association of Research Libraries, to which I shall refer further on, amply attest to this fact. The factors that have contributed to this development are well known: the increase in world publishing, the escalating costs of running libraries, and, simultaneously, shrinking or stationary budgets. These problems are now compounded by the drying up of Federal funding and the uncertainty of Foundation assistance.

It is evident that libraries, for a while at least, will have to stand on their own. While reading the excellent summary prepared by Carl Deal and William Carter describing past plans, commission reports, and blueprints for cooperative efforts, it occurred to me more and more forcibly that at this point it would seem more fruitful to start *ex novo* (or, more colloquially, from scratch) with a clear and hard inward look rather than seek delivery outside our own institutions. What, in fact, can libraries do on their own, individually and together? I suspect quite a good deal, if the appropriate cooperative patterns and arrangements can be set in motion. In his paper, Dr. Jones refers to a phrase now extensively used in the Department of Education: "creative retrenchment." I think that there is a lot of merit in this phrase and that we should take it up as a challenge and see how far we can go in making this period of retrenchment truly creative.

Three major areas will have to be addressed in a coordinated and cooperative manner during the years ahead: maintenance of adequate research resources; bibliographic control of these resources and rapid access to information concerning their location; and, ultimately, the preservation of the research materials of which we are the custodians. A rationally planned division of labor and the assumption of freely accepted responsibilities seem to be major conditions for the success of such an undertaking. Aside from these basic requirements, we have at our disposal today means that were not available to us when the Farmington Plan was initiated nearly three decades ago. The growing network of services for the rapid transmission and exchange of bibliographic information is furnishing us with a most powerful tool toward the establishment of truly national plans.

All the elements mentioned above are currently present in the system being developed by the Research Libraries Group. The model that these twenty-seven libraries have adopted is worth studying and watching. Prescinding from the proprietary aspects of the RLIN computerized network, the potential and pattern for a national system are definitely there. This is evident in the interest taken by the Task Force on Collection Development of the Association of Research Libraries in the RLG Conspectus. This fairly recent development points to a good chance that the Conspectus will be adopted by the Association of Research Libraries as the official instrument for a national survey of research collections and collecting policies.

This would be a major step toward a national system of information and toward a subsequent division of responsibilities. Basic to the system will be standardized descriptions of collecting levels and updated information concerning the current collecting policies of the research libraries involved. Equally basic to a satisfactory functioning of a national plan would seem to be a timely "alerting system" that would enable each individual library to make any change of policy or direction known to all other libraries participating in the plan so that they might take adequate action. Let us say that library X finds it impossible to continue a level of comprehensive acquisition in a certain field or subfield in which it had been traditionally strong and relied upon by other libraries. It would seem imperative that this information be made available as soon as possible so that the responsibility for the specific field or subfield might be reassigned. As you know, this system of notification and reassignment of responsibilities will form an important part of the cooperative collection development plan being implemented by the RLG.

While a viable system for the apportionment of collecting responsibilities is basic to any national plan, a system for sharing the cataloging workload involved in controlling and making known the materials acquired is perhaps even more desperately needed. As we all know, materials acquired through great effort and expenditure are of little use if left dormant in disorganized backlogs. Currently, many pieces of this very complex problem are beginning to fall into place, but there is still quite a way to go, and for the next few years the cataloging component of any national plan will continue to require a major, concerted effort. It is already quite clear, however, that any system or pattern that we might devise will require the most strict adherence to the standards necessary for the flow and exchange of computerized bibliographic data. I am

referring here, of course, to such national standards as AACR 2, the National
Level Bibliographic Record, Name Authority standards, or any other standards
that will be found necessary in a national network.

There exist today certain blocks to the free flow of bibliographic records. I
refer specifically to still unresolved financial and political problems basic to the
proprietary nature of the major utilities, chief among them OCLC and RLIN.
While the National Union Catalog can still provide an important national link, it
cannot, by its nature, provide the speed of information that an online national
system would furnish. A solution of these problems would constitute a most
significant breakthrough, and we must hope that a fair settlement will occur in
the not-too-distant future. As the dialogue continues, the interest of the Library
of Congress, the Association of Research Libraries, and the Council on Library
Resources could not be more explicit.

In this connection, a development of major significance was announced
only two weeks ago. The Council on Library Resources has awarded to the
Research Libraries Group a grant of $394,886 for the next phase of a project
that will involve the development and implementation of a standardized telecommunications link between the systems at RLG, the Washington Library
Network (WLN), and the Library of Congress. Upon implementation, the
Standard Network Interconnection (SNI) will enable users of either the Washington Library Network, the RLG's online bibliographic system, or the Library
of Congress to access the bibliographic resources of the other systems. The
announcement states, "the long-range implication of use of the SNI is that any
computer system will be able to connect with any other computer system to
create a nationwide bibliographic data base." By early 1983, this telecommunications link will make possible, in addition to the exchange of authority
data, the sharing of full catalog records, location and holdings data, and even
the transmittal of interlibrary loan requests.

What will be the role of the Library of Congress in this intensified search
for nationwide planning of research resources? Below are some of the major
areas in which the Library of Congress will continue, within the limit of its
fiscal capabilities, to perform its national responsibilities. Above and beyond
these specific areas, I should like to stress the deep commitment of this
institution to the establishment in the United States of viable plans for the
maintenance of research collections fully responsive to the national need.
While this is a historical position, we are fully cognizant of the fact that this
position has to be adapted to new means and new technologies. There are areas
where fully developed cooperative plans for collection development or cataloging would be of appreciable assistance to us, as they would equitably ease the
burden of the performance of our national responsibilities. There are also areas
in which we can supply other research libraries with a central reference point as
well as with a sense of continuity of commitment that cannot always be ensured
by other institutions.

As far as we can now foresee, the Library of Congress will certainly continue to pursue the following goals:

1. Maintain comprehensive research collections of official government publications, periodical literature, and monographic materials from Latin America, across the whole area and subject spectrum, except for technical agriculture and clinical medicine.

2. Continue the bibliographic control and distribution of cataloging data for as large a percentage of current receipts as fiscally feasible.

3. Continue to support and facilitate the exchange and distribution of computerized bibliographic data, while continuing its role in the establishment of standards and formats for their acceptance and transmission.

4. Whenever feasible, provide instruction in the application of standards and the preparation of bibliographic records suitable for computerized interchange.

5. Develop and expand Minimal Level Cataloging for certain monographs, serials, and microforms in order to extend more rapid bibliographic control to materials that would normally fall in the lowest—and slowest—cataloging priority.

6. Develop ''batch'' or ''group'' cataloging alternatives for pamphlet and report materials that could not, realistically, be cataloged individually.

7. Continue to sponsor and coordinate the cooperative microfilming of current and retrospective serials files, such as newspapers and official gazettes.

8. Encourage, sustain, and participate—either individually or in cooperation with national projects such as those sponsored by the RLG or the ARL—in working for a practical and feasible division of labor and for resource sharing plans for the acquisition, cataloging, and preservation of Latin American materials.

This last point, which involves the major areas of concern in any national plan, will require a considerable amount of concerted thought and the weighing and choosing of alternatives. Whether a division of responsibilities should be based on purely geographic lines, as proposed by the SALALM Committee on Inter-Library Relations, or whether ''subject'' or ''type of publication'' should also be added as important components in the scheme will have to be looked at carefully. From the point of view of the Library of Congress, for example, it would be of considerable help to know that another library was committed to the comprehensive acquisition of local histories, or popular fiction, or poetry from a specific country of Latin America. Similarly, in the area of cataloging it is possible that while a geographic division of responsibilities might supply a broad pattern of action, the key factor may actually become the speed in the creation of a catalog record and its input in a nationwide network.

As to the mechanics of acquisition, it is difficult to see how we could now duplicate projects as successful as those which the Library of Congress launched twenty years ago. The hopes we had in the 1960s for additional procurement centers in Latin America, Africa, and the Far East have completely faded, at least for the foreseeable future. A timely and free flow of information concerning procurement sources, prices, and availability of materials may go a long way in assisting interested libraries in their acquisitions programs. Reports from travelers will also help. Peter de la Garza, coordinator of the Library's Hispanic Acquisitions Program, will visit Colombia and Venezuela in the near future and we shall all profit from the information that he will bring back. It seems evident that cooperative patterns which lead to a well-formulated plan will have to be set in place with good will and a good deal of imagination. Above all, they should be based on a realistic appraisal of our individual strengths and fiscal capabilities, at least for the time being.

Ultimately, the test of any national plan for the development of Latin American collections, just as for other areas and fields, will be whether individual institutions will be willing and able to fit their own drives and mandates into a wider framework of commitments and obligations, be it the RLG model or an expanded ARL configuration. A number of area interest groups are now competing for the attention of their parent institutions and for Foundation funding. Beyond the Latin Americanists, there are the South Asianists, the West European Specialists, the librarians and scholars interested in the Far East, and those who devote their attention to the Near East, or the Soviet Union and the East European Block. In the past three decades this competition has been fruitful and creative insofar as it firmly established broad areas of legitimate concern.

In this current decade, however, it runs the risk of becoming a counterproductive pursuit unless these various groups can fit their own demands within a broader pattern of research libraries obligations and unless a clearer and better-articulated statement of need can be phrased. The massive acquisitions patterns of the 1960s and 1970s are no longer feasible or desirable. From long experience with major acquisitions programs, as well as through intellectual conviction, I feel that what is needed today in all fields and areas involving foreign acquisitions is a thoughtful and dispassionate reevaluation of what is essential for serious research in this country and a clear redefinition of parameters and policies. Any national cooperative plan for Latin American collection development will require this rethinking of needs and goals, as well as a blueprint of how best to accomplish our task.

18. Beware Also the Calends of March

John Rison Jones, Jr.

If I were at liberty, as a Federal employee, to choose a biblical text from which to speak to you this afternoon, undoubtedly that text would have to be taken from the Book of Daniel, and very probably a description of Daniel's descent into the den of lions. At least Daniel had some assurance that the Lord was with him and that he was merely undergoing a test of his personal faith.

In my case, I have no such assurance. Although your welcome has been warm and generous, I am not sure that the same "climate" will prevail as I make my exit from this room. My remarks will bring no comfort to those of you interested in a "National Level of Support for Collection Development," at least from the standpoint of Federal assistance from the Department of Education.

If Daniel was undergoing a test of personal faith, surely we are all undergoing a test of national faith compelled by the necessity of drastically reducing the need for Federal assistance in most areas of our national life. Perhaps a better "text" for me today might be the title of one of those marvelous volumes in the British Museum: "The Princely Dismal Calendar: Being The Bloody Almanack, for the Year of Our Lord, 1660, Fore-telling the strange catastrophes, Changes, and Revolutions that will befall most Princes, States and Commonwealths throughout Europe; and the Superlative Actions, designed by the Heavens, touching the Crowns, Scepters, ad Royal Diadems" (British Museum Entry 1260 and 999.)

As most of you are aware, there has been at least one major Federal area of support for the kind of activity that we are gathered here to discuss—Title II of the Higher Education Act of 1965, as amended, and, more specifically, II-C of the Act, the Strengthening Research Library Resources authorized by the Act. That program has provided grants to institutions with major research libraries that make "a significant contribution to higher education and research, that are broadly based and are recognized as having national and international significance for scholarly research, and that are in substantial demand by researchers and scholars not connected with the institution."

There is also a provision in Title VI of the new Act for our International Education Programs, formerly in Title VI of the National Defense Education Act of 1959. In these programs, the Secretary may make grants to institutions for the purpose of strengthening and operating graduate and undergraduate centers and programs which "will be national resources for the teaching of any

JOHN RISON JONES, JR.

modern foreign language, for instruction in fields needed to provide a full understanding of the areas, regions or countries in which such language is commonly used.'' The Act further stipulates that funds may be awarded for research and training in international studies and the international aspects of professional and other fields of study. The statute specifically allows the Secretary to include grants to centers having important library collections for the purpose of maintaining collections.

All of you are familiar with the broad outline of the Administration's Fiscal Year 1983 budget in which the Congress is asked by the Administration to terminate assistance under Title II for all programs related to College and Research Library Assistance and Library Training and Research. The Department of Education has further recommended congressional consent for the transfer of the International Education Programs and the Fulbright-Hays Programs to the International Communications Agency with a budget reduced from $26 million in 1981 to a proposed $10,314,000 in 1983. Obviously, the reduced level of funding has implications for the support of library maintenance.

Many reasons have influenced the Department's acceptance of the request to terminate library assistance and to reduce spending in the field of international education. The most compelling factor is the condition of the national economy and a need to reassess continued Federal support in most program areas. There is the strong conviction that the Federal Government operates in too many areas which are the legitimate concern of other sectors of the nation, primarily through the support and the backing that institutions can and should develop from the private sector. There is also the implication of a need for institutions to give priority to the flow of institutional funds and to begin to put into proper perspective what institutions need to support.

Part of our thinking in the Department involves the fact that with a diminishing dollar, there is a corresponding diminishing return on grants, especially small ones. What may have supported, for instance, the purchase of 1,000 volumes in the past, may very well only support 300 volumes at today's inflated book prices. This calls into question a wise usage of limited Federal resources. There is always an evaluation assessment, as well, which attempts to determine the impact of Federal assistance on higher education programs. Although there is possibly a significant enrollment of students at the graduate level in programs related to Latin American studies, we frankly do not see that enrollment as a dramatic increase over previous years. But this is hardly the place to discuss the relative priorities that students and institutions assign to specific areas of study. This is, and must remain, a factor and a gauge of Federal interest and potential involvement. Moreover, there are great Latin American Studies centers already in existence which enjoy local support and which enjoy constant institutional support not only for library acquisitions, but for an expansion of the range of offerings and for the general advancement of the field.

In my agency, we talk extensively about "creative retrenchment" as the Federal presence is withdrawn from so many areas of higher education where the field has come to expect an annual dollar support. Perhaps when the realities of that withdrawal are firmly fixed, people will engage in the kinds of "creative enterprises" that have contributed so greatly to our educational accomplishments in the past. And there are so many things that can be accomplished which do not require a Federal underwriting but do require an institutional commitment to our basic national goals of excellence. Several issues come to mind— and they are only suggestions and reflections from a rank amateur:

1. The continued refinement of OCLC (Ohio College Library Center) and RLIN (Research Library Information Network) to utilize the advancing technologies that we have to keep abreast of acquisitions. We simply need to know where things are located.

2. A reexamination of the need to proliferate. I do not presume to know much about your field, but I do know something about institutions, and I have a very strong professional conviction that it may be more in the national interest to stabilize and to plan for the expansion of some of our great centers rather than to develop more centers which will have a very uncertain future.

   Today there are more than 3,300 institutions of higher education—a dramatic increase from 1870, when we had less than 600 such institutions. Tragically, all of these institutions want to become involved in the next stage of development, that is, the two-year becoming a four-year; the four-year becoming a graduate school; and the graduate school advancing to national prominence.

   In an earlier day, when I was associated with an institution in the Southwest, the college President wanted me to build graduate programs in history and I had to ask, "Why? What is wrong with being the best undergraduate institution in the southwest? Do you have an idea of the cost of building a library for Hispanic studies?" Unfortunately, my advice was not taken. Our institution was in competition with the University of Texas at Austin. The funds that we were able to raise did allow us to make a significant choice about acquisitions. We elected to microfilm extensive portions of the Spanish Archives dealing with the Americas. At least we had a specialty that could and did attract young scholars. I have not been back on that campus for nearly eighteen years, and I can only hope that the library holdings are better now than when I left. My point, then and now, is that we should not have been in competition with another institution.

3. Is it too late for libraries to think about the consolidation of small separate holdings into a major regional center for studies? This would be enormously helpful for the researcher and would be in the national interest.

   In my graduate days when I was researching French foreign policy in the 1930s and its impact on European nations, there were only two great newspaper centers that I could have used effectively—in California and in New York. Both centers were totally inadequate because acquisitions virtually stopped with the depression.

I was fortunate to secure a Fulbright-Hays Fellowship to study at the University of Paris, but I found that even the great collections of the Bibliothèque Nationale and the British Museum were inadequate. I did find the Royal Institute for International Affairs—with the most complete collection in the world. No librarian told me of its existence; a fellow researcher had stumbled onto it! I tell this story to point out the importance of information—which you all recognize—and the need to provide those supportive services that allow research to thrive and grow.

I am a firm believer in thinking today about our future needs in informational terms and to think in broad regional concepts. I would like to think that what we have collected separately might be joined together in the interest of the advancement of research. If we cannot do that, and I understand the realities of separatism, we can make absolutely certain that we do not all collect the same things. We can develop diversity through intensive specialization—and this needs to be developed within regional terms because of the scarcity of dollars. We need to make absolutely certain that individual countries can be successfully covered regionally so that the broad parameters of research on Latin American countries can be accomplished. This will require a great deal of trust and cooperation. Unfortunately, there are few examples of such trust.

As we are all aware, it is not in the cards for all libraries to be great. Neither is it in those cards for us to engage in duplication. It can, and must, be prevented.

Also, I would suggest that this is true at all levels of institutional development, especially in the development of a comprehensive national level of support for collections. I would repeat an earlier statement, that development must be implemented in the absence of Federal support for the activity—at least for the present.

This is not a new source of frustration for librarians or historians. Ours is a civilization that does not place a good deal of emphasis on the past. As custodians of that past in printed form, librarians have always been creative. Hopefully, they can engage in "creative retrenchment" in this day of diminishing Federal support—and in this quest, they have the support of the Office of postsecondary Education.

I usually keep scraps of paper around the office with curious quotations from the past. There is the motto that I developed to get me through graduate school: "Never be encouraged; always give up!" Or there is that marvelous placard which I saw in Hyde Park many years ago: "Be a realist; demand the impossible!"

An appropriate quotation for those of us interested in library collections today might well be a paragraph I read in the *Chronicle of Higher Education* several years ago: "Every age leaves its mark. With temples, pyramids, gardens, cathedrals, tall ships, opera houses, galleries, libraries, laboratories and universities—successive generations have recorded their own creative aspirations and claimed the attention of generations to come. By looking at the best of what they left, we know what they sought to be. But what of our time?"

I sincerely hope that among our legacies for the future, there will be a splendid collection of materials on the Americas—and that librarians will have succeeded in this tremendously important quest.

19. Sharing Collection Responsibility and the Problem of Database Compatibility

Deborah Jakubs

The topic of this paper is of double importance to me, as a Latin American historian who has come face to face with the often frustrating and sometimes frightening difficulties involved in locating materials, and as a collection development librarian who has confronted the task of assuring future researchers of access to sources—perhaps just as frightening. A particularly vivid recollection came to mind as I read William Carter and Carl Deal's paper (Chapter 16) and may illustrate my point. A few years ago, in Buenos Aires, after weeks of trying to gain access to a complete run of a nineteenth-century Argentine newspaper, I was finally granted permission. The long-awaited moment arrived and the first dusty volumes were set in front of me. As I tentatively fingered the brittle pages, taking in their deplorable condition, all that went through my mind was the hope that someone, somewhere, had better copies or had had the foresight to microfilm such a rich source.

I was reminded of that incident as I read the comments of William Carter and Carl Deal regarding the "chronic neglect of fugitive and/or poorly formatted materials," remarkably rich sources that can slip away, "dismissed as ephemera." As the authors point out, efforts at organizing as a group to ensure that Latin American library materials of all kinds, in all forms, wherever published are collected and maintained at a high level despite dwindling funds for area studies, have been persistent and vigorous, if thwarted thus far in their ultimate goal. However, a national plan for collection development in this field seems closer than ever at the present time, when methods of evaluating in depth the holdings of our institutions are available and when it is more obvious than ever that serious steps must be taken to rationalize acquisitions. Even faculty members, notoriously loathe to go elsewhere to use research materials or to wait for a call from the interlibrary loan office, are realizing the need for a coherent and comprehensive program of cooperative collection development.

My contribution to this topic will address two main issues whose connection is not immediately apparent but which are critical to the successful implementation of a national plan for Latin American collections. The first concerns the experience of RLG and RLG libraries in the design and implementation of the collection development conspectus and its potential as a tool to assist SALALM in confidently devising a national plan. My second concern is the question of the compatibility of databases as it might affect the development of such a plan. I will address some of the current political and technical obstacles (the latter only in rather general terms) to the immediate linking of databases such as RLIN and OCLC. I should stress that the "problem" of the compatibility of databases, while naturally of interest to Latin American bibliographers, is a complex question of national scope and national concern. While we all would agree that a national linkage would be a boon to libraries, until it becomes an immediate possibility we must work around the "problem" as much as we can.

Even when RLG had only four members—Columbia, Yale, New York Public Library, and Harvard—in the days of "RLG I," prior to the acquisition of BALLOTS (Bibliographic Automation of Large Library Operations using a Time-Sharing System) and its subsequent conversion to RLIN (Research Libraries Information Network)—a Collection Development Committee was discussing the allocation of collection responsibilities for geographic areas, subjects, and forms of materials and was concerned with the placement of serial titles based on collection and program strengths within the consortium. Such planning became increasingly crucial and its effects potentially more far-reaching as more institutions joined the partnership and RLG I became RLG II. A greater number of libraries had more to share, on more levels and in more fields; they also had greater potential for rationalizing acquisitions in many areas to avoid or eliminate unnecessary overlap. RLG now has twenty-seven member-owners, and a standing Collection Management and Development Committee. Among their concerns has figured the development of an appropriate methodology for uncovering strengths and weaknesses in collections. This is a first, critical step toward assigning responsibility in any field and thus toward compiling a collection development policy statement for the consortium. The tool devised to provide this kind of in-depth and accessible information about the institutions' collections is called a conspectus. Since its first application to the field of East Asia it has proved to be invaluable for identifying so-called "endangered fields"—those in which too few or no institutions are collecting at a high enough level to support research. The analysis of data collected through use of the conspectus has also been useful at the level of individual institutions by allowing bibliographers to identify and remedy specific weaknesses in collections. A discussion of how the conspectus is used in collection evaluation may suggest ways in which a comparable tool would be helpful in organizing a national Latin American collecting plan.

The first test of the RLG conspectus involved East Asian collections throughout the U.S., at RLG institutions and the Library of Congress. Analyzing holdings in this field had high priority because of the disproportionately high costs of East Asian materials and the difficulty of their acquisition. The initial model for the conspectus was subsequently expanded and applied to other fields: Art and Architecture, Linguistics, Languages and Literatures, Philosophy and Religion, Sciences, History and the Auxiliary Sciences of History, Music, Economics, Sociology, Political Science, and South Asia. In the last field, both RLG and non-RLG institutions are participating in the compilation of data in light of the recognized danger to the integrity of South Asian collections posed by the termination of the PL480 program, and for the same reasons that East Asia received attention in the program.

How does it work? At RLG, generally in consultation with subject specialists and members of the Collection Management and Development Committee, a set of worksheets is developed for gathering data in a given field. These worksheets are designed along a broad subject outline, based on the LC classification schedules. Once the worksheets are distributed and approved, institutions are asked to supply two figures for each subject line or category; the first refers to the existing collection strength (ECS) and the second describes the current collecting intensity (CCI). Values run along a five point scale from zero, indicating no holdings or negligible holdings, and no systematic collecting policy in a field, to five, the comprehensive level, at which a library attempts to collect all significant works of recorded knowledge in all forms and in all applicable languages. The aim at level five is to be exhaustive. Between these two poles lie level one, minimal collecting beyond the most basic works; level two which indicates the collection of most up-to-date general materials; level three, which is the instructional support level for undergraduate and most graduate courses; and level four, the true research level collection. This level includes major published source materials required for dissertations and other independent research, in an appropriately wide range of languages.

The raw values supplied by institutions are further detailed or qualified by the addition of language codes and brief notes in which an institution may, for example, indicate a particular strength or special collection in a field. The data are currently maintained online at RLG by central staff, who can modify and update the conspectus. Once tabulated and verified, the data become the RLG Collection Development Manual. Work is progressing rapidly on an interactive conspectus file, a database that can be searched by institution, collecting level, field, and subfield. The file, which is now in test form, will allow institutions to compare their data online with those supplied by other institutions, and perhaps aid them in determining possible modifications in collection development policies in fields according to strengths reported elsewhere within the partnership. The file will also be of potential use in the area of shared resources/interlibrary loan, since a search could be done for collections at level four or five in a field to identify the likely owner of a given work.

Once the data have been collected, members of the Collection Management and Development Committee review the results, looking for "endangered fields." A subject is usually considered adequately covered if there are at least three level four or five collections in it. For each of these uncovered or undercovered fields, a decision is made by the committee regarding the need for assignment of primary collecting responsibility. This decision will be based on the importance of the field, the existence of level three collections within RLG, and on the accessibility of a research-level collection at a non-RLG institution. Analysis of the conspectus data usually results in the recommendation to assure coverage of a field, and subsequent querying of institutions regarding their willingness and ability to accept such a responsibility is carried out. Of course, attention is paid to local collection practices. When a library is asked to agree to maintain a level four or to upgrade its collecting policy to that level, it may refuse to do so, at which point the request will be made of another institution. Cases of refusing primary collecting responsibility are few in RLG, since achieving the main goal of a national collection development policy relies heavily on cooperation and in some cases may involve sacrifice.

The results of this ambitious gathering of data—at present the conspectus has addressed nearly 70 percent of the collections at RLG institutions—have been overwhelmingly positive. It has proved to be a way for librarians to better acquaint themselves with their own holdings and those of other institutions, and it has emphasized a healthy spirit of cooperation among them. Though not a perfect tool, it has been modified and improved with use, and has produced the desired results. It has also, at times, served as guidance for the group as a whole, as patterns have emerged during analysis of data by the Collection Management and Development Committee.

Assignments of primary collecting responsibilities in RLG have not approached the magnitude of whole countries' production or materials relating to an entire world area, although emphasis within individual institutions may shift as a result of studying the conspectus. The fact that the acquisition of most materials for area studies, among them Latin American studies, is done on a country basis cannot be denied, and certainly should be considered as holdings are evaluated. The SALALM committee on the use of the conspectus has dealt with this at its meeting. Within RLG, what has been deemed potentially "assignable"—in other words, materials and areas for which primary responsibility can be assumed or transferred in a relatively easy way—is only the difference between what is needed for instructional support and different degree programs at one level or another. Resources for instructional support cannot be stored off-site. The Collection Management and Development Committee, as a standing committee of RLG, is empowered to make recommendations concerning the assumption of primary collecting responsibilities to the Board of Governors (through the president or other senior academic officer representing his/her institution on the Board) but does not have the power to make those commitments itself. The Collection Management and Development Program is one of the several which underpin the cooperative basis of RLG.

The commitment of institutions to a serious investment of resources and agreement to participate in all the programs it includes are the two factors which make RLG different from any other network or consortium. Furthermore, it is the right and responsibility of the Board of Governors to sanction any participation of their respective institutions in cooperative schemes. These decisions are made in the interest of the partnership as a whole. For RLG institutions, the conspectus is an official link, a formal commitment to cooperation; for non-RLG institutions whose data have in the past been included in the conspectus (specifically for South Asia and Art and Architecture), the conspectus is an important source of information, to be used for comparative purposes.

The linking of databases, while opening a very large door to interinstitutional and interutility cooperation, is not going to happen as soon as one might prefer, although there are encouraging signs. Late in 1981, the Council on Library Resources approved a joint proposal for the study and development of a Standard Network Interconnection (SNI) among RLG, the Washington Library Network (WLN), and the Library of Congress (LC). The project covers the design, development, and implementation of a standardized telecommunications link among the systems of RLG, WLN, and LC to permit bibliographic applications on one system to exchange data with bibliographic applications on another system. The proposed project development will span sixteen months, and is a component of the Linked Systems Project (LSP), which also includes the ongoing work of the Linked Authority Systems Project (LASP).

As a result of this close coordination, once the capacity for the compatibility of systems is achieved (scheduled for April 1983), the first application of the link will be an authorities system. Once the initial mechanism is operational (phase one of the SNI), however, subsequent applications involving the sharing of other bibliographic data would not represent a major additional effort. Further technical detail on the functioning of the SNI is not appropriate here; however, one of its basic features may be of interest: a user logging on to his/her own system, will be able to communicate through it with another system. The links will therefore be: user to machine 1; machine 1 to machine 2; machine 2 to machine 1; and machine 1 back to user. In other words, the user will not "talk" directly to any system but his/her own.

Although at present no representative of OCLC is involved in the work on the SNI, it is certainly encouraging that the work is in progress. Currently the only ways to share bibliographic data are cumbersome, such as exchanging tapes containing machine-readable records. RLG has for some time been loading archive tapes for member institutions—a time- and resource-consuming process, but the best way currently available of sharing bibliographic data. RLG is committed to the exchange of bibliographic data on a mutually beneficial basis with any recognized entity, and takes no proprietary position regarding institutions' data in the RLIN database. RLG participates enthusiastically in the CLR project, along with WLN and LC, and looks forward to its completion in 1983, as well as to the development of future applications of the model. It offers great potential in the area of joint collection development along with the obvious benefit to shared cataloging projects. Regarding the participation of OCLC, I can only report that at a recent OCLC user group meeting a resolution was passed "to recommend to OCLC management that it investigate a limited area of cooperation on a programmatic basis with RLG designed to be of mutual and cost effective benefit to OCLC and RLG members, beginning with a Latin American cooperative cataloging project."

Work on links between RLG's RLIN system and local systems has also been successful. A terminal link has been developed that allows RLIN terminals to be used to access the local system at Pennsylvania State, and records are presently being transferred into that system. An adaptation of this mechanism is also being considered to link RLIN terminals with the local system at Northwestern, among others. This type of application, while constituting an important first step toward the distributed processing technical environment to which RLG is committed, is considered to be an interim arrangement prior to the implementation of the computer-to-computer link being developed under the grant from the Council on Library Resources.

The conspectus has been a versatile and useful tool for RLG, and would seem also to be appropriate for SALALM's efforts toward the development of a national plan for Latin American collecting. Gathering data on collection strengths and weaknesses via the conspectus is the first step toward determining the eventual distribution of primary collecting responsibilities, although careful analysis of the data must be the intermediate step. In no case has the Collection Management and Development Committee discussed assignment of Primary Collection Responsibilities (PCRs) without looking first at data reported by institutions. RLG is willing and indeed pleased to carry data on Latin American holdings for institutions participating in the SALALM project, but no decisions on the assignment or acceptance of PCRs can be made by RLG institutions except through the usual process of analysis by the Committee. Date reported by non-RLG institutions on their Latin American holdings can be used for informational and comparative purposes, as in the South Asian conspectus, but commitment of resources by RLG institutions must be made by agreement of the Board of Governors and for non-RLG institutions, a commitment may be made independently.

SALALM should proceed with the collection of data using the worksheets developed jointly by RLG central staff and Latin American bibliographers at RLG institutions, bringing together detailed information on the holdings of libraries wishing to participate. It is up to this group to provide the direction for the development of a national plan, and to formulate recommendations based on cooperative spirit and in-depth knowledge of collections. I hope that the result of the conspectus exercise will be a thorough and solid understanding of present collection levels and collecting policies, in anticipation of the day when interutility links are both technically and politically feasible. The efforts of SALALM and the cooperative awareness of RLG and non-RLG institutions in the area of Latin American studies are preparing the ground for a national plan; by proceeding along these lines we will be ready when the compatibility of databases is no longer a problem.

Annual SALALM
Bibliographies

Bibliography of Bibliographies
1982 Supplement

Haydée Piedracueva

CONTENTS

PREFACE

It is a pleasure to submit our *Annual Report on Latin American and Caribbean Bibliographic Activities, 1982*.

The purpose of this compilation is to call attention to recent bibliographies on Latin American topics. Included are bibliographies published as monographs or as articles in periodicals during 1980−81. There are also a few 1982 imprints. For serials publications such as *Anuarios bibliográficos* we have included the latest issue that came to our attention.

The entries are arranged alphabetically under broad subject areas. There is a section on Works in Progress. Author and subject indexes provide added points of access. Bibliographies appended to books or chapters in books, or to periodical articles, have been excluded.

The *Annual Reports* are the basis for the compilation of the *Supplements* to Gropp's *Bibliography of Latin American Bibliographies*. The Third Supplement, covering 1974−1979, is now at the press and will be published in the fall 1982.

This is my fourth year as editor of this paper, and the responsibility of its compilation should now go to other hands. I would like to express my deep thanks to the Chairman of the Committee on Bibliography, Dr. John R. Hébert (Library of Congress) and to the following members of the Committee whose contributions and cooperation have been so important in the past years: Paula A. Covington (Joint University Libraries); Mary Gormly (California State University, Los Angeles); Celia Leyte-Vidal (Duke University); Lionel Lorona (New York Public Library); Sara de Mundo Lo (University of Illinois at Urbana/Champaign); and Barbara G. Valk (University of California, Los Angeles).

Barbara Valk, Editor of the *Hispanic American Periodicals Index* (HAPI), suggested that HAPI indexers should send a copy of the indexing for articles that are bibliographies to this Editor, in order to expand our coverage of journals. Special thanks go to her and to all indexers that volunteered to send bibliographic information for inclusion in this paper.

My thanks also go to all SALALM members who have participated in this work.

National Bibliographies

Anuario bibliográfico colombiano "Rubén Pérez Ortiz." 1979. Compilado por José Romero Rojas. Bogotá: Instituto Caro y Cuervo, 1981.   (1

Anuario bibliográfico ecuatoriano. 1976/77. Quito: Univ. Central del Ecuador, Biblioteca General.

Includes *Bibliografía ecuatoriana*, 7.   (2

Anuario bibliográfico peruano. 1970/1972. Lima: Instituto Nacional de Cultura, Biblioteca Nacional, Centro Bibliográfico Nacional, 1979.   (3

Anuario bibliográfico puertorriqueño. 1978. Rio Piedras: Biblioteca General, Univ. de Puerto Rico, 1978.

Compiled by Gonzalo Velázquez.   (4

Anuario bibliográfico uruguayo. 1978. Montevideo: Biblioteca Nacional, 1979.   (5

Anuario bibliográfico venezolano. 1976. Caracas: Biblioteca Nacional, Centro Bibliográfico Venezolano, 1977.   (6

Bibliografía cubana, 1977. La Habana: Biblioteca Nacional José Martí, 1978.   (7

Bibliografía ecuatoriana. See: *Anuario bibliográfico ecuatoriano.*   (8

Bibliografía hondureña. (Books published in Honduras are listed in *Boletín de la Academia Hondureña de la Lengua*.)   (9

Bibliografía mexicana. No. 6, Nov./Dic. 1980.

México: Biblioteca Nacional de México, Universidad Nacional Autónoma de México, Instituto de Investigaciones Bibliográficas.   (10

Bibliografía nacional paraguaya. 1971/1977. Asunción: Univ. Nacional de Asunción, 1978.   (11

Bibliografía uruguaya. 1977. Montevideo: Biblioteca del Poder Legislativo, 1977. 2 v.   (12

Bio-bibliografía boliviana. 1979, con Suplemento de 1962 a 1978. Índice de materias 1962–1979. La Paz: Cochabamba, Bolivia: Ed. Los Amigos del Libro, 1981. 275 p.

Compiled by Werner Guttentag Tichauer.   (13

The CARICOM Bibliography; a cumulated subject list of current national imprints of the Caribbean Community member countries . . . v. 4, no. 1 and 2, 1980.   (14

Chile. Congreso. Biblioteca. *Boletín bibliográfico.* v. 4, no. 21/23, Jul./Dic. 1979. Santiago de Chile: La Biblioteca.   (15

(Includes a regular section in all issues, listing books published in Chile)

Ecuador; bibliografía analística. Año 2, no. 3, Jul. 1981. Cuenca: Banco Central del Ecuador, Centro de Investigación y Cultura.   (16

Guyanese national bibliography. Jul./Sept. 1981. Georgetown, Guyana: National Library.   (17

The Jamaican national bibliography, 1964–1974. The Institute of Jamaica, Jamaica, West Indies. Millwood, N.Y.: Kraus International Publications, 1981. 439 p.   (18

National bibliography of Barbados. Jul./Sept. 1979. Bridgetown: Public Library of Barbados, 1979.   (19

National bibliography of Haiti.

(Haitian imprints are listed in the journal *Conjonction*)   (20

Oficina de livros; novidades catalogadas na fonte. Jan./Dez. 1980.

São Paulo: Centro de Catalogação-na-Fonte, Câmara Brasileira do Livro.   (21

Peru. Biblioteca Nacional. *Bibliografía nacional; libros, artículos de revistas y periódicos.* No. 5/6, May./Jun. 1981. Lima: Instituto Nacional de Cultura, Biblioteca Nacional, 1981.   (22

Rio de Janeiro. Biblioteca Nacional. *Boletín bibliográfico.* v. 25, no. 3, 3er. trimestre 1980.   (23

Trinidad and Tobago national bibliography. V. 6, no. 2, Apr./Jun. 1980. Port-of-Spain: Central Library of Trinidad and Tobago and the University of the West Indies.   (24

Personal Bibliographies

Collective

Arizmendi Posada, Ignacio. *Gobernantes colombianos, 1819–1980.* Medellín: Editorial Albión, 1980. 263 p.   (25

"Bio-bibliografía de los colaboradores del presente número." *Revista histórica* (Buenos Aires) 2:6 (Ene./Jun. 1980) 219–220.

(Includes bio-bibliographies of Abelardo Levaggi, Alicia Vidaurreta, and Mark D. Szuchman.)   (26

Hogan, James E. "The contemporaries of António Francisco Lisboa; an annotated bibliography." *Latin American research review* 16:3 (1981) 138–145.

"Littératures." *Caravelle* 34 (1980) 177–178.

(Issue devoted to Ecuador, lists the works of eight Ecuadorian authors.)   (27

Mundo Lo, Sara de. *Index to Spanish American collective biography.* Boston: G. K. Hall, 1981–. V. 1: The Andean countries. 466 p. (*Reference publications in Latin American studies*)   (28

Sosa de Newton, Lily. *Diccionario biográfico de mujeres argentinas.* 2. ed. aum. y actualizada. Buenos Aires: Ed. Plus Ultra, 1980. 533 p.   (29

Individual

Exposición bibliográfica y documental Eduardo Acevedo Díaz, 1851–1921. Montevideo: Biblioteca Nacional, 1981. 85 p.   (30

Harmon, Robert Bartilett. *Architectural splendor in the sun—Mexico's Luis Barragan; a selected bibliography.* Monticello, Ill.: Vance Bibliographies, 1980. 13 p. (*Architecture series: bibliography*)   (31

Davies, Thomas M. "Jorge Basadre (1903–1980)." *Hispanic American historical review* 61:1 (Feb. 1981) 84–86.   (32

"Bibliografía bolivariana." *Revista* de la Sociedad Bolivariana de Venezuela, 2a. etapa 37:128 (Dic. 17, 1980) 113–133.   (33

Rivas Dugarte, Rafael Angel. *Simón Bolívar en publicaciones periódicas del exterior; materiales para una hemerografía.* Caracas: Centro de Estudios Latinoamericanos Rómulo Gallegos y Ministerio de la Secretaría de la Presidencia de la República, 1980. 238 p. (*Colección Manuel Landaeta Rosales*, 2)   (34

Bendfeldt Rojas, Lourdes. "César Brañas: por el mundo de su bibliografía." *Cultura de Guatemala* 1:2 (Jul./Dic. 1980) 81–124.   (35

184   HAYDÉE PIEDRACUEVA

Ambrogi, Marlise Vaz Bridi. "Trabalhos publicados (obras, artigos e resenções) acerca
   da matéria Camoniana no período de 1979—1980." *Revista camoniana* 2a. série, 3
   (1980) 243—247.   (36

Morales, Phyllis S. *Fray Angelino Chavez; a bibliography of his published writings,
   1925—1978.* Santa Fe, N.M.: Lightning Tree, 1980. 80 p.   (37

Perdomo de González, Mireya. *Bibliografía de Juan D. García Bacca.* Caracas:
   Universidad Central de Venezuela, Dirección de Publicaciones, 1981. 77 p.   (38

Gietz, Ernesto Gustavo. "Nómina de trabajos de Ernesto Gustavo Gietz, 1899—1981."
   Boletín informativo del Instituto Bibliotecológico (Univ. de Buenos Aires) 63 (Sept.
   1981) 7—13.   (39

Urquiza, Juan José de. "Eduardo Gutiérrez, el olvidado." *Revista Nacional de cultura*
   (Buenos Aires) 6 (1980) 27—42.   (40

Núñez, Dulce María. "Bibliografía de y sobre Dom Hector Inchaustegui Cabral."
   Eme-eme; estudios dominicanos 9:50 (Sept./Oct. 1980) 117—124.   (41

"Itinerario científico del Profesor Alejandro Lipschutz." *Araucaria de Chile* 10 (1980)
   8—11.   (42

Berger, Víctor. "Libros en preparación sobre José Carlos Mariátegui." *Hispania* 64: 1
   (March 1981) 134.   (43

Rovirosa, Dolores F. *Bibliografía Martiana del exilio, 1981.* Paper submitted to the
   XXVII Seminar on the Acquisition of Latin American Library Materials, Washington, D.C., March 2—5, 1982. 16 p.   (44

"Nicolás Matijevic (1910—1980)." *Revista interamericana de bibliografía. Inter-
   American review of bibliography* 31:1 (1981) 105—109.   (45

Rovirosa, Dolores F. *Ana Rosa Núñez; vida y obra.* 2. ed. Miami: Ed. Universal, 1981.
   34 leaves.   (46

"Bibliografía de Eunice Odio, 1945—1978." *Revista interamericana de bibliografía.
   Inter-American review of bibliography* 31:2 (1981) 207—214.   (47

Román Lagunas, Jorge. "Obras de Pedro de Oña y bibliografía sobre él." *Revista
   interamericana de bibliografía. Inter-American review of bibliography* 31:3 (1981)
   345—365.   (48

"Angel Palerm Vich, 1917—1980." *American anthropologist* 83:3 (Sept. 1981)
   612—615.   (49

"Bibliografía del Papa Paulo VI; biografía, cronología, bibliografía." *Efímeros* 4:8
   (Ene./Dic. 1979) 63—78.   (50

Chacón Tapia, Claudio. *Contribución a una bibliografía de Arturo Prat Chacón y el
   combate naval de Iquique.* Santiago de Chile: 1980. 76 leaves.   (51

Infante, Víctor Manuel. "Bibliografía e iconografía de Luis José de Tejeda (1604—
   1680)." *Revista nacional de cultura* (Buenos Aires) 2:7 (1980) 39—64.   (52

"Unikel, Luis (1932—1981)." *Diálogos* (Mexico) 17:2, no. 98 (Mar./Abr. 1981)
   p. 46.   (53

Virreira Sánchez, Efraín. *Bibliografía del Doctor Arturo Urquidi Morales, maestro de
   la juventud boliviana.* Cochabamba, Bolivia: Univ. Mayor de San Simón, Biblioteca
   Central Universitaria, 1980. 239 p.   (54

"Eva Verbitsky Hunt, 1934—1980." *American anthropologist* 83:4 (Dec. 1981)
   892—894.   (55

Exposición bibliográfica y documental Alberto Zum Felde, en el cincuentenario de la

publicación del Proceso intelectual del Uruguay, y crítica de su literatura. Montevideo: 1980. 71 p.   (56

Indexes

Academia de Ciencias de Cuba. *Revista de información científica y técnica cubana.* Año
12 no. 1, Abril 1981. La Habana: Academia de Documentación e Información
Científica y Técnica.
(Indexes Cuban journals in the sciences and technology)   (57
Actualidad bibliográfica iberoamericana (ABI). Año 3, no. 6, 1980. Madrid: Instituto
de Cooperación Iberoamericana.   (58
América indígena; 40 años. Indice general. México: Instituto Indigenista Interamericano, 1980. 3 volumes.   (59
Apuntes; revista de ciencias sociales. Indices de los números 1–10. Lima: Centro de
Investigación Universitaria del Pacífico, 1981.   (60
Auza, Néstor Tomás. *Correo del domingo (1864–1868)(1879–1880); estudio e índice
general.* Buenos Aires: Instituto Histórico de la Organización Nacional, 1980.
pp. 133–203.
(Separata de la Rev. Histórica, no. 5)   (61
Billick, David J. "Index to *Hispania*, volume 64, 1981." *Hispania* 64:4 (Dec. 1981)
740–750.   (62
"Boletín del Instituto Francés de Estudios Andinos." *Bulletin de l'Institut Français
d'Etudes Andines* 9: 1/2 (1980) 155–158.   (63
(The index covers Tomo 2–8)
"Contenido y autores de la Revista Estudios Sociales." *Estudios Sociales* (Chile) 24
(2o. trimestre 1980) 177–181.   (64
*Chicano periodicals index; a cumulative index to selected Chicano periodicals between
1968 and 1978.* Compiled by the Committee for the Development of Subject Access
to Chicano Literature, with an introductory essay by Felix Gutierrez. Boston: G. K.
Hall, 1981.   (65
Columbus Memorial Library. *Index to Latin American periodical literature, 1966–
1970.* Boston, Mass.: Columbus Memorial Library, OAS, 1980. 2 v.   (66
Cuadernos Políticos; revista trimestral de Ediciones Era. Indice de los números 1
(julio–septiembre de 1974) a 28 (abril–junio de 1981). México: Ed. Era, 1981. 16 p.
(Insert, Cuadernos políticos no. 28)   (67
"Diálogos; artes/letras/ciencias humanas; índice del volumen 16, enero–febrero 1980/
nov.–dic. 1981." *Diálogos* 16: 5/6, nos. 96/96 (Sept./Dic. 1980).   (68
HAPI; Hispanic American Periodicals Index. 1978. Editor: Barbara G. Valk. Los
Angeles: UCLA Latin American Center Publications, University of California, Los
Angeles, 1981. 749 p.   (69
"Indice de la Revista Areito, año 1980, vol. VI, nos. 21, 22, 23, 24." *Areito* 7:25
(1981) 58–59.   (70
"Indice general de Cuadernos dominicanos de cultura, 1943–1952." *Eme Eme;
estudios dominicanos* 9:49 (Jul./Ag. 1980) 79–103.   (71
"Indice general del año VI, números del 61 al 72 (julio de 1980) junio 1981–."
Cuadernos de comunicación 7:72 (Jun./Jul. 1981) 58–61.   (72

"Indice temático: INRA 1960–1963, Cuba (Internacional) 1963–1979." *Cuba internacional* 122 (Ene. 1980) pp. i–xxviii.   (73
(The index has also title: *20 años en Cuba*)
"Indice temático general de la revista del CERLAL (1972–1980). *Revista Noticias sobre el libro y bibliografía* 28 (Dic. 1980) 29–33.   (73a
"Mundo universitario; revista de la Asociación Colombiana de Universidades." *Mundo universitario* 17 (Abril/Junio 1981) 294–300.
(Covers nos. 1–16, Oct./Dic. 1972–Ene./Mar. 1981)   (74
"Nueva antropología; revista de ciencias sociales." *Nueva antropología* 3:12 (Dic. 1979) 153–158.   (75
"Revista de revistas." *Ciencias administrativas* 21: 58/60 (Ene./Dic. 1979) 85–132.   (76
Simbaqueba Reina, Luis. "Indice de materias y de nombres propios, Tomo XXXV, 1980." *Thesaurus* (Bogotá) 35:3 (Sept./Dic. 1980) 633–649.   (77
Valk, Barbara G. "SALALM Newsletter Index, Volume VIII." SALALM *Newsletter* 9:1 (Sept. 1981) 23–27.   (78
Zuleta, Ignacio M. "El nuevo Mercurio." *Revista interamericana de bibliografía. Inter-American review of bibliography* 31:3 (1981) 385–403.   (79

General Bibliographies

Latin America

Bibliographic guide to Latin American studies, 1980. Boston: G. K. Hall, 1981. 3 v.   (80
Boletín bibliográfico CERLAL 8:1 (March 1981). Bogotá: UNESCO, Centro Regional para el Fomento del Libro en América Latina y el Caribe.   (81
British bulletin of publications on Latin America, the Caribbean, Portugal and Spain. No. 65, Oct. 1981 (Annotated). London: Canning House, Hispanic and Luso-Brazilian Council.   (82
Butler, Erwin. "Spanish American books." *Booklist* 77:16 (Apr. 15, 1981) 1144–1146.
(Annotated)   (83
Butler, Erwin. "Spanish reference books." *Booklist* 77: 22/23 (Jul. 15/Aug. 1981) 1438–1441.
(Includes Latin America; annotated)   (84
CBA; Comentarios bibliográficos americanos. V. 14, no. 2 (Abr./Jun. 1982). Montevideo: CBA.   (85
Fichero bibliográfico hispanoamericano. V. 19, no. 1/2, Ene./Feb. 1980. Buenos Aires: Ediciones Turner.   (86
Hartness-Kane, Ann, and Richard D. Woods. *Latin America in English language reference books; a selected, annotated bibliography.* New York: Special Libraries Association, 1981. 49 p.   (87
Hartness-Kane, Ann. "Latin American reference materials for the college library." *Choice* 18:10 (June 1981) 1375–1388.   (88

Handbook of Latin American studies. V. 42: Humanities. Editor: Dolores Moyano Martin. Austin: Univ. of Texas Press, 1982. 911 p.   (89

Hébert, John R. "Bibliography and general works." *Handbook of Latin American studies 42, Humanities,* pp. 3–36.   89a

Hispanic Information Management Project. *Guide to Hispanic bibliographic services in the United States.* By the staff of the Hispanic Information Management Project and the National Chicano Research Network. Ann Arbor, Mich.: Survey Research Center, Univ. of Michigan, 1980.   (90

Institut fur Iberoamerika-Kunde. Dokumentations Leitstelle Lateinamerika. *Dokumentationsdienst Lateinamerika. Documentación latinoamericana. Ausgewahlte neuere literatur. Boletín bibliográfico.* 1981, no. 2. 11. Jahrgang 1981, nr. 2. Hamburg.   (91

"Investigaciones en curso y terminadas." *Revista interamericana de bibliografía* 31:1 (1981) 110–120.   (92

"Latin America 1981." *Current history,* Feb. 1981. (Whole issue is devoted to articles on Latin America)   (93

"Latin America, 1982." *Current history* 81: 472 (Feb. 1982). (Whole issue devoted to Latin America)   (94

Latin American studies in the Universities of the United Kingdom. No. 14, 1981. 47 p. London: Univ. of London, Institute of Latin American Studies.   (95

Matos, Antonio. *Guía a las reseñas de libros de y sobre Hispanoamérica. A guide to reviews of books from and about Hispanic America, 1978.* Detroit: Blaine Ethridge-Books, 1980. 1999 p.   (96

————. *Guía a las reseñas de libros de y sobre Hispanoamérica. A guide to reviews of books from and about Hispanic America, 1979.* Detroit: Blaine Ethridge-Books, 1981. 1688 p.   (97

Piedracueva, Haydée. *Annual report on Latin American and Caribbean bibliographic activities,* 1981. Submitted for the Twenty-Sixth Seminar on the Acquisition of Latin American Library Materials, Tulane University, April 1–4, 1981. 46 p.   (98

"Publicaciones recientes." *Chasqui.* (Regular section of this journal, lists recent titles on Latin America)   (99

"Publications of the Congress of the United States about Latin America." *Revista interamericana de bibliografía* 31:1 (1981) 194–196.   (100

"Publications of the OAS and its specialized organizations." *Revista interamericana de bibliografía* 31:1 (1981) 130.   (101

"Recent articles." *Revista interamericana de bibliografía* 31:1 (1981) 132–185. (Lists recent articles on Latin America)   (102

"Recent books." *Revista interamericana de bibliografía* 31:1 (1981) 121–129. (Regular feature, lists recent books published in Latin America or about Latin America)   (103

"Recent doctoral dissertations (on Latin America)." *Revista interamericana de bibliografía* 31:1 (1981) 186–193. (Regular feature)   (104

"La recherche latino-américaniste en France (1976–1978)." *Cahiers du monde Hispanique et Luso-Brésilien (Caravelle),* numéro especial, 1980. (Lists 112 theses on Latin American themes)   (105

"Registro de los estudios belgas y neerlandeses sobre América Latina." *Boletín de estudios latinoamericanos y del Caribe* 28 (June 1980) 113–118, and no. 29 (Dec. 1980) 105–106. (Regular section that appears in all issues)   (106

Sternberg, Rolf. "Selected geography texts on Latin America." *Latin American research review* 16:3 (1981) 272–275.   (107

Staff research in progress or recently completed in the humanities and the social sciences. No. 12, 1981. London: University of London, Institute of Latin American Studies.   (108

Individual Countries or Areas

Bibliografia de publicações oficiais brasileiras; Area Federal, 1975/1977. Brasília: Câmara de Deputados, Diretoria Legislativa, Centro de Documentação e Informação, Coordenação de Publicações, v. 1 (1975/77) –. 1981–.   (109

"Bibliography. Bibliografía." *Cuban studies/Estudios cubanos* 11:1 (Jan. 1981) 107–138. (This section appears in all issues of the journal and lists books and articles on Cuba)   (110

"Buenos Aires en sus libros." *Revista nacional de cultura* 6 (1980) 49–127.   (111

Butler, Erwin. "Dominican books." *Booklist* 78:6 (Nov. 15, 1981) 431–432.   (112

Butler, Erwin. "Mexican books." *Booklist* 77:18 (May 15, 1981) 1245–1246. (113

Caribbean Community Secretariat. Information and Documentation Section. *CCS Current awareness service . . . New additions.* No. 1–2. Jan.–Feb. 1980–. Georgetown, Guyana. (Books and articles on the Caribbean)   (114

"Caribbean studies in the Netherlands." *Boletín de estudios latinoamericanos y del Caribe* 29 (Dec. 1980) 99–103. (Regular section in all numbers of the journal) (115

Central America; a bibliography. 2. ed. Los Angeles: Latin American Studies Center, California State Univ., 1980. 112 p. (*Latin America bibliography series*, 2) (116

Central American accessions at the University of Kansas Libraries. No. 1, Nov. 1981– Lawrence, Kansas: Dept. for Spain, Portugal, and Latin America, Univ. of Kansas Libraries.   (117

Chavaria, Elvira. *Mexican American studies.* Austin: University of Texas, General Libraries, 1981. 15 p. (*Selected reference sources*, 17)   (118

Couyoumdjian, Juan Ricardo. "Fichero bibliográfico 1978." *Historia* (Santiago de Chile) 15 (1980) 365–418. (On Chile)   (119

Curação Public Library. Caribbean Collection. *Quarterly acquisitions list.* No. 4, Oct./Dec. 1981. Curação, The Library.   (120

"Documentación paraguaya." *Revista paraguaya de sociología* 18:50 (Ene./May. 1981) 181–195.   (121

Gladden, Earle M. "Haitian books." *Booklist* 77:10 (Jan. 15, 1981) 681–682. (122

Goslinga, Marian. "Recent books; an informative listing of books about the Caribbean, Latin America, and their emigrant groups." *Caribbean review* 9:4 (Fall 1980) 56–59. (This section appears in all issues of the journal)   (123

Instituto de Integración Cultural. *Catálogo bibliográfico de Antioquia.* v. 1– 1977–. Medellín, Colombia: El Instituto. (Annual publication, v. 3, 1980)   (124

Kuczynski, Pedro Pablo. "Recent studies of Peru." *Latin American research review* 16:1 (1981) 225–228.   (125

"Libros." *Revista de ciencias sociales* (Univ. de Costa Rica) 15/16 (Mar./Oct. 1978) 241–257. (Regular section, lists books on Costa Rica)   (126

Lidmilová, Pavla. "Bibliografía selecta." *Philologica Pragensia* 23:1 (1980) 13–20.   (127

Mead, Robert G. "Libros, artículos y revistas recientes en inglés sobre México." *Hispania* 64:1 (March 1981) 132–134.   (128

Merubia, Sonia. *Argentina.* Austin: University of Texas at Austin, General Libraries, 1981. 36 p. (*Selected reference sources*, 64)   (129

"Recent publications on Mexico." *The Mexican forum* 1:3 (Jul. 1981) 14–15.   (130

Research Institute for the Study of Man. *Accession list.* No. 20 (May./Oct. 1981). (20 p.) New York: The Institute.   (131

Schiltkamp, J. A., and J. Th. de Schmidt S. *West Indisch Plakaat boek.* 3–. Nederlandse Antillen: Bovenwinden Publikaties en Andere Wetten Betreaking Hebbende op St. Maarten, St. Eustatius, Saba 1648/1681–1861. Emmering (Amsterdam) 1980.   (132

Schon, Isabel. "Recent notorious and noteworthy books about Mexico, Mexicans and Mexican-Americans." *Journal of reading* 24:4 (Jan. 1981).   (133

Silva, Sonia T. Dias Gonçalves da. *Brasil; modernização e mudança.* Austin: Benson Latin American Collection, The General Libraries, Univ. of Texas at Austin, 1982. 2 p. (*Biblio Noticias*, 12)   (134

Silva, Sonia T. Dias Gonçalves da. *Brasil 70.* Austin: Benson Latin American Collection, The General Libraries, Univ. of Texas at Austin, 1981. 2 p. (*Biblio Noticias*, 11)   (135

U.S. Library of Congress. *Accessions list: Brazil.* V. 7, no. 5/6, May/Jun. 1981. Rio de Janeiro: Library of Congress Office.   (136

Vinci, Liliana F. *Contribución para una bibliografía sobre Córdoba.* V. 2. Córdoba: Univ. Nacional de Córdoba, Biblioteca Mayor, 1981.   (137

Woodward, Ralph Lee. *Belize.* Santa Barbara: American Bibliographical Center, Clio Press, 1980. xxi, 229 p. (*World bibliographical series*, 21)   (138

Subject Bibliographies

Agriculture

Boletín bibliográfico forestal chileno. No. 1, 1979–. Santiago de Chile: Corporación Nacional Forestal, 1980–.   (139

Catálogo colectivo regional de publicaciones periódicas em ciencias agrícolas e naturais de Minas Gerais. V. 1, no. 1–. 1980–. Belo Horizonte: Divisão de Informações Bibliográficas, Biblioteca Central de Univ. Federal de Minas Gerais.   (140

Commonwealth Agricultural Bureau, Slough. *Latin America; agricultural situation and development: Central America.* Slough: The Bureau, 1979. 28, iii p. (Its *Annotated bibliography*, no. RE 7)   (141

Instituto Interamericano de Ciencias Agrícolas. Centro Interamericano de Documentación e Información. *Documentos producidos por el Fondo Simón Bolívar.* San José, Costa Rica, 1980. 21 p. (*Documentación e informacion agrícola*, 84)   (142

Dyal, Donald H., and David L. Chapman. "Periodical literature of Hispanic American agricultural history: a bibliographical research problem." *Revista interamericana de bibliografía* 31:2 (1981) 215–226.   (143

Elso G., Sonia, and Verónica M. Bravo. *Bibliografía agrícola chilena.* v. 3: 1960–

1978. Santiago de Chile: Instituto de Investigaciones Agropecuarias, 1980. 258 p.   (144

"Informaciones periódicas sobre el henequén." *Yucatán; historia y economía* 5:25 (May./Jun. 1981) 64−70.   (145

Matos Mar, José M. *Bibliografía agraria peruana, 1957−1977*. Lima: Instituto de Estudios Peruanos, 1980−.   (146

Rodríguez Chaurnet, Dinah. "Estructura agraria y desarrollo agrícola." *Problemas del desarrollo* 9:44 (Nov. 1980/Ene. 1981).   (147

Vieira, Dirceu Justiniano. *Bibliografia sinalética sobre a cultura do algodão arbóreo* . . . Brasília: Empresa Brasileira de Pesquisa Agropecuária, 1980. 54 p. (Joint author: Elisabeth de Oliveira Serrano).   (148

Anthropology, Archaeology, Ethnology

Barrera Vázquez, Alfredo. "Four centuries of archaeology in Yucatan: a bibliographical essay." In: *Yucatan: a world apart*, edited by Edward H. Moseley and Edward D. Terry. 1980. 335 p.   (149

Mexico. Instituto Nacional de Antropología e Historia. *Informe 1979: 5 años de vida: evaluación 1975−1979. Proyectos especiales de investigación*. Mexico: INAH, 1980. 62 p.   (150

Oporto, Luis. Catálogo: *Materiales del Instituto Lingüístico de Verano sobre grupos étnicos de Bolivia, 1955−1980*. (Microfichas existentes en el C. D. A.). La Paz, Bolivia: Instituto Lingüístieo de Verano, Instituto Nacional de Antropología, Centro de Documentación Antropológica, 1981. 47 p. (*Serie Bibliografía antropológica*, 1)   (151

Valle Prieto, Ma. Eugenia. "Guía de antropólogos." *Nueva antropología* 4: 15/16 (Dic. 1980) 287−290.   (152

Economics and Business

Axline, W. Andrew. "Latin American regional integration: alternative perspectives on a changing reality." *Latin American research review* 16:1 (1981) 167−186. (Six books on the subject are reviewed)   (153

Baklanoff, Eric N. "Latin American economic history: economic vs. cultural interpretations." *Latin American research review* 16:3 (1981) 245−249. (Review essay)   (154

Bergquist, Charles. "What is being done? Some recent studies in the urban working class and organized labor in Latin America." *Latin American research review* 16:2 (1981) 203−223.   (155

"Bibliografía seleccionada sobre el nuevo orden económico internacional." *Revista de economía latinoamericana* 59 (Ene./Mar. 1980) 291−317.   (156

Brem, Walter. "Mexican oil: a guide to source materials." In: Ladman, Jerry; Deborah Baldwin, and Elihu Bergman, editors. *United States-Mexican energy relationship: realities and prospects*. Lexington: Lexington Books, 1981.   (157

Durand, Francisco. "La industria en el Perú: bibliografía." *Estudios andinos* 9:17/18 (1981) 195−246.   (158

Fitzgerald, E. V. K. "Recent writings on the Mexican economy." *Latin American research review* 16:3 (1981) 236—244.   (159

Hartness-Kane, Ann. *Business and industry in Latin America: directories.* Austin: Benson Latin American Collection, The General Libraries, University of Texas at Austin, 1981. 2 p. (*Biblio noticias*, 10)   (160

Hartness-Kane, Ann. *Latin America: economics and business.* (Updated ed.) Austin: University of Texas at Austin, The General Libraries, 1981. 28 p. (*Selected reference sources*, 23)   (161

Howe, Robert. *Foreign investments in Latin America: information sources in government publications. Supplement No. 1: February 1982.* 5 leaves. (Paper initially submitted for the Twenty-Sixth Seminar on the Acquisition of Latin American Library Materials, Tulane Univ., April 1—4, 1981).   (162

Lifschitz, Edgardo. *Bibliografía analítica sobre empresas transnacionales. Analytical bibliography on transnational corporations.* Mexico: Instituto Latinoamericano de Estudios Transnacionales, 1980. 608 p.   (163

Mexico. Secretaría de Programación y Presupuesto. *Catálogo de publicaciones oficiales (diciembre 1976—junio 1979).* Mexico: Secretaría de Programación y Presupuesto, Dirección General de Documentación y Análisis, 1980. 294 p.   (164

Pinzas García, Teobaldo. *La economía peruana, 1950—1978; ensayo bibliográfico.* Lima: Instituto de Estudios Peruanos, 1981. 156 p. (*Análisis económico*, 4)   (165

Ramírez, María Teresa. *Fuentes de información sobre energías no convencionales.* Bogotá: Fundación Mariano Ospina Pérez, Servicio de Documentación e Información, 1980. 77 p.   (166

Saint, William S. "The wages of modernization: a review of the literature on temporary labor arrangements in Brazilian agriculture." *Latin American research review* 16:3 (1981) 91—110.   (167

Schaffer, Ellen. *The Central American Common Market: a selected bibliography, 1975 to the present.* Washington: Organization of American States, 1982.   (168

Education

Cariola, Patricio. "Bibliografía anotada de experiencias participativas en el campo de la educación formal y no formal." *Socialismo y participación* 14 (Jun. 1981) 145—158.   (169

Dale, Doris Cruger. "Spanish-English bilingual books for children." *Booklist* 78: 1 (Sept. 1981) 53—55.   (170

"Enseñanza abierta: hemerografía." *Revista mexicana de ciencias políticas y sociales.* Año 26, nueva época, no. 101 (Jul./Sept. 1980) 139—195.   (171

Erziehung und Entwicklung in Lateinamerika: Auswahl bibliographie. Educación y desarrollo en América Latina: bibliografía selecta. Hamburg: 1980. xxiii, 225 p.   (172

Figueroa, Almaluces. *Bibliografía selectiva sobre tecnología educativa.* Rio Piedras, Puerto Rico: Escuela Graduada de Bibliotecología, Univ. de Puerto Rico, 1980. 15 leaves. (*Egebiana*, 1)   (173

Grossi, María Clara, and Ernesto Schiefelbein. *Bibliografía de la educación chilena,*

1973–1980. Santiago de Chile: Corporación de Promoción Universitaria, 1980.
335 p. *(Serie Documentos de trabajo)* (174

Lauerhass, Ludwig, and Vera Lúcia Oliveira de Haugse. *Education in Latin America: a bibliography.* Boston: G. K. Hall, University of California, Los Angeles, 1980. viii, 43 p. *(Reference series,* 9) (175

McKinnon, Linda T. (et al.). *Mexican American education fact sheets and mini reviews.* Las Cruces, N.M.: ERIC Clearinghouse on Rural Education and Small Schools, 1980. 18 p. (176

Oberg, Larry R. *Contemporary Cuban education: an annotated bibliography.* Stanford: Stanford Univ. Libraries, 1980. 40 p. (177

Silveira, Inalda. "Bibliografia sobre ensino rural." *Ciência & trópico* 7:2 (Jul./Aug. 1979) 335–340. (178

"Spanish language books for young adults and children." *Booklist* 78:1 (Sept. 1, 1981) 38–40, and 78:3 (Oct. 1, 1981) 190–191. (179

Valverde, Leonard A., (et al.). *Educating English-speaking Hispanics.* Washington, D.C.: National Association for Bilingual Education, 1980. 98 p. (180

History

Bendfeldt Rojas, Lourdes. "El Popol-Vuh: por el mundo de su bibliografía." *Cultura de Guatemala* 1:3 (Nov./Dic. 1980) 45–128. (181

Berger, Paulo. *Bibliografia do Rio de Janeiro de viajantes e autores estrangeiros, 1551–1900.* 2. enl. and rev. Rio de Janeiro: SEEC, 1980. 478 p. (182

Bibliografía histórica mexicana. V. xi, 1979. Mexico: El Colegio de México, Centro de Estudios Históricos, 1981. 289 p. Compilado por Luis Muro. (183

Bonilla, Heraclio. "The new profile of Peruvian history." *Latin American research review* 16:3 (1981) 210–224. (Bibliographic essay) (184

"Book reviews." *Hispanic American historical review.* (This section appears in all issues and contains reviews of books in Latin American history) (185

Centro de Estudios Puertorriqueños, New York. *Index to articles in the New York Times relating to Puerto Rico and Puerto Ricans between 1899 and 1930.* New York: Centro de Estudios Puertorriqueños, 1981. 94 p. (186

Cervo, Amado Luis. "Fontes parlamentares brasileiras e os estudos históricos." *Latin American research review* 16:2 (1981) 172–181. (187

Collier, Simon. "Allende's Chile: contemporary history and the counterfactual." *Journal of Latin American studies* 12:2 (Nov. 1980) 445–452. (Review of 12 books on the subject) (188

Di Genio de Carlomagno, Ana M. *Bibliografía municipal del Depto. de Montevideo.* Montevideo: Junta de Vecinos de Montevideo, Biblioteca José Artigas, 1980. 68 leaves. (189

Guia preliminar de fuentes para a história do Brasil: instituções governamentais no Município do Rio de Janeiro. Rio de Janeiro: Fundação Casa de Rui Barbosa, Fundação Getúlio Vargas, 1979. (190

Gutiérrez Solana, Nelly. *Corpus bibliográfico de la cultura olmeca.* Mexico: Universidad Nacional Autónoma de México, 1980. 135 p. (191

Hanke, Lewis, and Gunnar Mendoza. *Guía de las fuentes en Hispanoamérica para el estudio de la administración virreinal española en México y en el Perú, 1535–1700.*

Washington, D.C.: Dept. of Publications and Cultural Affairs, OAS, 1980. xi
523 p.   (192

Jáuregui C., Juan Heriberto. *Documentación existente en el Archivo Nacional de
Bolivia sobre rebeliones indígenas, 1780–1783.* La Paz, Bolivia: Centro de Investigaciones Históricas, 1980. 39 p. (*Serie Indices y catálogos*, 2).   (193

Lastaunau Rubio, Gabriel. *Fuentes para el estudio del Perú; bibliografía de biblio-
grafías.* Lima, 1980.   (194

Merubia, Sonia. *Argentine history.* Austin: Benson Latin American Collection,
The General Libraries, University of Texas at Austin, 1981. 2 p. (*Biblio
noticias*, 8).   (195

"Mexico." *Current history* 80:469 (Nov. 1981)
(Whole issue devoted to Mexico's current developments and events)   (196

Silvestrini Pacheco, Blanca, and María de los Angeles Castro Arroyo. "Sources for the
study of Puerto Rican history; a challenge to the historian's imagination." *Latin
American research review* 16:2 (1981) 156–171.   (197

Tutorow, Norman E. *The Mexican-American war; an annotated bibliography.* West-
port, Conn.: Greenwood Press, 1981.   (198

Valadés, José C. "Bibliografía: noticia para la bibliografía anarquista de México."
Historia obrera 5:20 (Segunda época) (Sept. 1980) 20–26.   (199
(Originally published in *La Protesta*, Buenos Aires)

Villegas, Carmen. *Bibliografía sobre colonización en América Latina.* Turrialba, Costa
Rica: CIDIA, 1980. 122 p. (*Documentación e información agrícola*, 80).   (200

Werlich, David P. *Research tools for Latin American historians; a selected, annotated
bibliography.* New York: Garland Pub., 1980. xvii, 269 p. (*Garland reference library
of social science*, 60).   (201

Humanities

Arellano, Jorge Eduardo. "Bibliografía de la pintura y la escultura en Nicaragua."
Boletín nicaragüense de bibliografía y documentación 39 (Ene./Feb. 1981) 82–
87.   (202

Chavaria, Elvira. *Chicano film favorites; old and new.* Austin: Benson Latin American
Collection, The General Libraries, University of Texas at Austin, 1981. 2 p. (*Biblio
noticias*, 12).   (203

Guyana. National Library. *Caribbean art and craft; a select list on Caribbean art and
craft, with emphasis on Guayana.* Georgetown: The Library, 1981, 39 p.   (204

Lozano, Eduardo. "Indian art of South America." *Latin American Indian literature* 4:1
(Spr. 1980) 52–63.   (205

Lozano, Eduardo. "Indian art of the Andean region." *Latin American Indian
literatures* 4:2 (Fall 1980).   (206

Millones, Luis. "Las religiones nativas del Perú: recuento y evaluación de su estudio."
Bulletin de l'Institut Français d'Etudes Andines 8:1 (1979) 35–48.   (207

Palen, Roberta R. "Weaving and traditional costume in Guatemala: a selective bibliography." *Revista interamericana de bibliografía* 31:1 (1981) 17–26.   (208

Reich, Peter L. "Algunos archivos para el estudio de la historia eclesiástica mexicana
en el siglo XX." *Historia mexicana* 30:1, número 117 (Jul./Sept. 1980) 126–133.
                                                                                             (209

194   HAYDÉE PIEDRACUEVA

Language and Literature

Allis, Jeannette B. *West Indian literature: an index to criticism, 1930–1975.* Boston:
G. K. Hall, 1981. xxxvii, 353 p.   (210

Carpenter, Charles A. "Modern drama studies: an annual bibliography." *Modern
drama* 24:2 (1981) 146–233.   (211
(Section on Hispanic drama: pp. 178–186)

Chamberlain, Bobby J. "A consumer guide to developing a Brazilian-literature reference library." *Hispania* 64:2 (May 1981) 260–264.   (212

Cobo Borda, J. G. "La nueva poesía colombiana: una década, 1970–1980." *Boletín
cultural y bibliográfico* 16: 9/10 (1979) 75–80.   (213

Coll, Edna. *Indice informativo de la novela hispanoamericana.* V. 4. Río Piedras: Ed.
Universitaria de Puerto Rico, 1980. V. 1: Antillas.–v. 2: Centroamérica.–v. 3:
Venezuela.–4: Colombia.   (214

Corvalán, Graciela N. V. *Latin American women writers in English translation: a
bibliography.* Los Angeles: Latin American Studies Center, California State University, 1980. 109 p. (*Latin American bibliography series*, 9).   (215

Ferrer Andrade, Guadalupe, and Ernestina C. Zenzes E. "Literatura y comunicación
(hemerografía)." *Revista mexicana de ciencias políticas y sociales*, nueva época,
26:100 (Abr./Jun. 1980) 157–172.   (216

Foster, David William. *Mexican literature; a bibliography of secondary sources.*
Metuchen, N.J.: Scarecrow Press, 1981. 412 p.   (217

"Literatura infanto-juvenil." *Oficina de livros* (Jan./Dez. 1980) 315–324.   (218

Lorini, Irma. *Catálogo de folletería minera del repositorio nacional.* La Paz, Bolivia:
Instituto Boliviano de Cultura, 1979.   (219

Masiello, Francine R. "Contemporary Argentine fiction: liberal (pre-) texts in a reign of
terror." *Latin American research review* 16:1 (1981) 218–224.   (220

Montes Huidobro, Matías. "Nueva generación." *Chasqui* 9:1 (Nov. 1979) 39–
74.   (221

Pluto, Joseph A. "Contribución a una bibliografía anotada de los estudios sobre el
español de Colombia, 1965–1975." *Thesaurus* 35:2 (May./Ag. 1980) 288–
358.   (222

Publicaciones del Instituto Caro y Cuervo; catálogo. Suplemento 1981. Bogotá: Instituto Caro y Cuervo, 1981. 7 p.   (223

Rivera de Alvarez, Josefina. "Genesis y desarrollo de la dramaturgia puertorriqueña
hasta los umbrales de la generación del treinta." *Revista del Instituto de Cultura
Puertorriqueña* 20:76/77 (Jul./Dic. 1977) 19–30.   (224

Rivero, Eliana. "Literatura chicana; introducción y contexto." *Areito* 7:25 (1981)
38–40.   (225

Rodríguez Rea, Miguel Angel. "Poesía peruana del siglo XX." II: 1921–1930. *Hueso
húmero* 8 (1981) 132–149.   (226

Rodríguez Rea, Miguel Angel. "Poesía peruana del siglo XX." III: 1931–1935.
Hueso húmero 9 (Abr./Jun. 1981) 148–158.   (227

Román Lagunas, Jorge. "La literatura hispanoamericana en Cahiers du monde hispanique et luso-brésilien (Caravelle), 1963–1979." *Cahiers du monde hispanique et
luso-brésilien* 35 (1980) 59–88.   (228

Valis, Noel. "Directory of publication sources in the fields of Hispanic language and literature." *Hispania* 64:2 (May 1981) 226–257.
(Includes a list of periodicals)   (229
Velasco, Ana María. *Literatura chicana en el exilio; índice general 1977/78/79/80.* Los Angeles, Calif.: Ed. de la Frontera, 1981.   (230
Wood, Richard E. "Current sociolinguistics in Latin America." *Latin American research review* 16:1 (1981) 240–251.   (231

Law

Albarrán V., Héctor. "Indice analítico y cronológico de los trabajos doctrinales y jurisprudenciales publicados en la Revista y Anuario de la Facultad de Derecho (1955–1979)." *Anuario*, Facultad de Derecho, Univ. de los Andes (Venezuela) 10 (1979) 561–583.   (232
Bibliografía sobre derecho de menores, legislación relativa a familia y a menores; codificación en material de menores y familia . . . Montevideo: Instituto Interamericano del Niño, 1980. 95 p.   (233
Bosque Paz, Gisela. *Libros—homenaje; índice analítico.* Caracas: Univ. Central de Venezuela, Facultad de Ciencias Jurídicas y Políticas, 1981. 25 p.   (234
Centro de Estudios Puertorriqueños, New York. *Preliminary guide to resolutions relating to Puerto Rico presented before the Annual Conventions of the American Federation of Labor, and articles, editorials and labor reports on Puerto Rico in the American Federationist, 1902–1930.* New York: Research Foundation of the City Univ. of New York, 1981. 20 p.   (235
Díaz Cueva, Miguel. "Bibliografía ecuatoriana sobre derecho societario." *Memoria de la Superintendencia de Compañías del Ecuador, 1964–1979.* (1979) 321–327.   (236
Olmo, Rosa del. "Indice bibliográfico de criminología latinoamericana." *Anuario del Instituto de Ciencias Penales y Criminológicas* (Caracas) (1976/77) 125–189.   (237
Pisani, María Auxiliadora. *Indice de legislación vigente (hasta 31-12-79).* Tomo V. Caracas: Inst. de Derecho Privado, Facultad de Ciencias Jurídicas y Políticas, Univ. Central de Venezuela, 1980. 238 p. (Vol. IV appeared in 1971)   (238
"Revistas reseñadas." *Boletín* del Instituto de Derecho Privado, Univ. Central de Venezuela 23/24 (Jun. 1980) 7–83.   (239
Villasmil de Losada, Helen. "Sección de bibliografía." *Boletín* del Inst. de Derecho Privado, Univ. Central de Venezuela 23/24 (Jun. 1980) 85–93.   (240

Libraries and Archives

Alanís Boyso, José Luis. "Los archivos históricos municipales de los Reyes La Paz, Chicoloapan, Chimalhuacán, Ixtapaluca, Atenco, Tezoyuca, Acolman, Nopaltepec, Axapusco, Temascalapa, Apaxco, Ayapango, Atlautla, Ecatzingo, Huixquilucan, Tlazala, Jilotepec, Metepec, Tenancingo y Tejupilco." *Boletín del Archivo General del Estado de México* 7 (Ene./Abr. 1981) 32–48.   (241
Alanís Boyso, José Luis. "Los archivos históricos municipales de Santa Cruz atizapan,

Temascalcingo, Villa Victoria, Tacámac, Polotitlán, Zinacantepec, San Martín de las
Pirámides, San Mateo Atenco, Xonacatlán, Otzolotepec, Jalatlaco, Joquicingo,
Texcaltitlán, Almoloya de Alquisiras, Coatepec Harinas y Tonatico." *Boletín del
Archivo General del Estado de México* 5 (May./Ag. 1980) 35–47.   (242

Alanís Boyso, José Luis. "Los archivos históricos municipales de Sultepec, Lerma,
Aculco, Villa de Allende, Temascaltepec, Donato Guerra, Amanalco de Becerra,
Jiquipilco, Texcalyacac, Temoaya, Zumpahuacan y Villa Guerrero." *Boletín del
Archivo General del Estado de México* 6 (Sept./Dic. 1980) 49–59.   (243

Banco Central del Ecuador. Biblioteca General. *Boletín bibliográfico* año 21, no.
64/65, 1981. Quito.
(Accession list of books acquired by the Library)   (244

Bazant, Jan. "Los archivos de notarías de Zacatecas." *Historia mexicana* 30:1, no. 117
(Jul./Sept. 1980) 134–136.   (245

Bibliografia brasileira de documentação, 1978–1980. Rio de Janeiro: Instituto
Brasileiro de Informação e Tecnologia, 1981.   (246

Buenos Aires. Universidad. Instituto Bibliotecológico. *Catálogo de la Biblioteca.
Obras. Suplemento 3.* Buenos Aires, El Instituto, 1980.   (247

Caillavet, Chantal. "Les archives équatoriennes." *Cahiers du monde hispanique et
luso-brésilien* 34 (1980) 171–175.   (248

Casa de la Cultura Ecuatoriana "Benjamín Carrión." *Guía del Archivo Nacional de
Historia.* Quito: Edit. Casa de la Cultura Ecuatoriana, 1981. 219 p.   (249

"Catálogo del Ramo Revolución Mexicana." *Boletín del Archivo del Estado de México*
5 (May./Ag. 1980) 48–51.   (250

Catálogos de documentos sobre el Instituto Literario del Estado Toluca. Mexico: Univ.
Autónoma del Estado de México, 1980. 98 p. (*Col. histórica*, B-6016).   (251

Dorn, Georgette Magassy. "Of libraries and bibliographies." *Latin American research
review* 16:3 (1981) 268–271.   (252

Flores, María G. *Mexican American archives at the Benson Collection: a guide for
users.* Edited by Laura Gutierrez Witt. Austin: The General Libraries, The Univ. of
Texas at Austin, 1981. vii, 74 p.   (253

Freudenthal, Juan R., and Héctor Gómez Fuentes. "Information and documentation in
Chile: progress report; bibliography 1974–1978." *Journal of the American Society
for Information Science* 31 (Nov. 1980) 445–448.   (254

García Mainieri, Norma. "Situación archivística actual en Guatemala." *Universidad
de San Carlos*, 2a. época, 10 (1979) 25–101.   (255
(Describes the holdings of several archives)

Garner, Jane. *Archives and manuscripts on microfilm in the Nettie Lee Benson Collection: a checklist.* Austin: The Univ. of Texas at Austin, The General Libraries, 1980.
48 p.   (256

Institute of Jamaica, Kingston. West India Reference Library. *The Catalogue of the
West India Reference Library.* Millwood, N.Y.: Kraus International Publications,
1980. 6 v.   (257

Kennedy Troya, Alexandra. *Catálogo del Archivo General de la Orden Franciscana del
Ecuador.* Quito: Banco Central del Ecuador, 1980.   (258

Lechuga Barrios, Carmen. "Sección catálogos: (El Archivo General del Estado de

México)." *Boletín del Archivo General del Estado de México* 7 (Ene./Abr. 1981) 52–54. (259

Lutz, Cristóbal H., and Stephen Webre. "El Archivo General de Centroamérica, Ciudad de Guatemala." *Mesoamérica* 1:1 (1980) 274–285. (260

Mexico. Archivo General de la Nación. *Catálogo de los ramos Oficio de Soria y Oficio de Hurtado*. Mexico, 1980. 84 p. (*Serie Guías y catálogos*, 58.

Compilado por María Elena Bribiesca Sumano. (261

———. *Catálogo del Ramo correspondiente de Virreyes Marquez de Croix*. Tomo III. Mexico: 1980. 95 p. (*Serie Guías y catálogos*, 56).

Compiled by María Elena Bribiesca Sumano, Rosa María Navarrete, and Elisa Cruz D. (262

———. *Catálogo del Ramo Escribanos*. Compilado por Abel González Flores et al. Mexico: 1980. 168 p. (*Serie Guías y catálogos*, 55). (263

———. *Directorio de burócratas en la Ciudad de México, 1761–1832*. Mexico: 1980. 301 p. (*Serie Guías y catálogos*, 52). (264

Compilado por Linda Arnold.

———. *Fondo Abelardo: Presidente Abelardo L. Rodríguez. Indice de series: Confederaciones, uniones y organizaciones*. Compilado por Angeles Suárez, Enrique Arriola Woog, Esteban Chavez, et al. (*Serie Guías y Catálogos*, 50) Mexico, 1980. (265

———. *Indice del Ramo Alcaldes Mayores*. Mexico: 1980. 2 v. (*Serie Guías y catálogos*, 53).

Compilado por María Elena Bribiesca Sumano. (266

——— *Ríos y acequias, mercados, abastos, y panaderías*. México: 1980. 102 p. (*Serie Guías y catálogos*, 54). (267

"Registro bibliográfico." *Boletim*, Biblioteca Mário de Andrade (São Paulo) 41:1/2 (Jan./Jun. 1980) 145–157. (268

"Atualização do acervo da Biblioteca Mário de Andrade."

Venezuela. Universidad Central, Caracas. Biblioteca Central. *Catálogo de obras ingresadas, enero–diciembre 1977*. Caracas: 1981. 390 p. (269

Villacís V., Eduardo. "Los índices del Archivo Histórico del Banco Central. Fondo Jijón y Caamaño. Tercera colección: Documentos. 9 volúmenes, 3,741 p. (1805–1875)." *Cultura* (Quito) 3:8 (Sept./Dic. 1980) 284–345. (270

Periodicals and Microforms

Annotated bilbiography of the present available Caribbean periodicals in the Public Library of Curaçao, Netherlands Antilles. Curaçao: The Library, 1981. 12 leaves. (271

Biblioteca Pública do Estado (Santa Catarina, Brazil). *Catálogo de jornais catarinenses, 1850–1980*. Florianópolis: Secretaria de Cultura, Esporte e Turismo, Fundação Catarinense de Cultura, 1980. 120 p. (272

Catálogo coletivo de periódicos do Estado de São Paulo em biomedicina. V. 1– 1977–. São Paulo, Universidade de São Paulo, Coordenadoria de Atividades Culturais, Divisão de Biblioteca e Documentação. (273

198   Haydée Piedracueva

Catálogo coletivo regional de publicações periódicas em ciencias sociais e humanidades de Minas Gerais. V. 1— 1979—. Belo Horizonte: Biblioteca Central da Univ. Fed. de Minas Gerais.   (274

Covington, Paula Anne. *Indexed journals; a selection of Latin American serials*. Submitted for the Twenty-Sixth Seminar on the Acquisition of Latin American Library Materials, Tulane Univ., April 1—4, 1981. Madison, Wisc.: SALALM Secretariat, Memorial Library, Univ. of Wisconsin, 1981. 21 p.   (275

Hodgman, Suzanne. *Microfilming projects newsletter*. No. 23, April 1981. Prepared by Committee on Acquisitions, SALALM, in the Memorial Library, Univ. of Wisconsin, Madison. 6 p. (XXVI Seminar on the Acquisition of Latin American Library Materials. *Working paper*, A-3).   (276

Lozano, Eduardo. *Cuban periodicals in the University of Pittsburgh Libraries*. 3d. ed. Pittsburgh, Pa., Univ. of Pittsburgh Libraries, Center for Latin American Studies, 1981. 94 p.   (277

Mace, Carroll Edward. "Libraries of Mérida, Yucatán, and a checklist of nineteenth-century serials in the Hemeroteca José María Pino Suárez." *The Americas* 38:2 (Oct. 1981) 249—267.   (278

"Un siglo de cultura dominicana; tabla cronológica (1844—1944)." *Eme Eme; estudios dominicanos* 9:52 (Ene./Feb. 1981) 85—116.   (279

Sonntag, Iliana L. "Sampling of new periodicals." *SALALM Newsletter* 9:2 (Dec. 1981) 12—13.   (280

Spain. Centro Nacional de Microfilm. *Publicaciones en microfilm/microficha*. Madrid: Instituto Bibliográfico Hispánico, 1980. 25 p.   (281

Universidad Federal de Goiás. Biblioteca Central. Seção de Periódicos. *Catálogo de periódicos*. Goiania: 1980. iv, 217 p.   (282

Zapata Cuéncar, Heriberto. *Antioquia: periódicos de provincia*. Medellín, 1981. 135 p.   (283

Politics and Government

Bustamante, Jorge, and Francisco Malagamba. *México-Estados Unidos; bibliografía general sobre estudios fronterizos*. 1. ed. Mexico: El Colegio de México, 1980. 251 p.   (284

Dahlin, Therrin C., Gary P. Gillum, and Mark L. Grover. *The Catholic left in Latin America: a comprehensive bibliography*. Boston: G. K. Hall, 1981. 350 p.   (285

Elite intelectual e debate político nos anos 30; uma bibliografia da revolução de 30. Coord.: Lucia Lippi Oliveira et al. Rio de Janeiro: Fundação Getúlio Vargas, MEC, 1980. 356 p.   (286

Fernández-Kelly, María Patricia. "The U.S.-Mexico border: recent publications and the state of current research." *Latin American research review* 16:3 (1981) 250—267.   (287

Fernández P., María Angélica, and María del Valle Stark O. "Instrumentos internacionales, Ministerio de Relaciones Exteriores de la República de Chile, Junio 1979— Marzo 1981." *Revista de legislación y documentación en derecho y ciencias sociales* 3:1 (Ene./Mar. 1981) 11—25.   (288

Finan, John J., and John Child. *Latin America; international relations; a guide to information sources*. Detroit, Mich.: Gale Research Co., 1981. (International relations information guide series, 11).   (289

Grindle, Merilee. "Armed intervention and U.S.-Latin American relations." *Latin American research review* 16:1 (1981) 207−217.   (290

LeoGrande, William M. "Two decades of socialism in Cuba." *Latin American research review* 16:1 (1981) 187−206.   (291

Portales, Carlos. *Bibliografía sobre relaciones internacionales y política exterior de Chile, 1964−1980*. Santiago de Chile: FLACSO, 1981. (*Documento de trabajo*, 108).   (292

Publicaciones editadas en español, 1980−1981. México: Centro de Publicaciones de Organismos Internacionales, 1981. 3 vols.   (293

Seckinger, Ron. "The Central American militaries: a survey of the literature." *Latin American research review* 16:2 (1981) 246−258.   (294

Science and Technology

Catálogo coletivo regional de publicações periódicas em ciencias biomédicas de Minas Gerais. Belo Horizonte: Divisão de Informações Bibliográficas, Biblioteca Central da UFMG. Vol. 1− 1980− .   (295

Erber, Fábio Stefano. "Science and technology policy in Brazil: a review of the literature." *Latin American research review* 16:1 (1981) 3−56.   (296

Valdivia Ponce, Oscar. *Bibliografía psiquiátrica peruana*. Lima, 1981. ix, 152 p.   (297

Social Sciences

Bailey, Juan, and Freya Headlam. *Intercontinental migration to Latin America; a select bibliography*. London: Univ. of London, Institute of Latin American Studies, 1980. 60 p.   (298

Bibliografía del folklore de Guatemala, 1892−1980. Guatemala: Dirección General de Antropología e Historia Guatemalteca, Univ. de San Carlos, 1980. 174 p.   (299

Centro de Estudios Puertorriqueños, New York. *Preliminary guide to articles in La Prensa relating to Puerto Ricans in New York City between 1922 and 1929*. New York: The Centro, Research Foundation of the City University of New York, 1981. 68 p.   (300

―――. *Preliminary guide to articles in Puerto Rican newspapers relating to Puerto Rican migration between 1900 and 1929*. New York: The Centro, Research Foundation of the City University of New York, 1981. 62 p.   (301

Delorme, Robert L. *Latin America; social science information sources, 1967−1979*. Santa Barbara, Calif.: ABC Clio, 1981. 288 p.   (302

"Dossier bibliográfico: periodismo y nuevas tecnologías." *Comunicación* 33/34 (Sept./Oct. 1981) 64−67.   (303

Feijóo, María del Carmen. *La mujer, el desarrollo y las tendencias de población en América Latina; bibliografía comentada*. Buenos Aires: Centro de Estudios de Estado y Sociedad, 1980. 59 p. (*Estudios CEDES*, v. 3, no. 1, 1980)   (304

Fundación Ecuatoriana de Estudios Sociales. *Pensamiento humanista y comunitario; bibliografía básica.* Quito: La Paz, 1979. 24 p.   (305

John F. Kennedy Library, Guyana. *Communications media: press, radio, journals; bibliography.* Georgetown: The Library, 1981. 15 leaves.   (306

Leon (Swadesh) Quintana, Frances, and Gilbert Benito Córdova. "The Chicano heritage" *American anthropologist* 8:1 (March 1980) 100–107.   (307
(Review article on 7 books on the subject)

Levine, Daniel H. "Religion, society, and politics; states of the art." *Latin American research review* 16:3 (1981) 185–209.
(Review article evaluates 7 books on the subject.)   (308

Mahan, Elizabeth. *International communication: access to the literature.* Submitted for the Twenty-Sixth Seminar on the Acquisition of Latin American Library Materials, Tulane Univ., April 1–4, 1981. Madison: SALALM Secretariat, 1981. 19 p.   (309

Nieschulz de Stockhausen, Elke. "Periodismo y política en Venezuela: cincuenta años de história." *Montalbán* 10 (1980) 715–911.
(Includes a catalogue of Venezuelan periodicals.)   (310

"Para una evaluación del impacto de las nuevas tecnologías de comunicación en Venezuela." *Comunicación* 33/34 (Sept./Oct. 1981) 79–83.   (311

Portes, Alejandro. "Migration, poverty, and the city in Latin America." *Latin America research review* 16:3 (1981) 225–235.   (312

"Recommended works." *Reforma newsletter* 2 (Spring 1981) 8–9.
(Books on Mexican Americans and minorities.)   (313

Wade, Ann E. *Guide to Latin American and West Indian census materials: a bibliography and union list.* London: SCONUL Advisory Committee on Latin American Materials, 1981– v. 1: Venezuela.   (314

Theses and Dissertations

Benseler, David P., and John F. Lalande, II. "Survey of doctoral degrees granted in foreign languages in the United States: Autumn 1979–Calendar year 1980." *The Modern language journal* 65:3 (Autumn 81) 311–315.
(Spanish languages and literatures: pp. 311–315)   (315

Buenos Aires. University. Instituto Bibliotecológico. *Tesis presentadas a la Universidad de Buenos Aires, 1979–1980.* Buenos Aires: 1981. 42 p.   (316

Buño, W., and H. Bollini-Folchi. *Tesis de doctorado presentadas a la Facultad de Medicina entre 1881 y 1902.* Montevideo: 1980. 246 p.   (317

Ceará, Brazil (State). Universidade Federal. Centro de Ciencias Agrárias. *Catálogo de teses do Centro de Ciencias Agrárias.* 1979–. Fortaleza: Univ. Federal do Ceará.   (318

Duport, Claudie. "Catalogue des theses et mémoires sur l'Amérique Latine soutenus en France en 1979 et 1980." *Cahiers des Amériques Latines* 31/22 (1980) 263–318.   (319

Epple, Juan Armando. "Tesis doctorales sobre literatura chilena en las universidades norteamericanas." *Literatura chilena en el exilio* 4:1 (Ene. 1980) 13–16.   (320

González, Nelly Sfeir de. *Doctoral dissertations on Latin America and the Caribbean:*

an analysis and bibliography of dissertations accepted at American and Canadian universities, 1966–1970. Urbana: Consortium of Latin American Studies Programs, 1980. xxviii, 201 p.

(*Publication*, Consortium of Latin American Studies Programs, 10)   (321

Hulet, Claude L. "Dissertations in the Hispanic languages and literatures, 1980." *Hispania* 64: 2 (May 1981) 330–337.   (322

(Annual feature in the journal.)

"Liste alphabetique des theses de troisième cycle soutenus en France en 1979 (toutes disciplines). *Cahiers du monde hispanique et luso-brésilien* 35 (1980) 207–215.

(Includes Latin America)   (323

"Positions et résumés concernant les theses de troisième cycle soutenus en France (1979) en droit, histoire, linguistique, littérature. . . . (etc.) de l'Amérique Latine." *Cahiers du monde hispanique et luso-brésilien* 35 (1980) 217–308.   (324

Revel Mouroz, Jean. "Note sur les recherches françaises-en sciences sociales sur le Mexique (1960–1980)." *Cahiers des Amériques Latines* 21/22 (1980) 7–22.   (325

"Teses defendidas na pós-graduação do departamento de letras da PUC-RJ." *Linguagens* (Pontifícia Univ. Católica, Rio de Janeiro) 1:2 (1981?) 129–134.   (326

Theses in Latin American studies at British universities in progress and recently completed. No. 14, 1981. London: Univ. of London, Inst. of Latin American Studies.   (327

"Trabajos de tesis de los graduados de la Univ. de San Carlos de Guatemala en 1978." *Universidad de San Carlos* (2a. época) 10 (1979) 305–367.   (328

Works in Progress

Anuario bibliográfico 1979. Buenos Aires, Ed. Librorama.   (329

Boletín internacional de bibliografía sobre educación. (A quarterly journal, to be published by UNESCO and the Comisión Española de Cooperación con la UNESCO.)   (330

Buenos Aires. Universidad. Instituto Bibliotecológico. *Catálogo de la Biblioteca. Obras.* Suplemento no. 4 is in preparation.   (331

Chatham, James R. List of dissertations in the Hispanic languages and literatures. (Title may vary.)   (332

Covington, Paula Anne. *Indexed journals; a selection of Latin American serials.* To be published by SALALM in its Bibliography series, no. 7, in Spring 1982.   (333

Espinosa Elerik, María Luz. *Bibliografía anotada y comentada de diccionarios técnicos y especializados, español-inglés.* Will be published by Whitston Pub. Co. in 1982.   (334

Freudenthal, Juan R. "Libraries in the West Indies."

Article to be published in the *Encyclopedia of Library and Information Science*, in 1982. Will include 148 entries.   (335

Latin American economic issues: information needs and information sources. To be published by SALALM, expected date: Spring 1982.   (336

McKegney, James C. *Computerized bibliography of 1808–1832 Mexican imprints.*

SUBJECT INDEX

AUTHOR INDEX

Bibliography of Microform Projects
1982

Suzanne Hodgman

Insofar as possible, we have attempted not to repeat any projects previously described, except those first reported in progress and now reported completed. An effort has been made to verify all entries, but where this has not been possible, we have tried to provide at least a workable form of entry.

INSTITUTION CODES

CSt-H	Hoover Institution on War, Revolution and Peace, Stanford University
CtY	Yale University
DLC	Library of Congress
MH	Harvard University
NjP	Princeton University
NN	New York Public Library

Adelante. Camaguey, Cuba. June, 1975–Dec., 1976. (2 reels: $40. Np2761)	Continuing project	DLC
América española. Cartagena, Colombia. Tomos 1–17; May, 1935–June, 1955. (182 feet; inc.)	Completed	NN
The American-Spanish War; A History by the War Leaders. Norwich, Conn.: C. C. Haskell and Son, 1899. 607p. (Film M 04335)	Completed	NjP
Annuaire du Brésil économique. Rio de Janeiro. 1912–1930/31. (2 reels: $40. 07243)	Completed	DLC
Argentine Republic. Dirección General de Estadística. *Anuario de la Dirección de Estadística. . .* Buenos Aires: 1893–1913. *Filmed with:* Argentine Republic. Ministerio de Hacienda. *Estadística de comercio y de la navegación.* Buenos Aires: 1880–1892. (20 reels: $360. 05770)	Completed	DLC
———. Dirección General de Navegación, Hidrografía, Faros y Balizas. *Tablas de marea.* Buenos Aires: 1941–1960. (263 feet; inc.)	Completed	NN
———. Ministerio de Hacienda. *Estadística de comercio y de la navegación.* Buenos Aires: 1880–1892. *Filmed with:* Argentine Republic. Dirección General de Estadística. *Anuario de la Dirección de Estadística . . .* Buenos Aires: 1893–1913. (20 reels: $360. 05770)	Completed	DLC
———. Ministerio de Relaciones Exteriores. *Boletín mensual. . .* Vols. 1–8, 1884–1891; vols. 1–48, 1903–1916. [Scattered issues lacking] (16 reels: $325. 39502)	Completed	DLC
———. Secretaría de Estado de Hacienda. *Memoria.* Buenos Aires: 1863–1940. [Scattered issues lacking] (22 reels: $475. 04935)	Completed	DLC
Bacon, Edgar Mayhew. *The New Jamaica; Describing the Island. . .* New York: Walbridge and Co., 1890. 243p. (Film M 04026)	Completed	NjP
Barricada. Managua, Nicaragua. July 25, 1979– Dec. 31, 1980. (4 reels: $95. Np 2985)	Completed	DLC
Belize Times. Belize City, Belize. Jan., 1966–Dec., 1968; Sept., 1975–Dec., 1978. [Scattered issues lacking] (7 reels: $130. Np 1825)	Continuing project	DLC
Bohemia. Havana. Jan.–Dec., 1977 (4 reels: $140). 1978–1980 (12 reels: $470)	Continuing project	Cst-H
Bolivia. Gaceta oficial. 1970–1979 (11 reels: $474. LL-02069). 1980+ (Est. per year: $60)	Continuing project	DLC
Brasil compre e vende. Brazil Buys and Sells. Manual da economia brasileira. . . Rio de Janeiro: 1940 (1 reel: $20. 07244)	Completed	DLC

Brazil. *Diario oficial. Estados Unidos do Brasil.* Section 1, part 1, 1971–1979 (171 reels: $5858. LL-02121); 1980+ (Est. per year: $1200); Section 1, part 2, 1971–1979 (40 reels: $1546. LL-02121); 1980+ (Est. per year: $250); Section 4, 1973–1978 (9 reels: $280. LL-02121; 1979+ (Est. per year: $80)	Continuing project	DLC
———. Instituto do Açucar e do Alcool. *Congressos açucareiros no Brasil.* Rio de Janeiro: Instituto do Açucar e do Alcool, 1949. 306p. (Film M 03998)	Completed	NjP
———. Ministério da Agricultura. *Boletim do Ministério da Agricultura.* Rio de Janeiro. Vols. 1–36, 1912–1947. [Scattered issues lacking] (15 reels: $295. 06812)	Completed	DLC
Buenos Aires. Museo Mitre. *Documentos del Archivo de San Martín.* Buenos Aires: 1910–1911. 12 vols. (3 reels: $50. 39385)	Completed	DLC
El Caimán barbudo. Havana. Nov., 1975–Dec., 1978 (2 reels: $70); 1979–1980 (1 reel: $39.50)	Continuing project	CSt-H
La Casa de las Américas. Havana. Jan.–Dec., 1977 (1 reel: $35); 1978–1980 (3 reels: $118.50)	Continuing project	CSt-H
Centro Naval, Buenos Aires. *Boletín.* Nos. 1/2-65*l*, Sept./Oct., 1882–Oct./Dec., 1963. [Scattered issues lacking] (19 reels: $440. 07612)	Completed	DLC
Chile. *Diario oficial de la República de Chile.* 1970–1978 (35 reels: $1123. LL-0205); 1979+ (Est. per year: $125)	Continuing project	DLC
———. Departamento de Economía Rural. *Boletín de informaciones agropecuarias.* Santiago. Vols. 1–134; July, 1942–Jan., 1954. [Scattered issues lacking] (4 reels: $75. 05748)	Completed	DLC
———. Ministerio de Relaciones Exteriores. *Boletín del Ministerio de Relaciones Exteriores, Culto i Colonización.* Santiago. 1896–1917. [Scattered issues lacking] (12 reels: $235. 39393)	Completed	DLC
Colección de historiadores de Chile y de documentos relativos a la historia nacional. Santiago. Vols. 1–50, 1861–1948; Index, 1931. [Vol. 46 wanting] (9 reels: $210. 04963).	Completed	DLC
Colombia. *Diario oficial.* 1821–1969 (245 reels: $6615. LL-02086); 1970–1977 (32 reels: $1298); 1978+ (Est. per year: $125)	Continuing project	DLC
———. Corte Suprema de Justicia. *Gaceta judicial.* Bogotá. Vols. 1–444, Feb., 1887–	Completed	DLC

Dec., 1972. [Scattered issues lacking] (49 reels: $985. LL-0303)		
Comercio exterior de Cuba. Havana. May, 1902–1936. (15 reels: $300. 06932)	Completed	DLC
El Conservador; órgano del Directorio del Partido Conservador de Colombia. Bogotá. Nos. 1–122, 124–308, 310–560; 1881–1884	Completed	CtY
Correio do livro. São Paulo. Ano 1–5; July, 1975–June, 1980. (78 feet)	Completed	NN
Costa Rica. *La Gaceta; diario oficial.* San José. 1970–1978 (47 reels: $1666. LL-02009); 1979+ (Est. per year: $225)	Continuing project	DLC
Criterio. Buenos Aires. 1977–1978. (1 reel: $20. 05999)	Completed?	DLC
Cuba. *Gaceta oficial* [Very incomplete]. 1964– Feb., 1969 (1 reel: $25. LL-02068); Feb., 1970–1977 (3 reels: $99); 1978+ (Est. per year: $35)	Continuing project	DLC
Cul-Po; cultura y política. Guatemala. Nos. 2–4; Feb.–June, 1975. (7 feet)	Completed	NN
Cursos y conferencias. Buenos Aires: Colegio Libre de Estudios Superiores. Años 1–29; 1931–1960. (3 reels; incomplete)	Completed	MH
Dedete. Havana. [Supplement to *Juventud rebelde*]	Continuing project	CSt-H
El Descamisado. Buenos Aires. May 22, 1973– March 19, 1974. (1 reel: $20. 97561)	Completed	DLC
Desco resumen semanal–DESCO. Lima. Año 3, nos. 54–102; Jan. 5, 1980–Dec. 30, 1980. (Film M S00488)	Continuing project	NjP
Dominican Republic. *Gaceta oficial.* 1865–1879 (7 reels: $130. 02423); 1970–1977 (15 reels: $766. LL-02087); 1978+ (Est. per year: $110)	Continuing project	DLC
Ecuador. *Registro oficial.* 1970–1979 (17 reels: $815. LL-02070); 1980+ (Est. per year: $80)	Continuing project	DLC
Fernández y García, Eugenio. *El Libro de Puerto Rico. The Book of Puerto Rico.* San Juan: El Libro Azul Publishing Co., 1923. 1188p. (Film M 04378)	Completed	NjP
Girón. Matanzas, Cuba. July, 1975–Dec., 1980. (3 reels: $55. Np 2695)	Continuing project	DLC
El Guatemalteco; diario de Centro América. 1970–1979 (39 reels: $1422. LL-02115); Index, 1971–1976; Vols. 192–204 (1 reel: $35); 1980+ (Est. per year: $200)	Continuing project	DLC

Haiti (Republic). *Le Moniteur; journal officiel de la république d'Haiti.* Port-au-Prince. 1862– 1957 (21 reels: $420. LL-02138); 1970–1972, 1975–1979 (6 reels: $262); 1980+ (Est. per year: $50) — Continuing project — DLC

Honduras. *La Gaceta diaria oficial de la República de Honduras.* Tegucigalpa. 1971–1979 (28 reels: $930. LL-02122); 1980+ (Est. per year: $150) — Continuing project — DLC

Industria; boletín de la Sociedad de Fomento Fabril. Santiago, Chile. Año 1–48, 1884–1931. [Scattered issues lacking] (17 reels: $350. 07277) — Completed — DLC

Instituto Histórico e Geográfico do Rio Grande do Sul, Porto Alegre. *Revista.* . . Vols. 1–29; 1921–1949. [Scattered issues lacking] (6 reels: $135. 06934) — Completed — DLC

Jornal dos municipios. Curitiba, Brazil. Oct., 1974– May, 1977. (1 reel: $20. 05919) — Continuing project — DLC

Junta de Estudios Históricos de San José de Flores, Buenos Aires. [*Publicaciones*]. Nos. 1–26; 1939– 1945. (1 reel) — Completed — MH

Jurisprudencia argentina. Buenos Aires. 1918– 1971. (137 reels: $2595. LL-0285) — Completed — DLC

Juventud rebelde. Havana. 1977–1980 (8 reels: $316) — Continuing project — CSt-H

Latin American Daily Post. São Paulo. Apr. 26, 1979– Sept. 1, 1980 (6 reels: $110. Np 2912) — Continuing project — DLC

La Luz; periódico político, literario e industrial. Bogotá. Nos. 1–366, 1881–1884. — Completed — CtY

Megafón. Buenos Aires. Años 1–3, nos. 1–16; 1975–1977 (38 feet) — Continuing project — NN

Mexico. *Diario oficial.* 1954–1959 (21 reels: $447. 02380); 1970–1978 (52 reels: $2255. LL-02093); 1979+ (Est. per year: $400) — Continuing project — DLC

———. Secretaría de Fomento, Colonización e Industria. *Anales de Ministerio de Fomento de la República Mexicana.* Tomos 1–11, 1877–1898. (3 reels: $75. 39444) — Completed — DLC

Mito. Bogotá. Apr., 1955–June, 1962. [Scattered issues lacking] (1 reel: $25. 07563) — Completed — DLC

Movimento. São Paulo. Nos. 236–286; Jan. 7, 1980– Dec. 28, 1980. — Continuing project — CtY

Nicaragua. *La Gaceta; diario oficial.* 1970–1978 (20 reels: $880. LL-02071); Subject index, 1970– 1974 (1 reel: $14); 1979+ (Est. per year: $27) — Continuing project — DLC

———. Ministerio de Hacienda y Crédito Público. *Memoria.* 1870/72–1940 (10 reels: $210. 07298) — Completed — DLC

Noticias de Guatemala. Guatemala. June, 1976– June, 1979. (3 reels: $55. 05974) — Completed — DLC

Nuevo amanecer cultural. Managua, Nicaragua. Nos. 1–30. *Filmed with: El nuevo diario.*	Completed	CtY
El Nuevo diario. Managua. Año 1, nos. 1–225; May 19, 1980–Dec. 31, 1980. (2 reels: $39.50 per reel)	Continuing project	CtY
Nuevo mundo. Buenos Aires. Tomos 3–7; 1973– 1977. (45 feet)	Completed	NN
Nuevo mundo israelita. Caracas. Feb., 1973–Dec., 1979. (3 reels: $65. 05940)	Continuing project	DLC
Opina. Havana. Nos. 1–6, 7–11, 13–17; July–Dec., 1979, Jan.–May, July–Dec., 1980. (Film M S00549)	Completed	NjP
Orbe. Havana. Año 1, nos. 1–3, 107; Mar. 13, 1931– March 25, 1933 (293 feet; incomplete)	Completed	NN
Orígenes; revista de arte y literatura. Havana. Año 10, no. 33–año 13, no. 4; 1953–1956 (Film M S00192)	Completed	NjP
Panama. *Gaceta oficial.* 1970–1979. (19 reels: $580. LL-02072); 1980+ (Est. per year: $65)	Continuing project	DLC
Paraguay. *Registro oficial.* 1974–1975. (8 reels: $364. LL-02139); 1976+ (Est. per year: $200)	Continuing project	DLC
Peláez y Tapia, José. *Historia de El Mercurio: un siglo de periodismo chileno.* Santiago: Talleres de "El Mercurio," 1927. 603p. (Film M 03942)	Completed	NjP
Perón, Juan Domingo. *Perón Speeches.* [Collection of items numbered 1–150.] (3 reels)	Completed	MH
Peru. *El Peruano; diario oficial.* 1968–1969 (13 reels: $270. LL-02073); 1970–1978 (87 reels: $2620); 1979+ (Est. per year: $150)	Continuing project	DLC
———. Ministerio de Fomento. *Boletín.* . . Jan., 1903–July, 1920 [Apr.–June, 1919 wanting] (11 reels: $225. 07450)	Completed	DLC
———. ———. *Registro oficial de fomento; minas, industria, beneficencia.* . . 1897–1917. [Scattered issues lacking] (13 reels: $270. 07417)	Completed	DLC
Pionero. Havana. [Supplement to *Juventud rebelde*]	Continuing project	CSt-H
Poesía de Venezuela. Caracas. May, 1963–1979. (1 reel: $20. 05982)	Completed	DLC
Prensa económica. Buenos Aires. Años 1–5; July, 1975–June, 1980. (189 feet)	Continuing project	NN
Puerto Rico. Commonwealth Board of Elections. *Estadísticas de las elecciones generales, 1904–1981.*	Begun: Oct., 1981	NjP
Que sucedió en 7 días. Buenos Aires. Nos. 1–293; Aug., 1946–Mar., 1968 [No. 208 wanting]. (7 reels: $155. 05740)	Continuing project	DLC
La República. Panama City, Panama. Jan. 16– Dec. 20, 1977; Aug., 1978–Oct., 1980. (22 reels: $445. Np 2740)	Continuing project	DLC
Revista de direito civil, commercial e criminal; publi-	Completed	DLC

Entry	Status	Code
* cação mensal de doutrina, jurisprudencia e legislação.* . . Rio de Janeiro. Vols. 1–153; July, 1906–June, 1945; Indexes. (35 reels: $795. LL-0294)		
Revista de educación primaria. Santiago, Chile. Vols. 8–35, no. 7; Sept., 1893–Sept., 1928 [Scattered issues lacking]. (4 reels: $85. 05755)	Completed	DLC
El Salvador. *Diario oficial.* 1847–1969. (296 reels: $5328. LL-02074); *Supplement,* 1847–1969. (12 reels: $216. 06778); 1970–1979. (69 reels: $3336. LL-02074); 1980+ (Est. per year: $380)	Continuing project	DLC
———. Dirección General de Estadística. *Anuario estadístico.* . . 1911–1950/1951. (7 reels: $150. 07240)	Completed	DLC
Saõ Paulo, Brazil (State). Departamento do Arquivo do Estado. *Documentos interessantes para a historia e costumes de São Paulo.* São Paulo. Vols. 1–91; 1895–1968. [Scattered issues lacking]. (10 reels: $195. 06933)	Completed	DLC
La Semana de bellas artes. Mexico. Nos. 109–161; Jan. 2, 1980–Dec. 31, 1980.	Continuing project	CtY
Semanario judicial de la federación. Mexico. Ser. 1–6, vol. 138; 1871–1968. [Ser. 4, vol. 36 and ser. 6, vols. 127–129 lacking] (223 reels: $4590. LL-0286)	Completed	DLC
Sociedad Geográfica de La Paz. *Boletín.* . . Nos. 1–69; 1898–Jan., 1947. [Scattered issues lacking] (3 reels: $65. 01319)	Completed	DLC
Solidaridad. Santiago, Chile. Nos. 85–107, Jan.–Dec., 1980.	Continuing project	CtY
Todo. Mexico. Nos. 1–616; Sept. 5, 1933–June 28, 1945. [Scattered issues lacking] (33 reels: $605. 06760)	Completed	DLC
Trabajadores. Havana. Vols. 1–8; Sept., 1971–Dec. 29, 1979. [Scattered issues lacking] (3 reels: $65. 05996)	Continuing project	DLC
United States. Library of Congress. Hispanic Foundation. *Hispanic Foundation Survey Reports.* Washington, D.C. Nos. 1–8, 1958–1959. (1 reel: $20. 05991)	Completed	DLC
Uruguay. *Diario oficial.* 1890–1969. (119 reels: $2618. 04270); 1970–1979 (42 reels: $1558. LL-02083); 1980+ (Est. per year: $190)	Continuing project	DLC
———. *Diario oficial. Sección avisos.* 1906–1969 (442 reels: $9724. 04434); 1970–1979 (111 reels: $4315. LL-02084); 1980+ (Est. per year: $600)	Continuing project	DLC
———. Ministerio de Relaciones Exteriores. *Memoria*	Completed	DLC

presentada a la honorable Asamblea General. . .		
1862−1946 [Incomplete] (10 reels: $180. 05715)		
La Vanguardia. Buenos Aires. Jan.−Dec., 1977	Continuing	CSt-H
(1 reel: $35), 1978−1980 (1 reel: $39.50)	project	
La Vanguardia. Santa Clara, Cuba. Aug., 1975−	Continuing	DLC
Mar., 1977. (1 reel: $20. Np 2667)	project	
Venezuela. *Gaceta oficial.* 1970−1979 (32 reels:	Continuing	DLC
$1126. LL-02075); 1980+ (Est. per year: $125)	project	
———. Ministerio de Fomento. *Memoria y cuenta.*	Completed	DLC
Caracas. 1863−1945. [Scattered issues lacking]		
(29 reels: $545. 07278)		
Villarino Cabezón, Joaquín. *José Manuel Balmaceda,*	Completed	NjP
el último de los presidentes constitucionales. . .		
Barcelona: Domenech, 1893. 494p. (Film 04336)		
Visão. São Paulo. Vols. 1−30, 1952−1971. (52 reels)	Completed	MH
El Zaguán. Mexico. Fall, 1975−Spring, 1977. (Film	Completed	NjP
M S00551)		
Zero hora. Porto Alegre, Brazil. Jan.−Sept., 1979.	Continuing	DLC
(9 reels: $190. Np 2762)	project	

Specialized Bibliographies and Reference Aids

Preliminary List of Guides and Directories of Latin American Libraries, Archives, and Information Centers

Celia Leyte-Vidal and Jesús Leyte-Vidal

CONTENTS

PREFACE

This bibliography has been compiled to focus attention on information resources in Latin America. By gathering together published guides and directories, we hope to assist the Ad Hoc Subcommittee on Compiling Directories of Latin American Libraries to establish priorities and guidelines for its future work. In assembling the list we relied on the OCLC On-line Union Catalog, the Library of Congress *Subject Catalog*, and Professor William V. Jackson's *Directories of Latin American Libraries*.

The bibliography is arranged alphabetically by country and by author or title within each country. Those guides treating more than two countries are listed first, under the heading "General." The entries are numbered consecutively. The hyphenated number at the *right* margin below the entry is the Library of Congress card number. The number at the *left* margin below the entry is the OCLC number. This information is included to aid retrieval of the records. The initials WVJ indicate that the information was taken from Professor Jackson's compilation.

Inconsistencies may exist in this work, as we have made no effort to verify and correct the entries. They are copied as they appear in the bibliographic tools consulted. In order to be as thorough as possible, we have in some cases recorded various editions of the same title. A name index follows the listing.

Our gratitude to Professor Jackson, to Nelly Gonzalez, and to Glenda LaCoste for their help in launching the project and bringing it to completion.

General

1. Asociación Latinoamericana de Instituciones Financieras de Desarrollo. *Directorio de unidades de información en las Instituciones miembros del ALIDE.* Lima, La Asociación, 1979 or 1980. 70 leaves.

    80-128625

2. Columbus Memorial Library. *Guía de bibliotecas de la América Latina.* Ed. provisional. Washington, Unión Panamericana, 1963. viii, 165 p. (Bibliographic series, no. 51)

    pa63-12/r81

3. Jefferson, A. A., and Alleyne, A. "Caribbeana resources in the English-speaking Caribbean." *Final report and working papers of the twenty-fourth Seminar on the Acquisition of Latin American Library Materials.* Los Angeles, University of California, June 17–22, 1979: 263–286.

4. Oliveira, Regina Maria Soares de. *Guia dos usuários da Classificação Decimal Universal (CDU) na América Latina: bibliotecas, centros e serviços de documentação. Directory of Universal Decimal Classification (UDC) users in Latin America: libraries and documentation-information centers and services.* Rio de Janeiro, Conselho Nacional de Desenvolvimento Científico e Tecnológico, Instituto Brasileiro de Informação em Ciencia e Tecnologia, 1977. 151 p. (FID publication, 558)

    79-119486

5. *Research guide to Andean history: Bolivia, Chile, Ecuador and Peru.* Contributing editors, Judith R. Bakewell et al. Coordinating editor, John J. TePaske. Durham, N.C. Duke University Press, 1981. xiii, 346 p.

    80-29365

6. Steele, Colin. *Major libraries of the world, a selective guide.* London, New York, Bowker, 1976. xix, 479 p.

    77-369002

7. Unesco. *World guide to science information and documentation services. Guide mondial des centres de documentation et d'information scientifiques.* Paris, 1965. 211 p. (Documentation and terminology of science)

    65-9614

8. Unesco. *World guide to technical information and documentation services. Guide mondial des centres de documentation et d'information techniques.* Paris, 1969. 287 p.

    72-16838

9. Unesco. *World guide to technical information and documentation services. Guide mondial des centres de documentation et d'information techniques.* 2d. ed. rev. and enl. Paris, Unesco, 1975. 515 p. (Documentation, libraries, and archives: Bibliographies and reference works, 2)

    75-325752

10. *World guide to libraries. Internationales Bibliotheks-Handbuch.* 3d. ed. New York, Bowker; Pullach/München, Verlag Dokumentation, 1970. 4 v.
1211667

11. *World guide to libraries. Internationales Bibliotheks-Handbuch.* 4th ed. New York, Bowker; Pullach/München, Verlag Documentation, 1974. 2 v.
1005009

12. *World guide to libraries. Internationales Bibliotheks-Handbuch.* Ed. by H. Lengenfelder. 5th ed. München, New York, Saur. 1980. xxv. 1030 p. (Handbook of international documentation and information, v. 8)
6592292

Argentina

13. Bahía Blanca, Argentina. Universidad Nacional del Sur. Centro de Documentación Bibliotecológica. *Guía: bibliotecas universitarias argentinas.* Bahia Blanca, 1967.
WVJ

14. Bahía Blanca, Argentina. Universidad Nacional del Sur. Centro de Documentación Bibliotecológica. *Guía de las bibliotecas universitarias argentinas.* 3 ed. Buenos Aires: Casa Pardo, 1976. 207 p.
77-568272

15. Deransart, Pierre. *Bibliothèques et systèmes documentaires en Argentine et au Brésil.* Le Chasnay, Institut de recherche d'informatique et d'automatique, 1977? 145 p.
78-363138

16. Giuffra, Carlos Alberto. *Guía de bibliotecas argentinas.* Edición preliminar. Buenos Aires, Fundación Interamericana de Bibliotecología Franklin y Comisión Nacional Argentina para UNESCO, 1967.
WVJ

17. *Guía de las bibliotecas universitarias argentinas.* Universidad Nacional del Sur, Centro de Investigaciones Bibliotecológicas. Buenos Aires, Casa Pardo, 1976. 107 p.
3050560

18. Matijevic, Nicolás. *Guía: bibliotecas universitarias argentinas.* Bahía Blanca. Centro de Documentación Bibliotecológica, Universidad Nacional del Sur. 1967. iii, 166 p.
68-90856

19. Matijevic, Nicolás. *Guía de las bibliotecas patagónicas.* Bahía Blanca, Centro de Documentación Bibliotecológica. Universidad Nacional del Sur, 1970. 43 leaves.
75-28756

20. Matijevic, Nicolás. *Guía de las bibliotecas universitarias argentina.* Buenos Aires, Casa Pardo, Centro de Documentación Bibliotecológica, 1976. 181 leaves.
3029350

21. Rio Negro, Argentina. Dirección Provincial de Cultura. Departamento de Bibliotecas. *Guía de bibliotecas de Rio Negro.* Viedma, Consejo Provincial de Educación, 1973. 57 p. (Publicaciones generales del Consejo Provincial de Educación, 4)
5123563

22. Universidad de Buenos Aires. Instituto Bibliotecológico. *Guía de las bibliotecas de la Universidad de Buenos Aires.* Buenos Aires, 1962. 51 p.
1651144

23. Universidad de Buenos Aires. Instituto Bibliotecológico. *Guía de las bibliotecas de la Universidad de Buenos Aires.* Buenos Aires, 1966. 64 p.

70-238241

24. Universidad de Buenos Aires. Instituto Bibliotecológico. *Guía de las bibliotecas de la Universidad de Buenos Aires.* 3. ed. actualizada. Buenos Aires, 1970. 87 p.

71-275791

Bolivia

25. Centro Nacional de Documentación Científica y Tecnológica. *Guía de bibliotecas, centros y servicios documentarios de Bolivia, 1973.* La Paz, Universidad Mayor de San Andrés, 1973. 113 p.
1200070

26. *Directorio de bibliotecas y centros de documentación de Bolivia, 1978.* La Paz, SYFNID, 1978. 109 p. (Publicación no. 1)
6989600

Brazil

27. Associação Paulista de Bibliotecários. Grupo de Trabalho em Bibliotecas de Ciências Sociais e Humanas. *Guia de bibliotecas de ciências sociais e humanas do Estado de São Paulo.* Ed. preliminar. São Paulo, 1973. 44 leaves.

75-574951/r76

28. Brazil. Instituto Nacional do Livro. *Guia das bibliotecas brasileiras.* 4. ed. Rio de Janeiro, 1969.

WVJ

29. Comissão Brasileira de Classificação Decimal Universal. *Levantamento dos usuários da CDU no Brasil.* Rio de Janeiro, O Instituto, 1975. 34 leaves. (Publicação avulsa - IBBD/CDU, no. 1)

78-383433

30. Fundação Instituto Brasileiro de Geografia e Estatística. *Guia das bibliotecas brasileiras, 1976.* Rio de Janeiro, Fundação Instituto Brasileiro de Geografia e

Estatística-IBGE, Instituto Nacional do Livro-INL, 1979. 11, 1017 p.
6588118

31. *Guia das bibliotecas brasileiras.* 1941– Rio de Janeiro, Secretaria de Planejamento da Presidência da República. Fundação Instituto Brasileiro de Geografia e Estatística, Diretoria Técnica.

80-646415

32. *Guia das bibliotecas do Estado de Minas Gerais.* 1977– Belo Horizonte, Conselho de Extensão da UFMG. Vols. for 1977– issued by the Conselho Regional de Biblioteconomia, 6a Região. 78-646033

33. *Guia das bibliotecas do Estado de São Paulo.* 1978– São Paulo, Secretaria de Cultura, Ciência e Tecnologia do Estado de São Paulo, Departamento de Artes e Ciencias Humanas, Divisão de Bibliotecas.

79-645196

34. *Guia de bibliotecas universitárias brasileiras.* 1979– Brasília, Ministério de Educação e Cultura, Departamento de Assuntos Universitários, Coordenação do Aperfeiçoamento de Pessoal de Nivel Superior.

80-642703

35. Rio de Janeiro. Instituto Nacional do Livro. *Guia das bibliotecas brasileiras.* Rio de Janeiro, 1941. 245 p. (Coleção B2. Biblioteconomia, 2)

41-15980

36. Rio de Janeiro. Instituto Nacional do Livro. *Guia das bibliotecas brasileiras, registadas até 31 de marcq de 1942.* 2. ed. Rio de Janeiro, Imprensa nacional, 1944. 475 p. (Its Coleção B2. Biblioteconomia, II)

46-1902

37. Rio de Janeiro. Instituto Nacional do Livro. *Guia das bibliotecas brasileiras, registadas até 31 de dezembro de 1952.* 3. ed. Rio de Janeiro, 1955. 678 p.

56-25294

38. Rio de Janeiro. Instituto Nacional do Livro. *Guia das bibliotecas brasileiras referente a 31 de dezembro de 1965.* Informe especial para o V Congresso Brasileiro de Biblioteconomia e Documentação a realizarse em São Paulo de 8 a 15 de janeiro de 1967. Rio de Janeiro, 1967. 21 p.
3652685

39. Seckinger, Ron, and Morton, F. W. O. "Social Science Libraries in Greater Rio de Janeiro." *Latin American Research Review*, XIV (1979), 180–201.

WVJ

40. Tavares, Maria Teresa Wiltgen. *Bibliotecas no Rio Grande do Sul, 1971–1972.* Porto Alegre, Governo do Estado do Rio Grande do Sul, Secretaria de Coordenação e Planejamento Global, 1973. 84 p.

79-350170

41. Uratsuka, Josefa Naoco. *Guia de bibliotecas de ciências sociais e humanas do*

*Estado de S*ão Paulo. São Paulo, Associação Paulista de Bibliotecários, Grupo de Trabalho em Bibliotecas de Ciências Sociais e Humanas, 1974. 61 leaves. Based on the preliminary edition of 1973.

76-460873

Chile

42. Centro Nacional de Información y Documentación. *Guía de bibliotecas y centros de documentación de Chile.* Santiago de Chile, Centro Nacional de Información y Documentación, 1972. iii, 120 p. (Serie Directorios, 1)
4367012

43. Centro Nacional de Información y Documentación. *Guía de bibliotecas especializadas y centros de documentación de Chile.* 2. ed. Santiago, Dirección de Información y Documentación, CENID, 1976. (Serie Directorios, 2)

WVJ

44. Sehlinger Peter J. *A select guide to Chilean libraries and archives.* Bloomington, Ind., Latin American Studies Program, Indiana University, 1979. 35 p. (Latin American studies working papers, 9)

80-108172

45. United Nations. Economic Commission for Latin America. *Directorio de unidades de información para el desarrollo: Chile.* Santiago de Chile, CEPAL, 1978. vii, 203 p.

79-110307

Colombia

46. Cali, Colombia. Universidad del Valle. Facultad de Arquitectura. *Guía de las bibliotecas y centros de investigación de Cali.* Ed. preliminar. Cali, 1961. 30 p.

66-86342

47. Colombia. Departamento Administrativo Nacional de Estadística. *La Biblioteca en Colombia,* 1964. 5. ed. Bogotá, 1966.

WVJ

48. *Directorio colombiano de unidades de información.* 1976– Bogotá, Impr. Nacional. (Serie Información y documentación)

78-641315

49. Florén Lozano, L., and Castañeda, J. *Guía de las bibliotecas de Medellín.* Medellín, Editorial Universitaria de Antioquia, 1966. 136 p.

68-111381

50. Programa Interinstitucional de Documentación. *Directorio de recursos bibliográficos del Valle de Aburrá.* Medellín, Programa Interinstitucional de Documentación, 1975. 22, 53 p.

79-128949

51. Rojas L., O. G., and Salazar Alonso, A. *Directorio colombiano de bibliotecas y*

centros de información y documentación. Bogotá, COLCIENCIAS, División de Documentación, 1973. vii, 187 leaves (Serie Directorios y repertorios—Colciencias, no. 2)

80-144458

Costa Rica

52. Consejo Nacional de Investigaciones Científicas y Tecnológicas (Costa Rica). *Guía de bibliotecas, archivos, servicios y centros de información y documentación en Costa Rica.* San José, Departmento de Información y Documentación, CONICIT, 1975.

WVJ

Cuba

53. *Directorio de bibliotecas de Cuba.* 1942– Compilado por Fermín Peraza Sarausa. Gainesville, Fla.; La Habana, Anuario Bibliográfico Cubano. (Biblioteca del bibliotecario, 2) Publication suspended 1953–1962.

44-35650

54. *Guía de bibliotecas de la República de Cuba.* 1976– La Habana, Biblioteca Nacional "José Martí."

76-235490

55. Havana. Biblioteca Nacional José Martí. Departamento Metódio. *Guía de bibliotecas de la República de Cuba.* 2. ed. aum. y corr. La Habana, 1966. 107 p.
1521607

56. Havana. Biblioteca Nacional José Martí. Departamento de Información de Ciencia y Técnica. *Guía de bibliotecas y centros de documentación de la República de Cuba.* 3. ed. La Habana, 1970. 101 p.
729307

Ecuador

57. Centro Latinoamericano de Documentación, Economía y Social. *Directorio de unidades de información para el desarrollo: Ecuador.* Santiago, El Centro, 1978. 52 p.
5530130

58. Preibish, Andre. *Directorio/guía de las bibliotecas en Ecuador.* Ottawa, National Library of Canada, Collection Development Branch, 1979. vii, 117 p.
6883915

Guyana

59. Stephenson, Yvonne. *A guide to library services in Guyana.* Georgetown, Guyana Library Association, 1972.

WVJ

Jamaica

60. Jamaica. National Council on Libraries, Archives and Documentation Services. *Directory of Information Resources in Jamaica.* Kingston, 1977.

WVJ

61. Richards, Judith E. *Directory of Jamaica Libraries.* Kingston, jamaica Library Association, 1967—.

76-367049

Mexico

62. Barbarena B., Elsa. *Directorio de bibliotecas de la Ciudad de México. Directory of Mexico City libraries.* 2. ed. corr. y aumentada. Mexico, University of the Americas, 1967. xxii, 259 p.

79-207319

63. *Directorio de bibliotecas de la República Mexicana.* 1962—. México, Secretaría de Educación Pública. Vols. for 1962—1970 issued by Departamento de Bibliotecas; 1979— by Dirección General de Publicaciones y Bibliotecas, Secretaría de Educación Pública.

80-641188

64. Mexico. Departamento de Bibliotecas. *Directorio de bibliotecas de la República Mexicana.* 2. ed. Mexico, 1965. 361 p.

65-70955

65. Mexico. Departamento de Bibliotecas. *Directorio de bibliotecas de la República Mexicana.* 5. ed. México, El Departamento, 1973. 335 leaves.
2744069

66. Mexico. Departamento de Bibliotecas. *Directorio de bibliotecas de la República Mexicana.* 6. ed. México, El Departamento, 1979. 2 v.
6073587

67. Ocampo, M. L., and Ortiz Vidales, S. *Guía de las bibliotecas en El Distrito Federal.* México, Talleres de El Nacional, 1943, 26 p.

43-12720

68. Peraza Sarausa, Fermín. *Directorio de bibliotecas de México.* Ed. de 1958. Habana, Ediciones Anuario Bibliográfico Cubano, 1958. 41 p. (Biblioteca del bibliotecario, 15)

58-38830

Panama

69. Peraza Sarausa, Fermín. *Directorio de bibliotecas de Panamá.* Ed. de 1948. Habana, Anuario Bibliográfico Cubano, 1948. 34 p. (Biblioteca del bibliotecario, 21)

49-16348

Peru

70. Agrupación de Bibliotecas para la Integración de la Información Socioeconómica. *Directorio de bibliotecas especializadas del Perú*. Lima, 1972.

WVJ

71. *Guía de bibliotecas del Sistema Nacional de la Universidad Peruana, 1974*. Datos compilados por Elba Muñoz de Linares. Lima, Consejo Nacional de la Universidad Peruana, Dirección de Evaluación de Universidades, Oficina de Evaluación, 1975. iv, 97 p. (Serie Informaciones Bibliotecológicas, 1)

77-573632

Puerto Rico

72. Alamo de Torres, Daisy. *Directorio de bibliotecas de Puerto Rico*. Rio Piedras, P.R., Asociación Estudiantes Graduados de Bibliotecología, Universidad de Puerto Rico, 1979. 100 p.

80-128849

73. Sociedad de Bibliotecarios de Puerto Rico. *Guía de bibliotecas de Puerto Rico*. Josefina del Toro, editora. Ed. revisada. San Juan, P.R. La Sociedad, 1971. 63 p. 4348585

74. Pagán Jiménez, Neida. "Caribbean Library Resources in Puerto Rico." *Final report and working papers of the twenty-fourth Seminar on the Acquisition of Latin American Library Materials*. Los Angeles, University of California, June 17–22, 1979: 193–198.

Uruguay

75. *Directorio de servicios de información y documentación en el Uruguay*. Montevideo, Uruguay, Biblioteca Nacional, 1981. 128 p. 8160183

76. Montevideo. Biblioteca del Poder Legislativo. *Bibliotecas del Uruguay*. Selección, textos y compilación, María Teresa Goicoechea de Linares, con la colaboración de Cristina O. de Pérez Olave y Lilian Fernández Citera. Montevideo, La Biblioteca, 1978. 252 p. (Serie de temas nacionales, 5)

79-102436

Venezuela

77. Martín, Olivia. *Directorio de bibliotecas venezolanas*. Caracas, Universidad Central de Venezuela, Dirección de Bibliotecas, Información, Documentación y Publicaciones, Departamento de Orientación, Información y Documentación. 1973. 99 p.

76-474325

Name Index

About the Authors

HENRIETTE D. AVRAM is Director for Processing Systems, Networks, and Automation Planning at the MARC Development Office of the U.S. Library of Congress.

WILLIAM E. CARTER is Chief of the Hispanic Division of the U.S. Library of Congress.

CLAUDIO DE MOURA CASTRO is associated with the Coordinação do Aperfeiçoamento de Pessoal de Nivel Superior (CAPES), Ministerio de Educação e Cultura, Brazil.

CARL W. DEAL is Latin American Librarian at the University of Illinois at Urbana-Champaign.

ROBERTO ETCHEPAREBORDA is Director of the Department of Cultural Affairs of the Organization of American States.

CHARLES S. FINEMAN is Humanities Bibliographer at the University Library, University of California, Santa Cruz.

JOHN FINZI is the Head of Collection Development at the U.S. Library of Congress.

JUAN R. FREUDENTHAL is Associate Professor, Graduate School of Library and Information Science, Simmons College, Boston. A lecturer, consultant, photographer, he has written innumerable articles on librarianship and information science in Latin America, the West Indies and Egypt. With his wife, Pat, he coauthored *Index to Anthologies of Latin American Literature in English Translation* (G. K. Hall, 1977). Dr. Freudenthal received his Ph.D. from the University of Michigan.

HECTOR GÓMEZ FUENTES is Professor at the Departamento de Bibliotecología, Instituto Profesional de Santiago, Chile. An expert in the area of informatics, he has published several articles on scientific and technical information in Latin America, and is the editor of *Bases de Datos Bibliográficas en Chile* (Universidad de Chile, Dept. de Bibliotecología, 1980).

LAURENCE HALLEWELL is the Latin American Bibliographer and Lecturer in Portuguese at Ohio State University Library. He was formerly Professor of Library Science at the Universidade Federal de Paraíba, Brazil.

SUZANNE HODGMAN is the Bibliographer for Ibero-American Studies at the University of Wisconsin-Madison. She is also the Secretary General of SALALM.

CECILIA ISAACS is Cultural Attaché at the Embassy of Colombia in Washington, D.C.

ALAN JABBOUR is Director of the American Folklife Center at the U.S. Library of Congress.

DEBORAH JAKUBS is associated with the Research Libraries Group, Inc.

RANDALL JOHNSON is a Professor in the Department of Spanish and Portuguese at Rutgers University.

JOHN RISON JONES, JR., is Deputy Director of the Office of Postsecondary Education, Office of Policy Development, U.S. Department of Education.

FREDERICK W. LANGE is associated with the Midwestern Archaeological Research Center at Illinois State University.

CELIA LEYTE-VIDAL is Monograph Cataloguer at the Perkins Library, Duke University.

JESÚS LEYTE-VIDAL is the Ibero-American Librarian at the Perkins Library, Duke University.

ELIZABETH MAHAN is Outreach Coordinator for the Council on Latin American Studies at Yale University. She received her Ph.D. in Communications from the University of Texas at Austin.

SONIA M. MERUBIA is Serial Records and Acquisition Librarian at the Benson Latin American Collection, University of Texas at Austin.

HAYDÉE PIEDRACUEVA is Latin American Bibliographer at Columbia University.

BARBARA G. VALK, President of SALALM in 1981–1982, is Editor of the *Hispanic American Periodicals Index* and Coordinator of Bibliographic Development at the UCLA Latin American Center.

JAMES W. WILKIE is Professor of History at the University of California, Los Angeles. He is Editor of the *Statistical Abstract of Latin America*.